Praise for
THE PIANIST FROM SYRIA

"A unique and affecting viewpoint on life in Syria before and in the midst of extreme violence."

—*Booklist*

"Ahmad shares a powerful account of his escape from Syria and the music that ultimately saved him. [A] deeply moving account of one man's struggle to survive while bringing hope to thousands through his music."

—*Publishers Weekly* (starred review)

"The moving story of a Palestinian musician and his family suddenly thrust into the perilous vortex of the Syrian civil war. Well-rendered and affecting, this is a fine delineation of the plight of an unwitting protagonist in the Syrian conflagration."

—*Kirkus Reviews*

"This moving memoir shows how, even after a grenade damaged his hand, music provides salvation."

—*Chatelaine*

"*The Pianist from Syria* is the inspiring tale of a man who risked his life to give a voice to many, offering them hope with his gift of music."

—*Washington Missourian*

"Written in an open, honest style, *The Pianist from Syria* is a testament to the resilience and beauty of ordinary people with simple dreams."

—*Booklistonline.com*

"I worry that people have become so numb to the suffering of others, but hopefully voices like Aeham's will provide a greater view of what it means to be Syrian, and what it means to be a refugee."
—Jade Anna Hughes, *From the Inside*

"*The Pianist from Syria* is relevant and timely, a story specific to Ahmad and his family while at the same time raising awareness of what must be an experience shared by many refugees from war-torn areas."
—*BookBrowse*

THE
PIANIST
FROM
SYRIA

— A MEMOIR —

AEHAM AHMAD

AS TOLD TO SANDRA HETZL
AND ARIEL HAUPTMEIER

TRANSLATED BY EMANUEL BERGMANN

ATRIA PAPERBACK

New York   London   Toronto   Sydney   New Delhi

ATRIA
PAPERBACK

An Imprint of Simon & Schuster, Inc.
1230 Avenue of the Americas
New York, NY 10020

First Atria Paperback edition March 2021

ATRIA PAPERBACK and colophon are trademarks of Simon & Schuster, Inc.

Certain names and identifying characteristics have been changed.

For information about special discounts for bulk purchases, please
contact Simon & Schuster Special Sales at 1-866-506-1949 or
business@simonandschuster.com.

The Simon & Schuster Speakers Bureau can bring authors to your live event.
For more information or to book an event, contact the Simon & Schuster
Speakers Bureau at 1-866-248-3049 or visit our website at
www.simonspeakers.com.

Interior design by Joy O'Meara

Map credit: Peter Palm, Berlin/Germany

Manufactured in the United States of America

10 9 8 7 6 5 4 3 2 1

Library of Congress Cataloging-in-Publication Data is available.

ISBN 978-1-5011-7349-3
ISBN 978-1-5011-7350-9 (pbk)
ISBN 978-1-5011-7351-6 (ebook)

Dedicated to my friend Niraz Saeid, who was tortured to death in Assad's prisons, and to Mahmoud Tamim, my brother, Alaa Ahmad, and to all the other political prisoners in Syria.

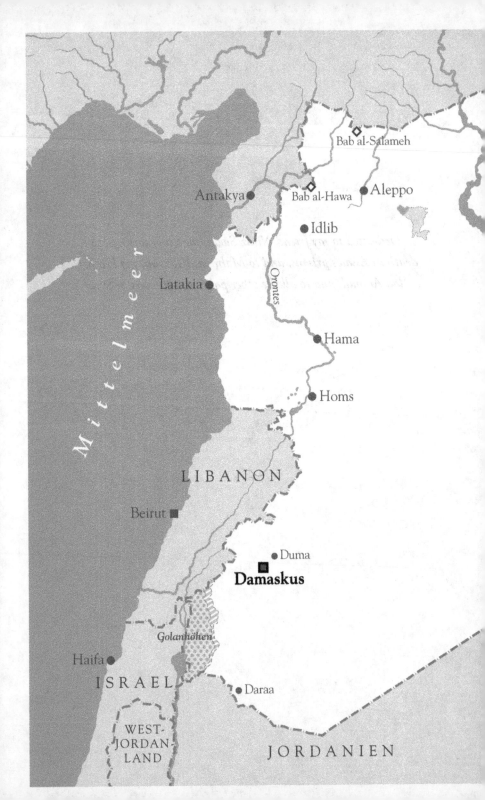

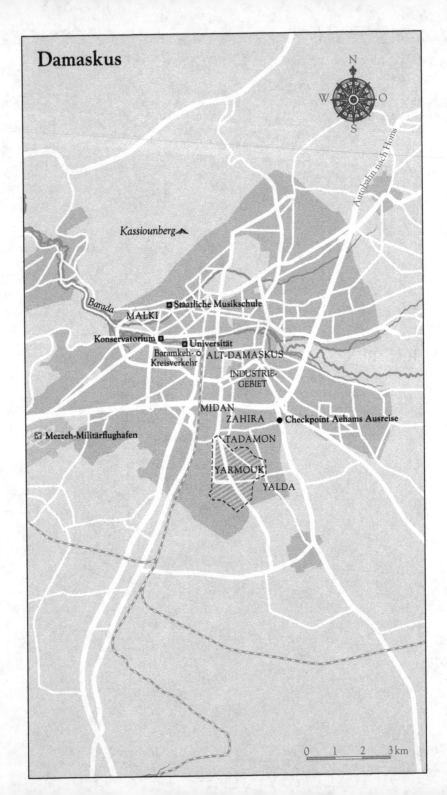

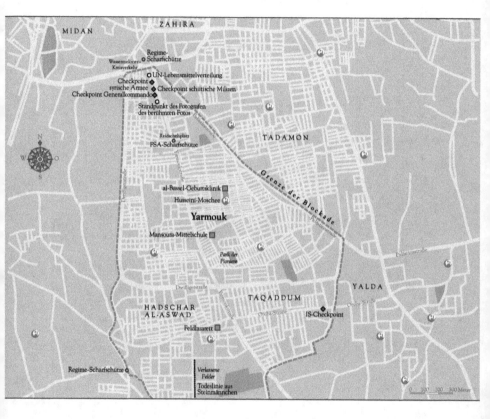

MIDAN   ZAHIRA

Regime-
Scharfschütze
Wassermelonen-
Kreisverkehr
UN-Lebensmittelverteilung
Checkpoint
syrische Armee   Checkpoint schiitische Milizen
Checkpoint Generalkommando
Standpunkt des Fotografen
des berühmten Fotos

TADAMON

Reidschehplatz
FSA-Scharfschütze

Grenze der Blockade

al-Bassel-Geburtsklinik
Husseini-Moschee

Yarmouk

Mansoura-Mittelschule

Park der
Pioniere

YALDA

Zweitligerstraße

TAQADDUM

HADSCHAR
AL-ASWAD

Oroba-Straße   IS-Checkpoint

Feldlazarett

Regime-Scharfschütze

Verlassene
Felder

Todeslinie aus
Steinmännchen

0   100   200   300 Meter

A photo can never really tell you what happened before or what came after. Like that picture of me sitting at a piano, singing a song amid the rubble of my neighborhood. It was reprinted by newspapers all over the world, and some people said it's one of the photos that will help us remember the Syrian Civil War. An image larger than war. But when I think back to that moment, I think of another image, superimposed on all the rest, an image of three birds.

That morning before daybreak I had gone out for water, together with my friends Marwan and Raed. Getting water was backbreaking work. We had to rise early and push a 260-gallon tank on a cart to one of the last working pipes in the neighborhood, then fill up the tank and push it back home.

We lived in Yarmouk, a suburb of Damascus. The armies of Syrian president Bashar al-Assad had cut us off from the rest of the world. We had no water, no electricity, no bread, no rice. By that time, more than a hundred people had died of starvation.

After my friends and I had delivered the water to our street, I decided to get some more sleep. But a little while later, my two-year-old son, Ahmad, whispered something in my ear and then playfully poked his tiny finger into my eye. Ouch! I jumped out of bed. Clearly, I wasn't going to get any more rest.

I decided to heat up some water with cinnamon—we had run out of coffee and tea a long time ago. But there was plenty of cinnamon, ever since a group of militants had stormed a local spice

depot. It hadn't seemed like such a bad haul at first, all this cinnamon, but think about it: Who needs cinnamon when you don't
even have bread or sugar? That's why it was ridiculously cheap.

Several months earlier, a few young men from the neighborhood had started a music group. We had been performing out
in the streets, standing around my upright piano. Every day, we
hauled it out on a cart, carefully steering it through the rubble.
We sang to escape the ever-present hunger that was gnawing at us.
Our performances were popular on YouTube, but the people in my
neighborhood could barely be bothered. And who can blame them?
When you're hungry, you can't think about anything else.

On that day, the two of us had agreed to meet with a photographer named Niraz Saied. Marwan and I began pushing the piano,
which was unbelievably heavy! Usually, there were six or seven of
us carefully maneuvering it through the torn-up streets. We turned
onto Palestine Street, which had once been a bustling commercial
center and was now deserted.

The damage there was staggering. The ruined buildings were
like concrete skeletons, giant tombstones reaching into the sky. Entire walls had been torn off, revealing the insides of various apartments, with pipes and cables sticking out. The street was littered
with heaps of rubble, with weeds growing among them.

I sat down at the piano and thought about what I should sing. I
had written dozens of songs in the past few months; they had simply poured out of me. Then I remembered a poem, scribbled on a
piece of paper, that a man had given me a few days earlier.

His name was Ziad al-Kharraf. In the old days, he sold honey
in our neighborhood. He was very cultured and educated, and he
used to be quite wealthy. I knew him only in passing. Ziad had a
doctorate, but I don't know in what. I do know that the honey was
merely his hobby. He used to take trips to the hills outside of town,
to meet with local beekeepers. Sometimes he even went abroad, to
countries like Yemen, where he would sample new blends of honey.
But that was then. Before the war.

Ziad had written the poem for his wife. She had been in the last weeks of pregnancy, and had transit papers for Damascus so that she could give birth to her child there. But something had gone wrong at the checkpoint: the soldiers wouldn't let her pass. Apparently, some bureaucrat had misspelled her name. She had to spend hours waiting while they tried to correct the error. When it became too much for her, she collapsed and fell onto her stomach. She died on her way to the clinic. The baby survived.

Ziad had loved his wife more than anything. They had married for love; it wasn't an arranged marriage. His wife had been his best friend. They had three daughters. Their new baby was their first son.

As the photographer was setting up his camera, a woman appeared carrying a tray. She had decided to make coffee for us, using the last bit she had, which she had saved for a special occasion. She wanted to share it with us and listen to the music. "What you're doing is very important," she said, pouring me a cup. I smiled at her with immense gratitude, savoring the wonderfully bitter taste of the coffee.

Then I noticed a chirping sound, and looked up to see three birds perched on a second-story balcony right across from me. It seemed a miracle, for normally birds vanish as soon as the shooting begins. Only very few of them find their way back to Yarmouk, and those are usually shot down because people are hungry. When I began to play, the three birds started singing again.

Everything came together for me—the chirping of birds, which I hadn't heard in so many months; the aroma of the coffee, which I had been longing for; the rage born out of hunger; my aching eye where my son had poked me; the lingering taste of cinnamon; my exhaustion from getting water that morning; and the haunted gaze of Ziad al-Kharraf when he'd asked me to make his poem into a song. Ziad's pain, the starving children of Yarmouk, and my brother's disappearance were all tearing at my heart. I was angry that the piano was out of tune, angry at my wounded hand. Closing my eyes, I began to sing, pouring all my despair into Ziad's poem.

My song became a cry, the cry of a man plunging into an abyss and giving voice to his descent into hell.

I Forgot My Name

I have lost my name
Its letters and its meaning
I have lost the words
That I need to sing my song

That was when Niraz must have snapped the picture.

Today people sometimes ask me: When you lived in that Palestinian camp, what color was your tent? Although Yarmouk was officially a "refugee camp," it was in fact a real neighborhood with real buildings. I used to own an apartment, a nice spacious apartment. I sold ouds, and my business had been thriving. But the war had destroyed it all. A grenade had cut the tendon between two of my fingers. A girl who had been standing next to my piano one day had been shot to death, and finally, the Islamic State had burned my instrument to the ground.

I would soon be exiled from Yarmouk, forced to leave my world behind. I would become one of those miserable gray figures, one of the millions who were now streaming into Europe. Some people think we only came to get a share of the wealth. But they don't understand us, don't know why we're forced to come. They're afraid of us.

And that is why I want to tell my story now in these pages. I want to raise my voice to dispel some of the fear and the lies. For pictures, too, can lie. Even if they contain a trace of the truth.

— CHAPTER ONE —

It begins with music. I must have been about two years old.

My bed was by a window; the sun was shining in. I remember my father lying next to me, playing the violin, his eyes hidden behind black glasses. The scroll of the violin was pressed against the mattress; the instrument's lower body was wedged under his chin. The violin bow came toward me, then swept back again. A sweet scent wafted through the room—there was a jasmine tree underneath the window. Pigeons were cooing in the birdcages outside as I listened with rapt attention to my father's music. I felt snug and happy.

I already knew that Papa was different from other men. He seemed to have no eyes, only black glasses that showed my reflection. He never went out by himself, but he knew every nook and cranny inside our apartment. At night, he would turn off the electricity to save money, and the apartment would become pitch-black. Whenever I had to use the bathroom, I called to him, and he would get up and guide me. He never bumped into anything, never knocked anything over. He always walked with calm, measured steps. And I trailed after him, stumbling, as if *I* were blind, not he.

Something else astounded me: Whenever my mother couldn't find something—the matches, for example, the potholders or the scissors—she'd ask him, "Abu Aeham, have you seen it?" And my father would say, "Look in the kitchen drawer, to the right." And that's where it was.

My father owned half a dozen canes but refused to use them, even though the streets of our neighborhood were dangerous for a blind person. The sidewalk pavement was uneven, cars were parked everywhere, and sometimes the workers cleaning the sewers would leave a hole uncovered for hours. Once, long before I was born, my father had been making his way along the sidewalk, feeling the ground with his cane, when suddenly he stumbled into one of these open holes. Disoriented and covered in the filth of the sewage basin, he realized he had lost a tooth. It was the last time he went outside by himself.

When I entered preschool at the age of three, I became his guide. He would take my hand, we'd start walking, and I would tell him what I saw: a car coming from the right, a pothole, a man running. After a few years, we no longer needed words. All it took was a small tug to the left or the right; he would always follow my lead. It was as if we were bound together by an invisible ribbon. As if my eyes were his eyes.

This is how we walked through Yarmouk, one of the most vibrant and crowded neighborhoods of Damascus. The buildings were raw, unfinished, unpainted, and the streets were always clogged, full of honking cars. Tiny alleyways branched off the main roads, narrow and crooked, barely wide enough for a person to pass through. Whenever my father and I made our way through this tangled web, we chatted about everything and nothing. Then, out of the blue, my father would say, "Turn here." And he was always right. We never got lost, not once. At times I wondered if he really was blind.

Some days we'd walk to the corner store to buy Alhamraa cigarettes, pungent and strong. He smoked two packs a day. Other days, we'd visit his favorite sister, Amina, who had studied biology. He loved to drop by for a cup of tea. Once, when his heart rate was suddenly and inexplicably elevated, I took him to the hospital. And every day, at eight in the morning, we went to my preschool together. After he dropped me off, he would visit a friend who lived around the corner. At eleven, he'd pick me up and we'd walk back home together.

My mother, who was a teacher at a local elementary school, would come home at noon each day. For lunch, we had *labneh*—a kind of yogurt cream cheese—served with bread and olive oil. Or *shanklish*, spicy cheese balls. Sometimes my father made me a fried egg. One day while doing so, he turned on the gas stove and poured oil in the pan, but then got distracted and went into the living room. Suddenly, there was the smell of burning oil. We both ran into the kitchen. The pan was engulfed in flames; the plastic handle had melted. Panicked, my father did exactly the wrong thing: he poured water onto the burning oil.

There was a small explosion and a giant cloud of smoke. "Get your pillow!" he yelled. I ran and brought it, and he used it to smother the fire.

We ran out into the streets, coughing. The neighbors had seen the smoke and came running: "Everything all right?" they asked, handing us bottles of water. When my mother came home and saw what happened, she scolded him: "Ahmad, haven't I told you a thousand times to wait until I get back?! You could have burned down the whole house."

"*Challas*, enough," my father said. "Let's go back in."

We began cleaning up the apartment. Finally, my mother said, "Abu Aeham, let's go out for food." I knew then that all was forgiven. My father's name was Ahmad, but she only ever called him that when she was mad at him. Most of the time, she called him Abu Aeham, a term of endearment: "Father of Aeham."

The person most upset about this mishap was my father himself. He couldn't believe this could happen to him! To him, the perfectionist! To him, who always planned ahead. He considered himself the master of his own destiny. When he was younger, he had trained to be a violinist, but then became a carpenter. Now he played the violin at weddings, in addition to building cabinets for the young couples. His two careers were intricately linked—just one crooked cabinet could spell the end of his wedding performances.

Only once did I see him hurt himself while working. Afterward, he kept sucking on his finger for hours, like a lion with a thorn in its paw. But he couldn't find the thorn. There was a tiny wooden splinter underneath his skin, and it had become infected. I used tweezers to pull it out.

My father had built all our furniture with his own hands. Everything seemed massive to me. Only the colors were a little off. I loved to climb on top of the large walnut cabinet and hide. One day, a television crew showed up and shot a small segment about my father, the blind carpenter of Yarmouk.

Another time, as we were walking down a street and I was directing my father this way and that, always trying to evade different obstacles, suddenly I heard a dull thud. My father had hit his forehead on an open window shutter. I had been looking down at our feet, without paying attention to what was right in front of us. His glasses had fallen off and he was bleeding from a cut on his forehead.

"Papa, I'm so sorry!" I yelled, and burst into tears. He was still clutching my hand, not wanting to lose his bearings. By then, passersby had noticed us; one of them bent down to pick up the glasses. The man shot me a nasty glare. My father put his broken glasses back on. One of the lenses had a crack. Someone gave him a handkerchief and he wiped the blood off his face. I was still crying. "It's all right, Aeham," he said. "It's all right, let's go home."

Back at home, he took rubbing alcohol and a cotton ball from a cupboard, sat down on a chair, and dabbed at his wound. We were both silent. I watched him timidly. It was my fault that he'd been hurt! But then he stood up, gave me a kiss, and said, "Aeham, don't worry! Things like this just happen; we can't avoid them."

In those years, we often went to Duma on the weekends, outside Damascus. Duma had always been a wine-growing region, even back in the days of ancient Rome. Everyone knew that Duma had the juiciest grapes in the whole Middle East. But Duma also had many new buildings and developments. My parents had bought a small condo there. Each month, my mother set aside a fifth of her salary to pay it off.

One morning, just after sunrise, my father and I were walking through the vineyards, along a small river and then up into the hills. Suddenly, one of the vintners who knew my father called out, "Ahmad! Come, my friend, let's have some tea!" And so we went to his house.

Islam tells us that God answers the prayers of the blind. Out in the countryside, where faith was extremely important, my father was always treated with the utmost reverence. We sat down under one of the gnarled vine trees. The farmer poured us tea. I leaned against the vine's sturdy trunk and filled my belly with sweet fruit. The grapes were dangling above my head, and the rays of the morning sun made them gleam. The two men discussed the world while I enjoyed the sparkling sunlight. This is one of my most cherished childhood memories.

When I was young, I used to draw my father as a stick figure with heavy black glasses. It's the only way I knew him. Did he even have eyes? And if so, what did they look like? I was curious. One day—I was already in elementary school—I asked him, "Papa, what happened to your eyes?" He looked astonished, then let out a loud, deep laugh. I joined in, high and clear, a countertenor to his baritone. "Do you really want to know?" he then asked. "I'll show you my eyes, but promise me you won't be scared." I promised, and he took off his glasses, slowly turning his head from right to left. "Papa . . ." I said haltingly. It was terrible.

His left eye looked gray and watery. The iris, the pupil, and the white uvea were fused into a dull, sightless ball. He had no right eye; there was only a hole. I learned that a student had accidentally run into my father when he was in elementary school, his index finger piercing Papa's eye, an accident that permanently robbed him of what little vision he had left. Before that, he had only been able to tell day from night, and only with his right eye. The eyeball had been so badly injured that it had to be removed.

I was shocked. My father, my all-powerful hero, had only one eye—and it looked terrifying. I almost cried. "I'll always be here for you," I stammered. "My eyes will be your eyes." My father put his glasses back on.

For a while, we sat together in silence. Then we couldn't bear it anymore, and we changed the subject.

When I think back on this moment today, in my apartment in Germany, it breaks my heart, for I left him and my mother behind in Yarmouk. I ran away.

Later I learned what had happened. When my father was eight years old, his eye had become infected. At the time, there were no doctors nearby, let alone eye specialists. Not then, not for a family of Palestinian refugees in a small village somewhere in Syria. My father said that several children had suffered from this illness—it must have been a virus. My grandmother made him herbal compresses. When that didn't work, she brought him to traditional healers, who were supposed to cure the problem with the wisdom of the ancients . . . and other mumbo jumbo. The infection only got worse.

His father, my grandfather, was Palestinian, and had been driven out of his homeland during the 1948 war, along with more than seven hundred thousand other refugees. My family was from Safad, where they had owned camels and sheep, and had grown figs, apricots, lemons, and oranges. They left everything behind, because they believed the war wouldn't last long. But it became impossible to return. In the end, my family ended up in Dili, a village in southern Syria. They had lost everything.

From then on, they all had to live in one room. The outside of the house was made of stone; the inner walls were made of dried mud. The women fetched water from a nearby creek, balancing the clay jars on their heads. In the midst of all this poverty, my grandparents married. A year after that, in 1952, my father was born, the first of ten children.

He knows what the world looks like because for the first eight years of his life he was able to see. If there was a cure, it was out of reach for him. A group of Bedouins tried to heal him by branding the back of his head with red-hot pieces of iron. To this day, he still has the scars. Then my grandmother brought him to a Gypsy tribe, who tried healing it with some kind of kohl pencil that they applied around his eye. My father suspects that the tiny grains of kohl destroyed the rest of his cornea. After all these ordeals, he was left with only five percent of his vision. He could tell darkness from light, but no more than that. He had to learn the world anew. He stumbled around like a toddler, bumping into everything. He was useless.

Eventually a group of nurses arrived in the village, conducting a vaccination campaign. They told my grandparents about a school for the blind in Damascus. One week later, a car pulled up in the village. The door opened to reveal Radia al-Rikabi—the daughter of Rida Pasha al-Rikabi, the prime minister of the short-lived Arab Kingdom of Syria, as it was known at the time. She had founded the Damascus School for the Blind, inspired by her blind brother, who had not only attended a university, but gone on to play violin on television.

Mrs. Rikabi spoke to my grandparents—and when she left, she took my father with her. He was petrified. Not only had he recently lost his eyesight, but he didn't know the place they were going to and had never left his native village before. Two hours later, they arrived at the school. My father was allowed to shower and was given new clothing and a clean bed. There were tables and chairs; everything was neat and well maintained. But for many weeks, his sightless eyes were filled with tears. He missed his parents, and thought they didn't know where he was.

Although my grandfather traveled there most weekends, whenever he was able to afford the long journey to Damascus, one of the women at the school had told him he wasn't allowed to talk to his blind son. He could only look at him from a distance; then he was asked to quietly leave again. But he always left expensive sweets for my father, who would wonder where they had come from.

He continued to feel terribly lonely. And then, one day, my grandmother came along with my grandfather to visit. When she saw her son, she rushed toward him, taking him in her arms and showering him with kisses. She could barely bring herself to let go of him. Everyone was in tears, and after that my father was allowed to spend weekends at home.

At the school, my father learned everything a blind person in our part of the world needed to know: how to read Braille and navigate unknown streets, but also how to weave wicker chairs and make carpets, brushes, and brooms. Radia al-Rikabi was like a mother to the students, mending their clothes and letting them sit in her lap. But she was also very stern: every night, she patrolled the dormitory, and if anyone hadn't washed their feet, there would be a scolding. That was something everyone was afraid of.

My father was infinitely curious, investigating everything with his hands. At first, he would secretly sneak into the workshop, but later he got permission from the headmistress. He built an airplane, a small carriage, even a pushcart—all made out of wood. Mrs. Rikabi often said to my father, "Ahmad, you have a great future ahead of you," and her words were an inspiration to him.

One day, a new teacher arrived at the school. A music teacher.

"What instrument do you like the most?" he asked my father.

And Papa replied, "Violin. I love the sound of the violin."

"If your parents buy you one," said the teacher, "I'll teach you."

That was just what my father wanted. So that weekend, when he visited his parents, he begged them to buy him a violin.

But they shook their heads. They were poor, and Grandfather said that a violin would cost as much as ten gallons of olive oil, about three months' worth of wages. On top of that, Grandfather didn't want Papa to become a musician, for in his eyes, musicians were no better than vagabonds or beggars, standing on street corners and playing for coins. "Do you want to end up like that?"

But Papa wouldn't give up. He was so intent on learning the violin that he eventually resorted to lying, telling Grandfather that everyone at school was supposed to play an instrument and that if you didn't have one, you'd be expelled. It worked! Grandfather would never allow his son to be kicked out of school, so he gave in. He borrowed money from relatives and bought a violin for my father—made in East Germany.

Once my father had his violin, he seemed to never put it down. Some days, he would practice as much as fifteen hours. Soon, he gave small performances, first at school and then in restaurants. He began to save money, and after he had graduated from school, he was able to pay for higher education, studying Arab literature at the University of Damascus. He asked some of his friends to read the textbooks aloud so that he could record them on cassette tapes, and whenever he had to take a test he brought a friend along, dictating the answers to him. Over the years, he accumulated thousands of tapes, which he passed on to other visually impaired students after he graduated. I've heard that even today they're still in circulation.

For a few years, he worked as an Arabic teacher, but he didn't take to it. Wanting instead to devote his life to music, he decided to build instruments. A blind instrument maker? Everyone thought he had lost his mind. A blind person shouldn't even be in a workshop! Surrounded by hammers, saws, drills, and other dangerous tools—even people with two healthy eyes hurt themselves all the time!

But my father was stubborn. With the help of his brothers, he bought wood, then began asking around at carpentry shops how each part of the process was done. He got himself some tools and started building his first oud—a potbellied Arabic instrument, not unlike the European lute. In fact, the lute is derived from the oud. Papa cut the wood, but his first oud came out crooked and useless. So he bought more wood. He trained himself to cut the sound holes with great precision. He learned how to glue the neck and the fingerboard. But he kept making mistakes, over and over again. Finally, after three years, he built his first functional oud.

And he kept at it. When his accordion broke, he took it apart to find out how it worked. The Western sound system divides each octave into twelve identical half-tone steps, whereas in the Arabic world, each octave contains eighteen quarter tones. After six months of toil, my father had turned the Western-style accordion into an Arabic one. Then people from all over Syria began approaching him to ask that he refurbish their instruments. There was only one other instrument maker able to do this kind of work, and he lived in Egypt.

One day in 1985, a young teacher visited him, requesting that he repair her Chinese accordion. A few days later when she returned to pick it up, my father chatted with her for a while, suggesting that she take accordion lessons from him. That woman was to be my mother.

An excellent soprano, she taught music and art at an elementary school and sang in the school choir. My father was quite impressed with her. At the time, he played in various bands and many women were interested in him, but he was always reticent. My mother, too, was very guarded. Whenever male colleagues approached her, she always declined. But my father impressed her. He seemed to be able to do anything. She almost forgot that he was blind. During those accordion lessons, they got to know each other, and after a while, they both realized: This is the person I've been looking for.

During one of their lessons, my father asked her if she wanted to be his wife. And she said yes.

Shortly after, he put on his best shirt and a pair of freshly pressed pants, and went to introduce himself to her parents. Her father was in favor of the match, but her mother was strictly opposed. So Papa left. "You can't marry a blind man!" her mother said. "He's handicapped! Do you want to be a nurse for the rest of your life?"

But my mother insisted. And my father wouldn't give up— thank God he was so stubborn! One day, he took his violin and played a song for his future mother-in-law. The evening ended with the whole family singing romantic pop songs by Fairouz, a famous singer from Beirut, who was my mother's favorite. Two months later, she agreed to the engagement.

One year later, on June 5, 1987, my parents married.

The following April, I was born.

I have a strong early image of my mother, and it's surprisingly clear: I'm sitting in a stroller at the farmers' market in Yarmouk. My mother had taken me shopping with her. People were shouting, vendors were haggling, it smelled of flowers and spices, of fish and overripe fruit—and I was in the middle of it all, a tiny prince on a tiny throne. I watched my mother go from booth to booth, choosing the best bell peppers here and the freshest parsley there. Then she pushed me to a nearby fountain—Damascus was famous for its many fountains—took some grapes, and washed them in the fresh water. Leaning over me, she put a grape in my mouth and said, beaming: *"Habibi!"* Darling. Then she gave me another grape. And a kiss.

In the mornings, before going to work, my mother often played a cassette by Fairouz, and would sing along in a cheerful duet before putting on her headscarf and leaving the house. And after lunch, she would often make music with my father. My father listened to pop music almost every morning, and by the afternoon, he had learned how to play the songs on his violin. After all, he was a wedding musician, and needed to be familiar with the popular hits of the day, so that people could dance to them. As my mother washed the dishes or folded clothes, she would sing along to Papa's music.

Arabic melodies modulate freely, and my mother was a master in playing with them and improvising variations. She sang when she cooked and she sang when she fed our canary, and the bird would often tilt its head and chirp along.

One day, after my father had finished building a new set of furniture, a large table with several chairs, my mother invited her colleagues from school over for dinner before he delivered it to his customers. She spent all afternoon in the kitchen, singing as she prepared the meal: hummus, baked potatoes, roasted zucchini, baba ghanoush, tahini, tabbouleh, *kafta*. She adorned the table with a cloth of Aghabani embroidery from her father, a lace vendor. It turned into an exuberant evening, and it was the first time I sat at a table.

Each night before I went to bed, my mother would read me

books she had chosen from her school library. I enjoyed the stories of Aladdin and the magic lamp, and of Sinbad the Sailor. And I loved listening to her speak in her elegant Arabic.

When I was three, my brother was born. A few days before his birth, my mother put my hand on her tummy, and I could feel his tiny kicks. "Feel how strong he is," said my mother. "He'll grow into a real rascal!" That turned out to be true. My brother's name is Alaa. Even before he learned to walk, he tried to lunge at me and bite me, pretending to be a lion. Once he had mastered the art of walking, his world expanded and he could pick fights with the neighborhood boys. He never listened to my parents. If he had, things might have turned out differently.

No one had ever done any civic planning in Yarmouk. It had simply sprung up in 1954, when the Syrian government resettled tens of thousands of Palestinian refugees there. Until then, everyone had been living in emergency shelters. An organization called UNRWA—the United Nations Relief and Works Agency for Palestine Refugees in the Near East—gave each refugee family three hundred Syrian pounds per room, and sometimes three bags of cement and ten wooden pillars. That's how the patchwork-like settlement grew into a real neighborhood.

Our building had been built the same way. Our front door, for example, was actually a barn door that my grandfather had bought from a scrap merchant. A smaller door had been cut into it. Our building seemed to constantly grow and change, but no matter what happened, that old door always remained. The small door constantly squeaked when we opened it. Every few years we painted the entire door white, because white doors—as we say in Syria—are a sign of good luck.

As a small child, I thought the doorknob was made of gold. Later I learned that it was only brass. Still, it must have had some value, because one day I heard a scratching at the door, and when I opened it, I saw a guy with a saw running away.

We lived on a street corner. On one side was a main road full of traffic, with a vegetable shop nearby. The other road was a small alley, only accessible to pedestrians. When I stepped out, there was a kiosk to the left that sold chewing gum, cola, ice cream, and trading cards. This is where we spent all our allowance. For some strange reason the kiosk was called Istiqama—Honesty. As children, we pondered this for hours. Why was the shop called that? The owner was anything but honest.

The chewing gum he sold us was old enough to crack your teeth. And since children aren't yet so good at math, he always cheated us. If you paid for five pieces of candy, he sometimes gave you only four, and you didn't realize it until later. Of course, if you confronted him, he denied everything. One day, I decided to pay him back for that. He had once again cheated me on chewing gum, but this time I went to my mother and told her everything: "He cheated me!"—"What?" she said, then marched straight out the door to confront him about it. When she came back, she brought me one more piece of chewing gum.

Our favorite games were *Dahhal* and *Tobbeh*. We could play for hours, either in the stairwell or out on the street. *Dahhal* was played by tossing marbles. We drew five lines and whoever succeeded with a good throw could take his opponent's most valuable pieces. *Tobbeh* worked like this: You put a pile of trading cards on the ground, pressed your hand on them as hard as you could, and then pulled back quickly, attempting to thrust them into the air. You were allowed to keep any card that landed on its back. We played this game until our fingers hurt. Which is also why my mother threw all my cards into the trash, afraid I would hurt my hands. I was so mad I threatened to never play the piano again, and finally she relented, going down to "Honesty" to buy me new trading cards.

There were six apartments in our building, one for my grandfather, one for us, and one for each of my father's four brothers. Right above us lived Uncle Mohammed and his wife, Aunt Ibtihal. My mother never got along with her. The two of them were always arguing! It only took the smallest spark to ignite a fire, and then their voices would rise to a crescendo.

We lived on the ground floor, and when the doorbell rang, it often fell on me to answer it. "Why is that?" my mother cried out. "Why are we the only ones answering the door? Why can't the fine lady and gentleman from upstairs be bothered?" She stomped upstairs to Aunt Ibtihal to complain. Crescendo, crescendo . . .

One time, some wood shavings from my father's workshop on the rooftop terrace had fallen through the window onto Aunt Ibtihal's clean white sheets. She showed up at our door, and it all started again. Sometimes one of the two women had claimed all the clotheslines on the rooftop and the other one was unable to dry her clothes. Once, an argument got so out of hand that Aunt Ibtihal took my mother's laundry and threw it down into the street. Furious, my mother did the same to hers.

"Hey, have you lost your minds?" someone called from below. "What's going on up there?" While the two of them were arguing on the rooftop, I had to go down to get everyone's clothes.

When I began playing the piano, I would often practice for half an hour before school. Aunt Ibtihal didn't like that very much. She would take a broom and knock on the floor with it. Stop it! My mother didn't appreciate this at all. One morning while I was practicing and Aunt Ibtihal was knocking, my mother stormed up, fully enraged. I heard a loud slapping noise and when my mother came back down, her hair was disheveled and her cheeks were flushed. "It's all taken care of," she said. Had they really slapped each other?

The men in the family paid no attention, quite deliberately. There's a saying in our part of the world: When women are arguing, the men should only nod and smile. Or at least keep out of it. You can only make it worse.

I think it was stress that made my mother lose her temper once in a while. She really had a lot to do. In the morning, she taught classes at school, then she had to do the shopping, the laundry, the cooking, and other household chores, and afterward she had to prepare her classes for the next day. Her husband was blind, and although he took loving care of us children, he wasn't able to contribute much else. But whenever my mother was relaxed, she was the most warmhearted and loving person imaginable.

The storm clouds came and went. The next day, the waters were inevitably calm again. It wouldn't ever have occurred to any one of us to move away and abandon the family, much less over a silly argument. Family is the most important thing there is. We all stick together. I, for my part, like Aunt Ibtihal very much, especially today. We often spend hours on the phone.

That makes living in Europe difficult for me at times—I'm so far away from my loved ones. It's even harder for my mother. It breaks her heart to not have her grandchildren around. Nowadays, I live in the German city of Wiesbaden. A few days ago, an elderly lady from Cologne visited us. She sat on the sofa and played with Ahmad and Kinan, my two sons. I took a picture of the three of them and sent it to my mother. It was meant to be a nice gesture, but seeing the kids just made her sad.

A few hours later she called me: "So, you have a new grandma now," she said, and I could hear that she was struggling against tears. I apologized to her. But she began weeping; then she started to curse the war, the bombs, and Assad, who had destroyed her life, who had driven us apart and taken her son Alaa. "This awful war!" she sobbed. "This awful war!"

There were no playgrounds in Yarmouk. My favorite thing was riding my red bicycle through the neighborhood, together with my best friend, Sadek. One day, we saw a toolbox standing by the side of the road. I thought my father could really use those tools, and since it didn't seem to belong to anyone, we put the toolbox on my bike rack and started pushing the bike back home.

Suddenly, a man called out, "Stop! Come back here! My tools!" He ran until he caught up with us. He was a handyman working in one of the nearby buildings.

"Where are your fathers?" he fumed. "I'll tell them you guys are thieves!"

"Please don't!" we called out. "Take your toolbox. It's all right!"

"Nothing's all right!" he yelled. "Where are your fathers? I'll show you!"

I knew that they put thieves in jail. Would I be sent to jail? I was scared. We pushed the bike home, followed by the angry handyman.

When he told my father the story, Papa scolded me: "Aeham! How could you do something like that?!"

"Papa, please, I took the tools for you!" I cried.

"Aha, so that's it!" yelled the man. "You're in it together!"

My father was shocked. It took him a while to convince the handyman otherwise.

Today I chuckle when I think about this story . . . and others like it.

It's astonishing: Whenever I think of my childhood, the sun is always shining; I don't remember a single rainy day. I still remember the scent of the flowering jasmine and the smell of the olive soap that I washed my face with each morning. I remember the heat in the summer, the honking cars, the cries of the vegetable vendor, the sounds of soccer balls getting kicked against our wall.

Other fathers never had time for their children. They toiled from morning to night, and when they didn't have to work on Fridays, they were too tired to play with their kids. The next morning, they went to mosque, and after lunch, everyone went out for a walk together. Then the fathers went to a café to meet their friends, brothers, cousins, and when they came back, the kids were already asleep. No wonder that later on, the kids only talked about their mothers. They barely saw their fathers.

My father was always there for me. He bottle-fed me, changed my diapers, cleaned up, and tidied the room. He answered thousands of questions: Papa, why are we refugees? Why are we Muslims? Is there a God? Later on, he even talked to me about sex. In the Arab world, this kind of conversation is unthinkable between fathers and their sons.

A lot of other boys were afraid of their fathers, who were strict and would beat their kids. But I remained my father's helper, and he remained my friend.

— CHAPTER TWO —

My father wanted to enroll me at the State School of Music in Damascus. But first I had to pass the entrance exam. As the big day approached, Papa became more and more nervous. "Sixty more days," he said to me one morning. "Then it'll be time for your test." And so began a slow countdown. Thirty days, then twenty, then ten, and so on. He smoked even more than usual, a sure sign that he was tense. With only three days remaining, he enlisted his friend al-Chadra, the keyboard player in his wedding band, to accompany him on a test run, to scout the best route to the school. He left nothing to chance.

Each year in summer, during the school holidays, when Damascus was glowing with heat, when the night brought no relief and most people spent the day at the beach or dozed in the shade, a man named Solhi al-Wadi held his entrance exams, determining who would be admitted to his school. Solhi al-Wadi was a famous conductor. The heat worked in his favor. He wanted only the most diligent students, the most talented, the most ambitious.

Al-Wadi had almost single-handedly established classical music in Syria. He was a cellist and had trained at the Royal Academy of Music in London. In 1962, he founded the State School of Music in Damascus, or the Arabic Institute, as it was officially called. In 1970, Hafiz al-Assad, the father of Bashar al-Assad, took power in a coup. The regime wanted to appear open-minded, and al-Wadi was in the right place at the right time. In 1990, two years after I was born, al-Wadi opened the State School of Music. From then on, young Syrians could study the piano, trombone, or oboe here at home, without having to travel abroad, to cities such as New York; Montpellier, France; or Heidelberg, Germany.

Each year, more than a thousand children applied for one of the one hundred openings at the State School of Music. In theory, anyone who passed the entrance exam had a right to be admitted. But in practice, the school was incredibly elitist. Most of the students were the children of government functionaries or millionaires, of well-respected artists and intellectuals. Still, my father wanted to try to get me in. He had plans for me. He didn't want me to play the fiddle at weddings: he wanted me to perform on a grand piano in concert halls. To him, my entrance exam was the gate to Paradise.

I knew al-Chadra, the keyboard player. Ever since I was four years old, he had been a regular visitor at our home. He had given me lessons on my father's old Casio keyboard. We played scales, études, simple chords. And then my father sat down with me for an hour each afternoon and we practiced together.

On the big day, I put on a clean T-shirt, then my father and I climbed into a minibus and took off. Damascus has a network of small public buses connecting the whole city. Papa and I had left much too early. Traffic in Yarmouk was dense, as always—even the Midan market was full of cars. When we had to switch to another line at Baramkeh Circle, our minibus at first didn't come. We must have waited half an hour. My father grew increasingly impatient. He wrung his hands and paced back and forth.

"We have to take a taxi!" he fumed. "But I don't have enough money. Damn!" I've never seen him that nervous before. He constantly opened the glass window on his watch—made especially for blind people—and felt the time.

Finally, the minibus came. The journey continued, albeit haltingly.

"Papa, let's practice at home," I said to my father. "It's too far. We're losing time. I could be practicing the keyboard." He remained silent and tense.

I looked out the window and realized I'd never been in this neighborhood. The streets were wider and much quieter than what I was used to. I saw people from different countries on the sidewalks, and more and more women without headscarves. At a tree-lined street, we finally got out of the minibus. Everything was calm and well maintained. We were in Jisr al-Abyad, the embassy district, one of the most exclusive areas of Damascus. I saw villas towering behind wrought-iron fences, framed by fragrant rosebushes.

Once again, my father flipped open the glass window of his watch, then cursed quietly. We started to hurry, and when I could finally see the school building, he asked me, "Are there people waiting outside?"—"No."—"Dammit!" We ran the final stretch toward the ivy-covered villa, rushed up the stairs, entered the lobby—and saw that we had come in time.

A line of people went through the entire building. Fathers and mothers with their children. We took our place in line.

Now I was getting nervous. On our way here, I had seen something puzzling: A black Mercedes had pulled up and a chauffeur had emerged, opening the back door. A boy, no taller than I, had stepped out of the car. In Syria, you had to be richer than God to afford a Mercedes. Why would a grown man hold the door open for a little kid? I told my father what I had seen. "Probably the son of some government bigwig," he replied curtly. I was more confused than ever.

For the rest of the time, we were silent. My father was too nervous to talk to me. One child after the next was called into the examination room. Finally, after almost three hours, it was my turn. I opened the door.

In the middle of the room stood a curved wooden box. It was a grand piano, but I had never seen one before. Three men and a woman sat behind a table. Another man stood by the window, his hands in his pockets—Solhi al-Wadi, the school's director. I found it odd that he didn't move. Weren't you supposed to shake hands when you greet someone?

One of the men at the table addressed me.

"Where are you from?" he asked me.

"Yarmouk," I replied.

"Do you play an instrument?"

"Yes. Keyboard."

He stood up, went over to the grand piano, hit a key, and asked me to sing the same note. And again. And again, two dozen times. Then his hand tapped out a rhythm on the table. I repeated it.

And that was all.

The woman turned to me. "You live in Yarmouk?" she asked.

"Yes."

"And you play keyboard?"

"Yes."

"Hmm . . ." she said.

What did that mean? I had no idea, but it didn't seem good.

The man brought me to the door, opened it—and my father came stumbling in. He almost fell; he only just caught himself. Apparently, he couldn't bear the tension, so he was listening at the door. It was an embarrassing moment. The whole situation probably could have been handled more gracefully, but this wasn't that kind of place. "You were listening in?" Solhi al-Wadi scolded my father. "That's not permitted!"

"I'm sorry. I'm Aeham's father," he said.

At that moment, everyone seemed to realize that he was blind. Al-Wadi calmed down. "It's all right," he said, relenting a bit. "Quite all right."

My father asked when the results would be announced, then we went outside and began our long journey back to Yarmouk. Papa was silent. Perhaps he was worried I might have failed. I thought about everything that had happened that day. The chauffeur, all the huffing and puffing, the principal scolding my father. I didn't like it there.

A few days later—almost no one in Yarmouk had a telephone back then—my father went to the grocery store on our street and called the school. But the secretary there told him he would have to come by in person—the results were posted inside the building.

So, the next day, we took another minibus across town. Al-Chadra, the keyboard player, went with us. We needed him. My father was blind and I hadn't learned how to read yet.

The results were posted on a noticeboard on a wall. Some thirteen hundred children had taken the exam that year. The list was endless. And for some reason, the names were not sorted alphabetically. Al-Chadra kept searching for my name. My father became increasingly tense; his knees were practically shaking.

"Did you find him?" he asked al-Chadra. "Did you find him?" Finally, on the seventh or eighth sheet of paper, al-Chadra saw my name: "Aeham Ahmad, sixty percent. Failed," he read.

"What?" my father called out. People turned to look at him. The heart of the world stood still.

"Are you sure?" he asked al-Chadra.

Our friend took another look.

"No, sorry!" he said. "I misread. Aeham *Hamada* got sixty percent. *Our* Aeham . . . ninety-nine percent!"

The heart of the world began beating again. My father laughed, a deep, booming sound. It echoed through the lobby, then up the stairs and into the summer sky. Once again, everyone turned to look at us. Ninety-nine percent! Normally, only the children of high-ranking government bureaucrats got grades like that. Certainly not some unwashed Palestinian boy from Yarmouk! On the way home, we were euphoric.

When we arrived, my father told everyone in the building. "Aeham did it!" he said, cheering. "Tonight we'll be celebrating!" And when night fell, all my uncles and aunts and cousins crowded into our small apartment. My father called out to each new arrival, "Aeham did it! He did it!"

My mother served lemon-flavored ice cream and tea while my father stood in the living room playing wedding songs on his violin. Our guests sat in a circle, singing and clapping, and doing little dances with their hands. For the first time since I've known him, my father's eyes seemed to be laughing. But perhaps it was just my imagination.

I didn't quite understand all this commotion, but I was happy. I liked ice cream, and that night, I didn't have to stay at home and practice on my keyboard: I was allowed to go outside and play soccer with my cousins until well into the night.

Classes began in the fall. The first thing we did was solfège, a traditional vocal exercise from France. The teacher gave us music sheets, and we had to sing each note: "Do, do, re, re, mi, mi . . ." The entire first year was devoted to singing. We wouldn't learn an instrument until our second year.

But before I could start singing, we had to buy the solfège textbook. It was imported from France and terribly expensive. The book cost five thousand Syrian pounds, around ten dollars, about the monthly salary of an average employee in Syria. My father asked the school personnel if he could simply make photocopies of the book. Out of the question, they said. We were hoping to buy a used copy, but we couldn't find one. As a result, I wasn't able to attend the first three classes. I had to wait until the end of the month, when my mother got paid. Only then were my parents able to buy the book.

Our solfège teacher was a wonderful elderly lady named Nadia, who treated all of us forty children very lovingly, like a mother. She sang in a beautiful, warm soprano. If someone forgot to transcribe their musical notes at home, she didn't yell. No, she gently reminded them to bring the homework in for the next class.

"You have a beautiful voice!" she sometimes said to me. I continued singing with renewed confidence:

Do mi do mi do mi sol fa re do re mi re
Do mi do mi do mi sol fa mi re do
Re mi re mi fa mi re
Mi fa mi fa sol fa mi
Do mi do mi do mi sol fa mi re do.

I sometimes talked to Sham, a girl from my class. But she was the only one I knew. The music school was like a club for rich kids. The parents brought their children, then waited for them, and at the end of the day, everyone got into taxis or cars and took off. Only my father and I trudged to the bus stop and took the minibus home.

On days when I didn't have music classes, my father practiced solfège with me in the afternoon. He would sing a motif and then have me improvise on it.

"Why is that important?" I asked him.

"It's very important!" he said. "You can turn any humble melody into a sweeping symphony. It's the language of music. Once you're fluent in it, you have complete freedom."

After half an hour of practice, he made us black tea. Papa always drank his tea very strong and sweet, heaping five spoonfuls of sugar into each cup. He let the leaves float in the pot, turning the tea dark and bitter. When you drank it, you had to pick bits of leaf off your tongue and lips. Normally, I wasn't allowed black tea. Only during our singing practice did he pour me a cup. Then we sang for another half hour, and then I was finally allowed to go outside and join my friends.

After the first year of music school, we had to take another test. This time, we had to sing notes by sight and clap a rhythm. Then the teachers decided which instrument we'd be assigned: guitar, drums, flute, cello, or piano. This time, our parents were with us. The lady administering the test asked my father what instrument he had in mind for me.

"Piano," my father said with a firm voice.

"Piano?" the woman asked. "You have a piano at home?"

"Yes," my father said. But that was a lie.

"If your son wants to learn to play keyboard, that's no problem. There's another music school that offers keyboard lessons."

"No. Piano."

"Very well. I'll send one of our teachers over to take a look at your piano," the woman said.

My father nodded.

There was no way out anymore. Years ago, when Papa had convinced Grandfather to buy him a violin, the instrument had cost three months' worth of wages. But a piano was even more expensive: it would eat up a whole year's salary. My father borrowed money from every relative he had and began a frantic search for an affordable instrument. An acquaintance had a lead: The man's wife was a pianist from Ukraine, and she knew a lady who still had an old Russian piano in her basement, a "Ukraina." Apparently, it was still in the box it had come in. The lady wanted three thousand dollars for it.

One of our neighbors owned a pickup truck and drove us to the lady's home. Six of us went down into the basement—my father, four of my uncles, and myself. We saw a gigantic wooden crate. The men tried to lift it—and started cursing. None of them had ever seen a piano, let alone tried to carry one. When they were moving the crate up the stairs, they started cursing and complaining.

"Ahmad, you're insane! What are you going to do with this giant box?" they said. "You're throwing away good money. What did you say you paid for this?"

"It's a piano! For Aeham!" Papa told them in a soothing voice. "And as a thank-you for your help, I'll play my violin for you whenever you want!"

The men were arguing so loudly that the Ukrainian lady peeked down and asked if everything was all right.

Somehow, we managed to maneuver the box onto the back of the pickup. When we arrived in front of our building and lifted it out, a throng of people crowded around us; everyone was curious. We carried the box into our apartment. But when we were inside, we realized that the piano wouldn't fit through the door to my room. My uncle Mohammed, a bricklayer, had to break open the doorframe. We moved the piano in, then he repaired the damaged wall.

I tested the keys. They were all out of tune. The piano had never been tuned. The next day, my father managed to get in touch with a piano tuner. There weren't many in Damascus. "No, I'm not going all the way to Yarmouk," the man said brusquely. "It's too far."

My father didn't like it when someone talked down to him. But what could he do? He began pleading, until the man finally relented.

"All right, I'll make an exception," said the piano tuner. "My next opening is in six months." In addition, he asked for a fee of fifty thousand Syrian pounds—about a hundred dollars. My father almost dropped the receiver. He didn't have that kind of money. Also, we couldn't possibly wait that long. So he hung up and tried calling other piano tuners. To no avail.

Then, my father did what he had always done in situations like that: he taught himself how to do it.

He carefully removed the wooden sound box and felt around until he found the wrest plank, which held the piano's tuning pins. He asked a welder to make a tuning key for him. He worked at night, when the noise in our building and on the street had quieted down. He gently plucked the strings with his fingernails, then listened, then made adjustments. He canceled all his performances and guzzled countless cups of sweet black tea. Meanwhile, I slept peacefully in my parents' bed. And then, one day, he was finished.

Soon, it was time for the school's piano tester to come. People who don't know Yarmouk sometimes think that it's a dangerous area. There are many Palestinian groups like Fatah and Hamas, always marching around, shouting slogans, pumping their fists into the air and waving flags. The man from the music school said he wanted to park his car outside Yarmouk. My uncle Amin had to go pick him up.

The man greeted my father, nodded at me, and took his seat at the piano. He played every key, all seven octaves, going note by note, first playing every C, then every D, then all the Es, and so on. After that, he tested the pedal. Meanwhile, my father stood in the doorway, listening.

"Very good," the man said at last, then he closed the lid. "It's well tuned."

My mother had prepared a meal for him: tabbouleh, a finely chopped salad of tomato, parsley, bulgur wheat, and mint; *maqluba*, a dish of meat, rice, and vegetables; and kibbeh, made with lamb and bulgur wheat. We all lounged on pillows in the living room. The man ate with gusto.

"I want to apologize to you," he suddenly burst out, directing this to my father. "I'm the piano tuner you called a few weeks ago. I was arrogant and treated you unkindly. I'm sorry."

My father smiled. As I said, he hated being condescended to. Now he was enjoying his victory.

"The piano is tuned wonderfully," the man added. "Who did that?"

My father smiled and shrugged, but he said nothing.

At last, my piano lessons could begin. Three times a week, my father and I went all the way across the city to the music school. If traffic wasn't too heavy, it took us ninety minutes each way. My father dropped me off with Rana Jneid, my first teacher. Later we both took the minibus back.

I didn't like Rana Jneid. She never smiled at me, she never gave any praise, and it was impossible to please her. If I was ever late, if my bus had been stuck in traffic, she would always yell at me. But if she was the one who was late, which happened often, she floated into the room, all dolled up as if she were going to a dance. Then she curtly said, "Go ahead." Not a word of apology.

At each lesson she wore a different dress, scuttling down the corridors in her high heels. Back in those days, everyone had Nokia cell phones with interchangeable cases, and there were dozens of colors and themes to choose from. Rana Jneid always color-coordinated with her dress. Whenever she wore a blue outfit, for example, she had a matching blue cell phone case.

Normally, pianists don't have long fingernails. It makes it harder to play. Except, of course, for Rana Jneid. Her fingernails were long and blue—like her dress—and they scratched across the keys.

One day I played an étude by Czerny for her. Carl Czerny was a student of Beethoven and a teacher to Liszt. His pieces were particularly hard to master. Generations of piano students have struggled with his compositions, and I was no exception. Rana Jneid was standing behind me as I played. Then I heard the beeping of a cell phone. I turned around and saw my suspicions confirmed: while I was toiling away at the piano, she was playing with her phone.

It had taken me two hours to get here, and now my teacher wasn't even listening to me. I played louder, hoping to gain her attention. Forte, fortissimo . . .

Suddenly, there was a knock at the door. "Come in," said Rana Jneid. A girl named Sandybell came in. She was older than me, a proper young lady. She wore a dress and high heels. I had heard that her father owned a paint factory. Sandybell was one of the privileged kids who were dropped off here by a chauffeur. Her parents had been nonchalant enough to name her after a cartoon character: *Hello! Sandybell* was a popular manga show.

Out of nowhere, Rana Jneid acted like a completely different person. She smiled at Sandybell. "How nice to see you," she gushed. Then she discussed Sandybell's next private lesson with her.

Sandybell left, and at once, Rana Jneid's warmth was gone. She motioned for me to keep playing while she turned her attention back to her cell phone.

I was deeply annoyed. What gave her the right to treat me like a second-class citizen? To act like I was worthless? Why did I have to deal with her status issues?

I remember running into Sandybell one other time. Again, I had a lesson with Rana Jneid in the small practice room. But I kept making the same mistake, always at the same place. Rana Jneid lost it. "You're an idiot!" she called out. "You just don't understand! C major! Not C minor!"

She threw the music sheets off the music stand. The sheets hovered in the air for a moment, then they gently slid to the ground.

I began gathering them. As I was crawling on the floor, there was a knock at the door. Sandybell entered. At first, I only saw her expensive pumps. She gave no indication that she even noticed me. She only wanted to know when her next private lesson was scheduled. Then she left. By then, I had collected all the sheets. But Rana Jneid ended the lesson. "You need to practice more!" she snapped at me.

For two years, Rana Jneid bullied me. I never heard a single word of encouragement from her. On several occasions, she told me to simply quit the piano, that I just wasn't good enough. I told my father. He went with me to the next lesson. He wanted to talk to her. He even brought her a little gift.

"Please be understanding of Aeham," my father said, oozing charm. "I promise you, he will practice more." But even his efforts only improved her behavior for a short while.

The music school made me unhappy. I didn't like going there. I simply didn't belong in that world.

After two years, my father gave in and sought a meeting with the school's deputy principal.

"Please don't misunderstand," he began. "Rana Jneid is an excellent piano teacher. But somehow, she and Aeham don't click. Would it be possible to assign him a different teacher?"

The music school charged no tuition, which meant that you couldn't make any demands. The man pondered what my father had said.

"Really, it's entirely our fault," my father cooed. "My son simply can't understand her, but he so desperately wants to continue his musical education."

I was assigned a new piano teacher.

Her name was Cosette Bakir—I wondered if her parents had named her after the character in Victor Hugo's *Les Misérables*. She was no better. Bakir had studied in France, but she was a terrible pianist. She played choppily, like a child. On top of that, she was condescending and unfriendly. One time, while playing a piece by Mozart, I made a mistake, and she hissed at me, "Again!" I made the same mistake. Her voice grew harsher: "You don't understand. Again." I made the mistake a third time. "Why do you keep making the same error?" she snapped at me. "What are you, some kind of parrot?"

No small wonder that I was grateful for Irina Ramadan. She was the piano player who was married to my father's friend and through whom we bought the piano. Irina had studied at the Tchaikovsky National Music Academy in Kiev, before she met her husband and moved to Damascus with him. She was tall, blond, and elegant. She didn't work and had no children. Maybe that was the reason why she treated me like her own son. *"Chhhhhabibi,"* she called me lovingly, drawing out the "ch" with her thick Russian accent.

She taught me the true meaning of music. She taught me how to listen to the pieces, how to find their exuberance or melancholy. With her, I forgot my joyless Syrian teachers who only paid attention to my mistakes, who seemed intent on smothering any joy I might take in music. Her fingers rushed playfully and boisterously across the piano keys. Music that had seemed stifling suddenly became free of heart. With her, I felt my playing become lighter and unconstrained, like the effortless flow of a Mozart sonata.

"Bach is like our daily bread," Irina Ramadan impressed upon me. "He's the foundation of everything. Without Bach, something is missing."

Another time, she told me, "You can't own Beethoven. You can only explore Beethoven."

Or: "Keep playing Czerny, you'll learn a lot about composition."

One day, when I came to her, I saw her drinking a red juice.

"Irina, may I have some of that juice?" I asked.

"No," she said. "It's not good for children."

"Then why do you drink it?"

"Because I like it. Let's get started now."

"But if it's not good for children, it can't be good for grown-ups either."

"Enough. Let's play."

Now I was curious. I kept asking her about the mysterious juice, but she always evaded my questions. Finally, I asked my father about the red juice. Why was it so alluring to grown-ups but bad for children? He laughed out loud. "Aeham, she was drinking wine! Alcohol!" So that was it! Alcohol. My father never touched that mystery juice.

I visited her every Monday for five years. When you're that young, your teacher is everything to you. If you like your teacher, you give it your best. If you don't like your teacher, you lose your passion. "Very good, Aeham," Irina Ramadan said, full of praise. Then she rewarded me with a piece of dark Russian chocolate. "*Chhhhhabibi*, before your next test, eat a piece of chocolate, it will make you happy."

At long last, she had to return to her home country. During our final lesson, she had tears in her eyes. "Promise me that you'll never give up music," she said. "Music is a miracle; it will always be there for you." I nodded.

"And promise me that you'll never forget me." I promised.

— CHAPTER THREE —

Every day, my mother and I went to the same elementary school. She was a teacher there, and I was a student. For me, this was highly problematic. I stuck out. Is he dressed properly? Did he comb his hair? Did he do his homework? Ugh! I wanted to be just like the others. But it was impossible. Whenever I misbehaved in class, my teacher would scold me: "I'll tell your mother."—"Why can't you tell my father?" I would say. "Like the other kids?"

Syrian schools had an almost military feel to them. If you forgot your homework, if you disrupted class or if you caused any trouble, you had to hold out both hands, palms up. Then you were given a few whacks with a small cane. After each recess there was a muster. We had to line up and stand straight while the principal made an announcement.

And each Saturday morning—the first weekday in Syria—we all had to gather to salute the flag and sing the Syrian national anthem. I would sit at a keyboard on a small stage and play the melody. Fifteen hundred boys were singing:

The great blossoming plains of Syria are like noble towers
They touch the highest sky
Such a land that blossoms in its glowing suns
Is like heaven itself

I didn't like this kind of music. All that clanging brass reminded me of military marches. But what could I do? I was the only keyboard player in the school, not to mention the son of a teacher. I couldn't very well back out.

One day, during recess, I got into a fight with another boy. He pushed me, I pushed him back, and soon we were both tussling. He ended up falling down and hurting his face. He touched his bleeding lip—and pulled half a tooth from his mouth. Crying, he ran to a teacher.

At the end of the next recess, we were standing in line, and my mother got on the small stage, held up my opponent's tiny piece of tooth, and said, "Aeham has hurt one of the other boys. As you know, he is my son. Therefore, it is up to me to punish him."

I stepped forward, tears in my eyes. "But he started it," I said pleadingly. "If someone pushes you, you come to me," my mother replied. "But you can't just start fighting." Then I had to hold out the palms of my hands, and she administered three short strokes with a small cane. In front of everyone.

I went back to my class, crying. It didn't hurt much at all, but I felt humiliated. How could my own mother do this to me?

In the afternoon, when we were home, I cried and asked her why she had done this. "I had to, Aeham," she said. "Or they would have thought that I favor you. And that would have been very bad for both of us." Wait, what? I had no idea what she was talking about.

The next Sunday, everything was as it used be. The boys were singing, I sat at the keyboard, the flag was raised. When the final chords had faded, my mother went to the microphone and said, "Aeham has been accompanying us on the keyboard for two years now, and he's been doing a very good job. We should thank him for playing." She began to clap. Fifteen hundred boys joined in.

For the first time in my life people applauded me. Did I enjoy it? I'm not sure anymore.

After sixth grade, I went to middle school. The principal was a terrible man, quick-tempered and always eager to yell at people. The teachers were afraid of his explosive rage, and the students were terrified of his punishments. The school was financed by the UNRWA, which meant there was no compelling reason to play the Syrian national anthem. But the principal insisted. He was Palestinian, but he was so eager to assimilate that he had even joined Assad's Baath Party. Each Saturday morning, the students stood ramrod straight in the schoolyard, singing the national anthem, accompanied by a trumpeter, a drummer, and a keyboard player—me. It seemed I just couldn't escape the marching music I hated so much.

One morning I came too late. I had bought sweets by the school gate and had forgotten about the time. Then I saw that the gate was closed. Any other student could have simply climbed over the wall and discreetly taken his place in the row of pupils. No one would have noticed. But not me. "Where is Aeham Ahmad?" the principal called from the stage. He summoned my homeroom teacher, but he could only shrug his shoulders. "How dare he come late!" the principal said, enraged.

That's what the others had told me. While all this was going on, I was still outside, banging against the school gate. Finally, the groundskeeper came. "I'm the keyboard player," I said. "Please let me in!" He reluctantly opened the gate and walked me toward the stage. The principal glared at me, his eyes gleaming with rage. "How dare you come too late!" He nearly leapt at me. "This is an affront! The hymn celebrates our country!"

"It's not our country," I murmured.

"What?" the principal snapped. But he had heard me loud and clear. And probably the others had as well, because the microphones were turned on. A second affront in one day. He launched into a lengthy discourse. Syria! Homeland! Acceptance! Integration!

Fatherland! And so on and so on. When he was finished, he ordered us to sing the hymn. He led with a forceful voice:

Guardians of our homeland, peace be upon you
Our proud spirit can never be conquered
The native home of Arabism is a sacred shrine
As the throne of the sun is an invincible kingdom

Two hours later I heard an announcement on the PA: "Aeham Ahmad, please come to the principal's office." Was I afraid? No. What could possibly happen? The worst-case scenario was that he would ask my father to come in and that he would complain about me. Other children might shake in their boots at the thought, because their fathers would let them have it. But I knew Papa would be on my side.

Just as he had been before. One time, during music class, I had refused to play Middle Eastern music. That afternoon I had an exam at the music school, and it was just too much to try to squeeze these two completely different musical systems into my brain. Like I said: In the Western world, an octave is divided into twelve half tones, and in the Eastern Hemisphere into eighteen quarter tones, which is why classical Arabic music can't be played on a piano or a guitar. In my view, it was very reasonable to not play Arabic harmonies that day. But my music teacher was irate, and the principal summoned my father.

A short while later, Papa was in the principal's office. He agreed with the music teacher on all points. "Yes," he said. "Aeham has made a mistake. He shouldn't have refused, and it won't happen again. Thank you for teaching him Arabic music."

But when we walked home together a little later, he said to me, "You can do what you want, but be respectful to your teachers."

This kind of support was an incredible gift. I was allowed my own opinion, and I didn't have to fear his wrath.

The door to the principal's office was open. I went in and stood in front of his desk. Of course, no one offered me a seat. The principal launched into yet another political lecture, and it was considerably longer than the first. Hospitality! Gratitude! Friendship between nations! And so on. Once again, I wasn't paying any attention.

On the principal's desk were three small flags: the Palestinian flag, the Syrian flag, and one more flag that I didn't recognize. It was dark blue, with a circle of yellow stars in the middle. Whose flag was that?

When the principal had finished his tirade, I asked him about it. "Oh, that's the flag of the European Union," he told me. "Our school receives funding from Europe." Europe? "Great!" I said. "I should play the European anthem next time!"

I knew the piece well—I had practiced it in my piano lessons. Beethoven's "Ode to Joy." I loved its blissful exuberance. It was so different from the plodding militarism of the Syrian national anthem.

"Or I could play a piece by Mozart," I said, getting carried away. "The 'Rondo alla Turca'! Mozart's Piano Sonata no. 11, third movement, 'The Turkish March,' one of his best-known melodies. It's so buoyant!"

"Out of the question!" the principal said.

"Let me try it," I insisted. "Do you know the 'Rondo alla Turca'? It's wonderful."

The principal stared at me, enraged that I dared to contradict him. I wanted to provoke him, of course, but what could he possibly do? I was being friendly and respectful, and all I'd done was suggest playing classical music. Europe! Mozart! That wasn't something the principal could punish me for. So he sent me away.

A few Saturdays later, I actually went through with it. I just couldn't help myself. The students were lined up, standing straight, and we three musicians were playing the Syrian national anthem. The brass was clanging, the flag was flying. But when it was over, I simply continued playing—Mozart's "Rondo alla Turca," bouncy and delicate. Many of the students laughed, and it seemed that the military strictness was crumbling.

"Aeham! Stop it!" my music teacher hissed at me. "Right now! Stop it at once!"

I stopped. Did the principal realize what I had done? I couldn't be sure. He began giving his weekly speech. Order! Discipline! Punctuality! He didn't appear to have noticed.

"I hate practicing!"

"Stupid piano!"

"I want to be like other kids!"

"I'm a Palestinian. What do I care about Mozart?"

"I want to play soccer with the others!"

This happened more and more often. The older I became, the less I felt like practicing piano. One afternoon when I was in middle school, I complained:

"I need more free time! I don't want to play anymore! I hate my teachers, I hate the music school, I hate music. I hate that damn piano!"

My father was silent.

"I'm not a machine!" I fumed. "Every day it's the same thing! Practice, practice, practice. Can't you say something else for a change?"

"Don't talk like that to me," my father said.

"You're blind," I snapped at him. "What do you know? You can't even play soccer."

"You're hurting my feelings," my father said. "Stop it."

"I'm going outside to play soccer," I told him.

My father thought about it for a moment, then said, "I'll join you."

"You? You want to play soccer?"

He insisted. We went down to the street. Some of my friends were already there, kicking a ball around.

"I'll be the goalie," my father said.

And he was. I cautiously kicked the ball in his direction. At that moment, he jerked his body around—and deflected! Next came a low shot—goal! Then a medium shot—he heard it coming and caught it. He was able to deflect several balls like that. I couldn't believe it.

"You see?" he said after the game. "I'm blind, but I can still catch a ball. Anyone can play soccer." I looked at his glasses in embarrassment. "But not anyone can play piano. I want you to come on up and continue practicing." So I did.

A few months later I was sitting at the piano and didn't feel like practicing. Again. I was irritated, and slammed my palm down on the instrument. "I don't want to be a pianist!" I ranted. "I want to be a normal kid! Who the hell goes to that music school? Rich kids! A chauffeur drops them off. And me? Everybody hates me. I don't want to do it anymore! I've had enough."

My father got up and left the room, then I heard him going downstairs. A short while later he returned with some of my friends who'd been playing soccer.

He turned to them. "I'll give anyone who can play something on the piano ten pounds."

The first kid sat down at the piano. "I can't play," he said. "Try anyway," my father encouraged him. "Just play a little something." The boy had never seen a piano before, and he plunked around a little. Then the next kid took his seat. All of them had heard me practice when they were playing soccer outside, and knew how effortlessly I played "Für Elise," my fingers practically flying across the keys.

When the boys had left, my father said. "You should be proud of your achievements." I was silent. His medicine had an effect. At least for a few months.

With each day in middle school, our concentration slipped as our thoughts began spiraling more and more around one specific topic:

girls. Who were they? What were they thinking? How could we meet them? Would they like us? How could we impress them? Did you see *this* girl, *that* girl? What should I say to her? And what happens next?

Before school, after school, during recess—soon, we boys talked about nothing else. Girls! We were all feverishly looking forward to eighth grade, when sex ed was on the curriculum and the teachers would explain to us how children were made.

I participated eagerly in those discussions, but I didn't quite understand all the commotion. To me, girls were much less mysterious. After all, I constantly met them at the music school, I sang with them in the choir, I stood in line with them while waiting to take a test.

The girls' school was on the same street as the all-boys school. When classes ended at noon, life began. We burst out of the school gate, babbling wildly. Some of the boys tore off their dark brown school shirts, revealing colorful T-shirts. Others put gel in their hair and walked around in front of the girls' school.

The girls came out of the gate, just as eager as we were. Some wore headscarves, some didn't—it all depended on the girl and her family. Some took out their makeup mirrors and put on powder and lipstick. Both hair gel and lipstick were strictly prohibited inside the school.

The boys whistled at the girls, the girls giggled, and some of the more daring boys went over to talk to them. The most adventurous among us soon had girlfriends. Having a girlfriend meant that you were allowed to accompany a girl on her way home and talk to her. But sometimes a girl changed her mind, first going out with one boy, then with another. And sometimes the boys got into a fistfight over the femme fatale, who enjoyed being the center of attention.

I admired the other boys. But I just wasn't able to emulate them. Colorful T-shirts? Hair gel? That wasn't me. My pants and shirts were as dull as my haircut. Instead of sending me to a barbershop, my father cut my hair himself. I had a bowl cut, and felt like a donkey among horses.

But one day on my way home, I saw a girl who caught my eye. She wasn't the prettiest one, and she didn't wear as much makeup as the others. Perhaps she didn't feel the need to be the center of attention. I liked that. Maybe she wasn't all that different from me. She always walked home by herself, looking around absentmindedly, as if in a dream. One day our eyes met, and she quickly averted her gaze. My heart seemed to burst. Should I dare speak to her? If so, when? I took heart and went over to her.

"*Marhaba,*" I said to her, hello. She stared at the ground. She seemed very shy, but at least she had stopped walking.

"Marhaba," I said again, and held out my hand.

"My father says I'm not supposed to shake hands with boys."

"You know, I go to a music school, and girls and boys are in the same class. We always shake hands. There's nothing to it."

"No, I can't," she said, then turned around and walked off.

I went home blushing. I had finally approached a girl! But I'd been rejected. It felt like someone had slammed a door in my face. After that, I gave up trying.

I became lazy and sullen again about practicing. "What good does it do, playing the piano?" I snapped at my father one afternoon. "What good is it? Why should I care about Mozart?"

"I want you to learn a language anyone can understand," my father said. "We're refugees. We can't return to our homeland. I want you to be international."

"But we live in Yarmouk! In Yarmouk! In Syria." I'd had enough. "I quit," I said, standing up and slamming the piano lid down.

My father stayed calm. He always stayed calm. He thought for a moment, then he said, "You're coming with me tonight. We'll play at a wedding together. Be ready at around six."

Right, I thought. Some kind of joke. I didn't believe him and went outside to join my friends. But at six o'clock, he said, "Let's go."

"I'm tired, I don't feel like it," I said.

Suddenly, he yelled at me. It was one of the few times in his life he had done that. "You're coming with me!" he said, explosively loud. I got scared and gave in. So we went.

At a Palestinian wedding, women and men celebrate separately. The groom joins his friends and the men of the family on the one side; the other side is reserved for the bride and her girlfriends, the mother, aunts, and cousins. Both men and women dance the *dabkeh*, but apart from each other. The dabkeh is an Arabic line dance, popular all across the Eastern Mediterranean. The dancers grab each other's hands and shoulders, undulating back and forth, and forming a line through the room.

The wedding took place on a rooftop terrace. It was a mild night in May. Several hundred men had come. I set up my keyboard. I was happy to see al-Chadra there, the man who had given me my first music lessons. When the band was ready, my father took the microphone. "We are proud to present our new keyboard player tonight, Aeham Ahmad," he said, and gestured toward me. Some of the men applauded, but others were jeering: "He's just a kid! Since when do kids play at weddings?" My father just grinned.

I didn't know any of the songs. There was no sheet music, and we had never practiced together. "No problem," my father had said. "When I give you the signal, you just play chords: A minor, C major, A minor, C major, and so on. Most of the songs are based on those two chords. When I give you the next signal, you take a pause."

We began. I played A minor and C major chords until my father nodded at me. I paused and looked at the men, all of them dancing exuberantly. My first performance! I had the jitters, but I loved it, I loved the attention. It felt great to see everyone dancing to our music. Then came my father's next signal: A minor, C major, A minor.

Around midnight, my father and I went home. He put two hundred and fifty Syrian pounds into the palm of my hand, almost five dollars. My first wages! I was beaming. Everyone had clapped for me, and on top of that I had earned money! I decided to buy a new soccer ball.

However, at the end of the night, I realized that my father had turned the volume of my keyboard almost completely down. No one had heard me. But I didn't care. The performance, playing in a band . . . I had loved every moment of it.

I spontaneously decided to become a wedding musician. For weeks and months, I pleaded with my father to take me with him again. "Good idea, Aeham, we'll do that," he said. But when the time came, there was always a reason why it wouldn't work that night. But next time! Promise!

In the end, he never took me to another wedding again. But he had managed for me to make my peace with music. I hated playing the piano a little bit less. And I continued practicing.

— CHAPTER FOUR —

Meanwhile, my father had become a sought-after piano tuner. He had an excellent ear, he charged reasonable prices, and it didn't take him six months to show up for work. I often went with him. First, I brought him to his customers and then I tested the piano he had just tuned, to hear how it sounded. And this is how I learned about the world of Damascus's upper class. In Syria, wealthy people were cut off from the rest of the country, as if they were on a distant planet.

One day, we found ourselves in the salon of a man whose name inspired fear. One of the men who had done the dirty work for the old Assad. A man who had the blood of thousands on his hands.

Of course, I didn't know any of that back then. I only knew that my father was oddly tense that afternoon. We started our journey at an intersection outside Yarmouk. A huge BMW with tinted windows picked us up. My father took a seat in front; I sat in back. We drove off. I had never been in such a big car.

We passed the neighborhood where the music school was, then we drove uphill. In Damascus, the farther up the hill you live, the more money you have. The wealthiest live high up, on the slopes of Mount Qasioun. At the very top, Assad had one of his villas.

I had never been in this neighborhood before. The houses were set back from the street, the properties were larger than anything I had seen, and the lawns were deep green and well watered. The car stopped. A checkpoint. This was something else I hadn't seen before: armed men stopping us. Who were they? They didn't seem to be soldiers, but they also didn't look like ordinary policemen. The chauffeur lowered his window.

"Who are these guys?" one of the armed men asked. He seemed to be in charge.

"A blind man and his son. They're supposed to tune the boss's piano," replied the chauffeur. The commander motioned for us to get out. He started with my father. Papa had to take off his jacket, crouch down, and open his mouth wide.

Then he was allowed to get back in the car.

The commander turned to me: "Why are you here?"

"I'm guiding my father."

"Where are you from?"

"Yarmouk."

"I still don't get it," he said. "Why is your father bringing you?"

"I'm supposed to play the piano, to test the sound."

He seemed interested in that; he wanted to know where I studied. Then he asked, "Are you Palestinian?"

"My father is. I guess that means I am as well."

He grinned. I was allowed to get back in the car.

We drove on, and after a while came another roadblock. Once again, it was manned by armed guards in strange uniforms. This time, they said we could stay in the car, but the chauffeur had to get out. The men patted him down. He had to open the trunk, and one of the guards examined the underside of the car with a mirror, like the kind dentists use, only much larger. I was surprised—wasn't the chauffeur one of them?

We drove on. I saw men with Kalashnikov rifles standing at the street corners. We stopped at a wrought-iron gate with gilded ornamental spires. Two armed guards opened the gate from the inside. The car came to a halt in front of a second, massive fence made of metal. The chauffeur brought us to a door. The door was opened from inside. I heard several loud snapping and clicking noises as the dead bolts were opened one after the other. We entered—and found ourselves in Europe.

Two smiling women greeted us. One of them was blond. They both wore their hair uncovered. The lawn was perfectly manicured. In the back, I could see a swimming pool. There were several luxury cars in the parking lot, Mercedes and BMWs. The two women led the way. I took my father by the hand. We entered the house through arches overgrown with roses.

I could feel my father's tension. He was petrified. But there was no way out. It would seem suspicious if we turned back now.

The entrance hall had floors of white marble, and paintings of idyllic landscapes adorning the walls. To the left was a bar with colorful liquor bottles; farther to the back was a statue. Its hand was broken off. It seemed to be thousands of years old. On the left and right sides of the room, a vast set of stairs led to the second floor. And in the middle of the entrance hall stood a huge concert piano.

I had never seen an instrument like this. It was a Steinway Model D, worth almost two hundred thousand dollars, made in Hamburg and New York. This was the instrument we were supposed to tune. My father opened the piano cover and braced it. I opened the lid and played a sonatina by Mozart. The piano sounded crisp and clear. No comparison to that old music box we had at home.

Then I noticed a change in the air. The two women suddenly straightened. I paused. A man came down the right side of the stairs leading a girl by the hand. She had red hair and was dressed in a sweatsuit. The man had a gray mustache and gray, slicked-back hair, and was wearing a black suit and a white shirt.

He slowly clapped his hands. "Bravo, bravo!" he called. "Welcome! How are you?" He approached me and shook my hand.

"I'm Aeham Ahmad, and that's my father," I hastily replied. The man looked only at me, not my father. It made me uncomfortable.

"Where did you learn to play piano so well?" he asked me.

I told him of the music school.

"Excellent!" he boomed. "So young, and such a fine pianist already."

He asked me a few more questions, then finally turned to my father and shook his hand.

Sometimes it seemed my father couldn't hide his feelings very well. Maybe because he was blind. In any case, I could always tell what he was thinking; his face was like an open book to me. And I knew that, in this moment, he was afraid. He tried to hide it. He reminded me of a turtle pulling its head in. He didn't want to talk, he wanted to do his job and not make any mistakes. He just wanted to get out of here in one piece.

"The piano is excellently tuned," my father said cautiously.

Not really, the man explained, which was why we were supposed to tune it again. Also, one of the hammers was defective, could we please take a look at it?

"The two ladies"—they flinched when they heard this—"will take care of you."

Then he turned away and went back up the stairs. The girl in the sweatsuit, probably his granddaughter, stayed downstairs. She sat on one of the steps and looked at us.

My father began his work, silently and stoically. I handed him the tools. I could feel his tension. I had no idea who this man was, but judging by my father's discomfort, he must have been dangerous. My father repaired the hammer and began tuning the piano. He plucked a string, listened to its sound, and adjusted it with his tuning key.

The red-haired girl kept watching us. Every once in a while, I would look at her, our eyes would meet, and then I would quickly look away again.

For three hours, my father worked in silence. The blond woman served us orange juice in heavy crystal glasses. Then, as we packed up our things, the girl approached us.

"Is it your piano?" I asked.

She nodded and sat down on the piano bench.

"Where are you taking classes?"

"A teacher comes to the house."

"How long have you been playing?"

"About a year and a half." She began playing a song. It sounded amateurish.

Again, I was surprised. A private instructor, an expensive piano—why wasn't she able to play better?

The owner of the house must have heard us talking, and came downstairs and stood behind the girl. My father explained what he had done.

"Very good," said the man. "What do I owe you?"

"It's all right. Thank you for allowing us to visit you," my father said.

"I'm certain your boy could use the money, even if you can't."

The man pulled out his wallet, took out a bundle of bills, and handed it to me. I was surprised, but I took the money.

We said good-bye, then we were driven back. My father and I were both silent. I didn't dare give him the money; I was afraid the chauffeur would see it. He might tell his employer, and he in turn might become angry because he had given the money to me, not my father. So I didn't move. But once we were at home, in our living room, I handed my father the bills. They were moist from my sweat. The man had paid us twenty thousand Syrian pounds, almost four hundred dollars. For us, it was a fortune.

My father began to pump me for information. He wanted to know everything. What did the man look like? What did the house look like? The two women? The guards at the checkpoints? Did I notice anything else?

"This man is dangerous. Don't talk to anyone about this," he implored me. "Not to anyone! In Syria, the walls have ears."

It was a popular saying. We all knew that state security was everywhere. Just one disparaging remark about a minor government bureaucrat was enough to get people arrested. Some victims languished for years in the government's torture chambers. And there was another saying, "Not even God himself would dare to slander Hafez al-Assad."

I asked my father what the man's name was.

"One day I'll tell you. But not now," my father said.

Years later, I learned his name, Mustafa Tlas. From 1972 to 2004 he had been Syria's secretary of defense, one of the old Assad's closest confidants. He was known to spread hideous anti-Semitic conspiracy theories and was said to have made a fortune smuggling weapons and antiques.

Our visit to his villa had intimidated me so much that for months, I believed government spies were watching us. After all, we had been in the boss's house. Had we made a mistake? Had we become suspicious? Every time I stepped outside, I kept an eye out for anyone observing us. But I never saw anyone.

— CHAPTER FIVE —

For more than six years my father accompanied me to the music school. The bus left Yarmouk and drove through a new development called Zahira, then past the gigantic Midan market and the junkyards of Senaa, an industrial part of town. At Baramkeh Circle we switched to another bus, continuing through the downtown area, past the university, changing buses again at the President Bridge, crossing the Barada River—no more than a thin trickle in summer, but in winter a mighty stream. Finally, on our third bus, we entered the elegant embassy district, where the music school was located.

We were used to traffic jams. Often, the bus moved at a snail's pace. On some days, nothing moved. If, for example, there was an accident somewhere, then all the drivers were stuck, furiously leaning on their car horns. The heat made the road seem blurry, and we would be sitting in our minibus, drenched in sweat, wedged between other sweaty passengers. Everyone was getting more and more nervous, because everyone was missing their appointments. In my mind, I could already hear my piano teacher scolding me. The minutes were ticking away ever so slowly.

Then we decided to get out. We had to somehow get around the traffic jam. We pushed open the bus door and snaked our way through the sea of cars. Sometimes it took us half an hour to reach the source of the traffic jam—the accident. Usually, we saw dented cars, bystanders, and two men screaming at each other. The traffic police always took the side of the man paying the highest bribe.

Sometimes the opponents even attacked each other with their fists. We hurried on to the next bus.

At the end of each semester, students at the music school had to give a recital. You could only fail it once. My father and I tried our best to be on time. But one time, I must have been eleven years old, traffic was more hellish than ever and we moved forward inch by inch. When the bus arrived, I jumped out and ran into the school building, then bounded up the stairs.

A lady was descending toward me, elegantly dressed. I knew her: Colette Khoury, granddaughter of the former prime minister. She was a famous writer of feminist novels as well as a board member of the school.

"Why are you running like this?" she asked as I tried to rush past her, flushed and sweating.

"I have an exam, I'm much too late," I said, wheezing.

"You need to catch your breath." She looked me up and down. "You can't play like this. I'll talk to your teachers."

She went into the examination room and announced that Aeham Ahmad—A.A., always first in the alphabet—would play after the letter *C* today. Then she smiled at me and left.

There weren't many days when I liked being at the school, but that was definitely one of them.

At age eleven, I was assigned a new piano teacher at the school, my third one. Like my earlier teacher, her name was also Irina and she was from Russia, but her last name was Boloushouk. Ever since Syria's independence in 1946, our country had had close ties— diplomatic, military, and cultural—to the Soviet Union, and later to the Russian Federation. I liked Ms. Boloushouk. She was very friendly. Her Arabic was terrible, but she always smiled at me. Sometimes she asked me to write down what she said on a notepad, and she thanked me by giving me pieces of Russian chocolate. Just like Irina Ramadan used to do.

One of the first things she did was this: She hung a clock above the piano in her practice room. She didn't like it when people were late. In the Middle East, time is a flexible thing. Someone says they'll visit sometime in the afternoon, but then doesn't arrive until 6 p.m. I never liked that. Irina Boloushouk wouldn't accept it either. On the other hand, if the Damascus traffic had once again collapsed completely and I rushed into the room covered in sweat, then she told me in a kind voice, "It's all right, Aeham. Take a deep breath and tell me how you are today!"

Because it wasn't easy to get my bearings after a journey like that. Playing the piano is hard work, even for the most talented musicians, and I never was one of those. If you're tense, you just can't get the sound right. Then your playing becomes robotic and dry; you stumble through the music with stiff hands. Each attempt to wrestle with a piece of music is doomed to failure.

So. Once more, from the beginning. Take a breath. Relax your joints, let your hands go soft, let them hover above the black-and-white landscape of the octaves, loose and free. Let your fingers gently descend. Find the right moment, let the current of the music take you. Let it become your heartbeat. Throw your fingers onto the keys like an artist splashing paint.

By that time, I had learned to play more sophisticated pieces. For six months, Irina Boloushouk had me practice Rachmaninoff's Prelude in G minor, op. 23, no. 5, a difficult piece with a complex rhythm. The prelude seemed to dance across the keyboard from bass notes to treble, through all keys and tonalities. My hands had to perform countless seamless transitions, and it was exhausting just to hit the right keys, like mastering a high-wire act.

Day by day, I worked on the piece, line by line. First, I only sang the notes. Then I worked on the left hand. Slowly. Then a little faster. Then the right hand. Then both hands, very slowly. A little faster. If I made a mistake, I had to start over. And over, and over, and over. Twenty, thirty, a hundred times. Then on to the next line. Then the next sheet. Then I had to put it all together. Another mistake! Start over. Try making it sound more alive. Week in, week out. It was like building a house from pebbles.

When I was thirteen, my father bought me a cheap mountain bike, fairly sluggish and with small, twenty-inch tires. Most of the time I had to ride standing up, and that is how I got to school from then on, 7.5 miles across the city. Riding a bike in Damascus was extremely dangerous. Cars and minibuses were jostling all around, and I was right in the middle of it all. It was glorious.

Because from then on, I didn't have to sit idly in the bus anymore, sweating nervously. From then on, I could just keep pedaling and have a good idea when I'd arrive. It took me an hour and forty minutes to get there. My father still gave me money for the bus fare. He said to keep it, a bit of extra pocket money.

Only once did I miss school—when a minibus cut in front of me and I ran into it. The bus's rear light was damaged, and so was my front tire. But I was unharmed. The driver was angry. I gave him all the money I had on me, then I pushed my bike back home. There was no point in going to class after this. But apart from that, I was always on time. During the last year of school, a teacher named Vladimir Tsaritzky asked me if I wanted to be his student. He taught at the conservatory as well. I felt honored, and I happily agreed. He was a hulking giant, around sixty, with green eyes and blond hair and the build of a wrestler. He wore his shirts partially open and I could see a white wooden crucifix buried in his chest hair. He was an Orthodox Christian. And he had a weakness for women. Whenever Sandybell came clicking past in her high heels, he stared after her with hungry eyes.

I liked him. He was an excellent pianist and was very direct, wearing his heart on his sleeve. He wasn't as two-faced as many of my countrymen. In Syria, people will smile at you and stab you in the back. With Tsaritzky, I began enjoying classical music again, sonatas by Mozart and Beethoven, and études by Czerny. There was no getting away from Czerny. Tsaritzky made me start from scratch, beginning with my basic technique. We played scales and arpeggios, and we worked on my articulation. Too much staccato on your left! Try using it like a bow. Place your hand lower, put your thumb and fingers a little higher. This way, you can lower your arm, you don't have to keep hovering as you play. And lighter on the keystroke! Lead with your arms, the hands will follow. Things of that nature.

One time, we had our class at the conservatory. I could hear Tsaritzky from far away. He was hammering ecstatically at the keys. I knocked. The fortissimo continued; he didn't seem to have noticed me. I pushed down the door handle, went in, and took a seat. Tsaritzky was playing a Steinway piano, deeply and passionately. It was as if he was devouring the instrument. Each time he leaned forward, his wooden crucifix clicked against the piano. After a while, there was a loud snapping noise: one of the strings broke.

He stopped, then turned to me, as if awakening from a dream: "Hello, Aeham." And we began our class.

One time, I heard an announcement by Solhi al-Wadi, the school's all-powerful headmaster, coming over the loudspeakers: All students report to the lobby, please.

I went and took my place amid the crowd. Al-Wadi stood in front of a wall. I could see a footprint on it. Someone must have been standing there and leaning his foot against it.

"Who did that?" al-Wadi hissed. "This isn't your home! It's not my home either! This is the Damascus Music School! You have no right to ruin the walls like that. Who did this?"

No one came forward.

One after the other we had to step forward and lift our feet. Al-Wadi compared the soles of our shoes with the print on the wall. And he found the culprit, a young violin student, who turned pale with fear.

Al-Wadi delivered a long tirade—and expelled the boy.

In my tenth year at the music school, I had to take a final exam. Everything went wrong, absolutely everything. But in the end, it turned out all right. Or at least well enough. I learned a lesson from that.

The disaster began to unfold two days before the exam. Two of my uncles had a huge fight. I could hear them from my room, their angry, never-ending argument. Aunt Ibtihal still didn't like it when I practiced for hours. She no longer thumped the broom against my ceiling, but she stomped down the stairs and slammed the large door downstairs shut—so hard that the whole building shook. Then she stomped back up again.

It was summer. My exams were always in the summer. At around noon, the power sometimes went out, because everyone turned on their air conditioners. The light in my room went out, and the fan stopped working.

The bus drivers of Damascus always put towels around their necks, drenched in ice water, to cool down. I wasn't allowed to do that. My father had forbidden it, for fear of ruining the piano with water.

And then the old carpenter down the street, Abu Fathi, died. The funeral lasted three days. On the first day, hundreds of plastic chairs were carried outside and placed on the sidewalks in front of our buildings, so that everyone could see the body wrapped in a white shroud. Loudspeakers were set up, a sheikh read the obituary, and all day long, friends and neighbors came to pray. On the second and third day, they started playing prerecorded suras from the Quran over the loudspeakers. You could hear them throughout the whole neighborhood. It was unthinkable, of course, to interrupt a funeral with music. It was all right to play when a child was born, but music at a time of mourning would have been inappropriate.

On the fourth day, my father went over and explained the situation to Abu Fathi's son. He told him that I would have my final exam at the music school in a few days—would I be allowed to practice? He allowed it. My father closed all the windows and fastened the right pedal. Which meant that I was playing a muted piano in sauna-like conditions. It was impossible to practice the articulation of the pieces, and that would be a large part of my final grade.

In other words: I was miserably ill-prepared.

On the day of the exam, I left an hour early on my bicycle. I didn't want to arrive sweaty and out of breath.

But on the way there, the bicycle chain popped off. What could I do? I had to put it back on by hand. It popped off again. And again. When I finally arrived at the school, I hadn't only lost a lot of time—my fingers were now covered in oil.

As always, I parked my bike a few streets away; I didn't want anyone seeing it. Then I ran toward the school—and into Vladimir Tsaritzky, my teacher. He said hello and asked me if I felt ready. I shrugged. Then he noticed my fingers.

"Aeham! You can't go into an exam like that! Quick, wash your hands!" he called, and gave me a paper towel.

That was what I had been hoping to do! In about ten minutes, it would be my turn to play—I was always first. I ran through the building and into the bathroom. When I opened the faucet, nothing came out!

In the summer, the water was regularly turned off for a few hours each day. It could happen at any point. But did it have to happen now! I took the paper towel that Tsaritzky had given me and rubbed my fingers with it. But the oil wouldn't come off. So I rubbed my fingers on my pants, because you couldn't play with oily fingers. You'd leave oil on the keys.

Other kids came to their final exam freshly showered and in black suits. I entered the room dirty and sweaty. Six instructors were waiting for me.

"Aeham, what happened?" the new headmaster asked me.

Solhi al-Wadi had suffered a stroke several years ago. The new principal didn't just look like the old one, he was also just as stern.

"Nothing," I said.

"That's not true!" he said, sounding irritated. "Are you a mechanic now?"

I didn't respond.

"Well?" he went on. "What happened?"

So I told him. I explained that I had come here on my bike and my chain had popped off. That I had been biking here for the past three years.

For a moment, everything was silent. Then he stood up and approached me. I took a few cautious steps toward him, having no idea what to expect, and prepared for anything. But not this: he hugged me.

He must have been touched that I had biked for years all across town, just to be able to go to class. He must have understood how much effort it cost me just to be here. I was certainly not the most talented pianist, but I never gave up. Other kids took this school for granted. But my father and I had to fight for the privilege to come here. It seemed like at that moment he understood.

I was touched as well. All too often, I had felt rejected here. All too often, I had been made to feel like I didn't belong. Why hadn't someone hugged me earlier? I would have loved the school. I would have loved music.

The headmaster gave me a box of tissues. I continued cleaning my fingers, then I began playing my pieces, Czerny, Beethoven, Sibelius. In truth, I wasn't particularly good that day. But I did it. A few days later, I was surprised to learn that I had gotten a grade of 80. I couldn't believe it. There were other students who were better than me, and they had scored only 65. Was my grade a belated welcome?

On the way back home, I was in a great mood, feeling that something had ended and something new was beginning. I cheerfully worked the pedals of my bike as I made my way through the Damascus traffic. I felt free.

— CHAPTER SIX —

In the years before my final exam, as I was getting more and more unruly and less willing to practice the piano, my father had yet another brilliant idea: he began to pay me for practicing.

At the time, my friends got around seventy-five Syrian pounds each week for pocket money, a little more than ten cents. It was enough money to snack on falafel three times a week. My father paid me the same amount for each hour of piano practice, treating it like paid work. If I practiced a lot, I could easily make over a thousand Syrian pounds a week, almost two dollars. I suddenly had as much pocket money as a rich kid. The money was enticing. So I began playing more.

But becoming a musician? I never considered that for one second. I wanted to build a house, get married, start a family. For some reason I had the idea of buying property in Dili, in the south of Syria, where my father was born and where my grandfather, after fleeing from Palestine, had leased his first plot of land. I wanted to go back to my roots, even though we had all been uprooted.

"I want to buy land with my savings," I said to my astonished father one night. But he didn't laugh; he asked me what I meant. Then he thought about it for a moment and said, in all seriousness, "All right, let's drive to Dili and look at property."

I had saved about twenty-five thousand Syrian pounds, almost fifty dollars, collecting the bills in a small box. During one of the next weekends, I took the money with me. We took a bus south and got off two hours later in Dili, at the gates of Daraa. For half an hour, we walked over dirt tracks, past olive groves and thorny bushes. My father had made an appointment with a man who had property for sale.

We greeted him. It's a good thing my father didn't tell him that I was the prospective buyer, for he probably would have laughed. No, Papa asked the man to explain everything, and then they negotiated the price. My father haggled him down to a hundred and fifty thousand Syrian pounds, about three hundred dollars.

I was speechless. So much money! For this far-flung, shabby plot of land! My savings would have probably bought no more than a few olive trees. On the ride back, I sat at the window, brooding, looking out over the dry landscape. But my father kept encouraging me. "Keep practicing piano, keep getting good grades. I'm planning on opening a music store. Then we can work together, and I can buy you an apartment."

What was he talking about? We had almost no money.

A few months later, he asked me to accompany him—he wanted to look at a store. Years ago, he had known a carpenter named Abu Nisar, who had applied for a job with him. But Abu Nisar didn't want to hire a blind man and had sent my father away. Now Abu Nisar had passed away. The carpenter's shop had shut down and the sons were arguing about the inheritance. The empty store was for sale, for a fraction of its worth.

By that time, real estate prices in Yarmouk had exploded. The former refugee camp had turned into a popular shopping area. People were competing for limited space to open new stores. Around 650,000 people lived in Yarmouk, and hundreds of thousands came every day to do their shopping. Yarmouk and Palestine Streets were full of brightly lit stores, one next to the other. Buying a medium-size storefront could cost you thirty million Syrian pounds, around sixty thousand dollars. Renting a store cost about two thousand dollars a year. Several building owners even rented out their entrance areas, that's how lucrative it was.

The fabric stores closed at midnight, electronics stores at 4 a.m., and the giant DVD shops and many restaurants were open all night. The *souq*—the market—was a spice mecca. Here, you could find aromas from all over the world. And that wasn't all. More than a hundred jewelers and gold traders were competing with one another. The scents of grilled street food hovered above the throngs of people. That was Yarmouk! Alive, vibrant, laughing, pulsating to the heartbeat of an unstoppable future.

The store we were going to see was on the other side of Yarmouk Street, in an area full of workshops—carpenters, locksmiths, blacksmiths. We met Abu Nisar's son in front of a dust-covered metal roll-up gate. Apparently, it hadn't been opened in years. He had a large key chain, and it took him a while to find the right key. He bent down, put it into the massive padlock—and nothing happened. He tried again. Nothing. The lock was rusty.

"Aeham, go and get some oil," my father said to me.

I went into the workshop next door, where they made aluminum window frames. I asked to borrow a small bottle of oil, then I brought it to Nisar. He put a few drops into the lock, tried again—and click! It opened. As he pushed up the rattling metal gate, my father smiled quietly. He saw with his ears, and evaluated rooms by sound. He seemed to like what he heard here.

The store was dark. I went inside—and stumbled. I had not seen the two steps leading downstairs into the workshop. Nisar walked ahead of me and turned on the light. I was amazed. The room was gigantic.

"Papa! This is much too large for my twenty-five thousand—" I started to say.

I didn't get any further. "Shhh," my father hissed at me. I understood. Nisar didn't need to know any of this.

We began inspecting the old workshop. Abu Nisar's sons had already sold all the machines. The floor was covered with wood shavings, and the walls were black from soot. Whenever it was cold, Abu Nisar had lit a fire in a barrel, then he had worked in the midst of all that soot and pollution. No wonder he had died at age fifty.

My father went through the room toward the right-hand wall.

"Careful," I said. "The wall is dirty."

But he continued. He felt the wall, put his ear against it, and listened. Then he went to the left wall and did the same thing. Again, he gave a knowing smile. We said good-bye to Nisar.

On the way back, he explained to me what he had done. He had wanted to check if he could hear the neighbors. If so, the walls were too thin and the neighbors might be bothered when we played music in the store. But he had heard nothing.

A few days later, Nisar came to sign the contract. Half of the purchase price had to be paid at once. I realized that my parents had been saving money for a long time. They had put the money in a wooden safety box that my father had built into their massive wardrobe. Now, in front of my astonished eyes, he put seven hundred and fifty thousand Syrian pounds—almost fifteen hundred dollars—on the table and asked me to sign the contract.

His father-in-law had lent him the money for the next payment. Like most Syrians, my grandfather didn't have a bank account. Instead, he had used his savings to buy gold and jewelry for his wife. He gave my father a gold chain worth another thirty-five thousand dollars. My father would have to repay him with a similar chain within one year.

We began renovating. My father had not a penny left, so we did everything ourselves. The floor was useless, and because Papa didn't want to compromise the height of the room, he and Uncle Sadik decided to tear the flooring out. Each Friday, Uncle Mohammed came to help us. They shoveled debris onto a pushcart, then my father and I brought it far outside Yarmouk, to a dumpster. It took an hour per load. After two loads, we were completely exhausted.

For half a year, we worked each weekend. My brother, Alaa, hardly did anything. Sometimes he tagged along and reluctantly helped a little for about an hour, then he would get into an argument with my parents and leave. One time, when friends of mine had come along to help and my brother sat around playing games on his cell phone, I confronted him. He angrily got up and shoved me to the ground.

"How can you do this?" I yelled. "In front of my friends!"

"You're not my boss!" he grumbled. And with that, he was gone.

How I miss those fights today!

When all the debris had been carted out, my father installed electrical wiring. A proper electrician could have done it in two days. My father needed several weeks. But it was the first time he had done anything like this. We painted the walls in three different colors, with leftover paint that an acquaintance had given us. Uncle Mohammed tiled the floor with bright granite. After that, the shopwindow was delivered. And last but not least, we put up a sign above the door. Two men attached it, and I looked on with pride: AEHAM'S MUSIC SHOP, it said, visible to everyone. My father solemnly handed me the keys.

The first thing we sold, a few days later, was a *risha*, a pick used for the strings of the Arabic oud. We sold it for five Syrian pounds, a little less than a cent. But a few years later, Aeham's Music Shop was booming, and we had hundreds of students. My father had 450 ouds built each month in a separate workspace, to be shipped to Dubai and from there all over the world. And we would always remember: It all began with a pick.

— CHAPTER SEVEN —

And then I discovered music. Previously, I had played piano only because my father wanted me to. I simply obeyed him, wanting to be a good son. And yes, there had been moments when I was gripped by ambition and tried my best to become a brilliant pianist. But in truth, it was never something I was passionate about.

But now, at age sixteen, I had an awakening. I suddenly understood that I had begun to learn a beautiful language. And now I wanted to explore it more deeply.

The year 2004 was to be a fateful one for me. I began going to high school, which was the most terrible place I had ever set foot in. The teachers were inept and the majority of the students were ignorant and brutal. All they thought about was getting laid and getting stoned. I skipped school as often as I could, climbing over the high wall. I would get on my bike and escape—to our store. In the mornings, the shop was closed, which meant I had a place of my own. An incredible luxury.

No one was ever alone in Yarmouk, the most crowded and noisy neighborhood in all of Damascus. Our apartment was small, and my brother and I shared a bunk bed—he was on top and I was on the bottom. Whenever I practiced piano, my father would listen in. The moment I played something other than Beethoven or Bach, he'd scold me: "Aeham, that will get you nowhere, please stick with classical music." In his view, playing piano wasn't meant to be fun. For him, it was serious business. He was always looking to the future—to the admissions test at the conservatory, which was still a few years away. So I had to play Beethoven and Bach. All day, every day. Jazz? Arabic music? A waste of time. "First, my son, you need to practice for the test," he said. "You can have fun later."

But when I was alone in our shop, I could play any music I wanted. Or all of it together, in my own pop-jazz-Arab fusion.

Just a short while ago, my father had had to cajole me into practicing. Now I couldn't get enough. On some days, I played for five hours.

My hero in those days was Ziad Rahbani, a political commentator and satirist from Lebanon, a gifted composer and a virtuoso jazz pianist. He had started at age sixteen, writing songs for his mother—Fairouz, the great diva from Beirut. I wanted to be like him. I began to dream: What if I became a musician after all? If I stood on huge stages, applause all around me?

Besides the changes in my own life, Syria, too, was changing dramatically. In 2000, when I was twelve, Hafez al-Assad died, and his son Bashar came to power. The dictatorship was just as brutal as before, and the torture chambers were as full as they'd ever been, but to some extent the regime loosened the chains a little bit. When the old Assad was in power, you could go to jail for even having a television antenna on your roof. They were afraid you might be watching foreign TV stations. Bashar was less strict. He allowed his subjects to watch satellite TV, buy cell phones, and surf the internet, even though many websites were blocked.

In 2003, when I was fifteen, the first season of *Star Academy* was shown on satellite TV. It was a casting show, produced in Beirut and broadcast all over the Arab world, from Mauritania to Iraq. Many people in Syria saw music as something dubious—God forbid you wanted to become a musician! But with *Star Academy* and later the Arabic *SuperStar*, a whole generation was swept up by the glamour of pop music. Countless young people suddenly wanted to learn an instrument—and suddenly, they all looked to me . . . a pianist.

My grades, meanwhile, were taking a nosedive. Until then, I

had been a halfway decent student—my mother had seen to that. My elementary and middle schools had been administered by the UN, and the teachers there made good salaries and were highly motivated. But at my new high school, the teachers were paid next to nothing, just like everywhere in Syria's state-run schools. They earned around five thousand Syrian pounds per month, around ten dollars. It was barely enough to live on. No wonder, then, that many teachers weren't particularly interested in their jobs. Many of them just wanted to get private students for after-school tutoring, since that's where the real money was.

My high school was located outside Yarmouk, and was attended by both Syrians and Palestinians. To me, it was like a jail. The only freedom you had was during recess, but you were constantly bullied. Some of the kids smoked hash; others secretly drank Armenian gin from a flask, or sipped "Simo"—a Syrian cough syrup whose effects were like codeine. The walls of the schoolyard were defaced with obscene words and drawings. And in the three years I went there, I only once dared to enter the bathrooms.

In the middle of the schoolyard was a basketball hoop. This is where the bully from my class administered his brutal punishments. His henchmen would grab you by the arms and legs and ram you—legs spread wide—against the pole of the hoop. I tried to stay away from these people. I avoided looking at them and tried my best to not cross paths with them. Still, one time, they got me.

"Hey, Aeham, what are you looking at!" one of the boys called. And then he said to his boss, "I think he needs a lesson."

"Yeah!" the boss cheerfully agreed. Then they grabbed my legs and dragged me to the pole. Luckily, no one was holding on to my arms, so I was able to cushion the impact with my hands. But it hurt for days.

This was their idea of fun. Sometimes, however, things would get serious. At times, someone would pull out a knife and cut their opponents, to teach them a lesson. Was there a teacher looking out for us? A principal who punished them? Nowhere in sight.

The bully from my class also bestowed a nickname on me. *Fijle,* he called me, Little Radish, because I was so small and skinny. Everyone called me that and I hated it.

But in one respect I was fortunate. Someone had chiseled some makeshift steps into the school wall, which turned out to be my escape from hell. Whenever things got tense and no one was looking, I'd climb over the wall, jump on my bike, and ride back to Yarmouk. There I would quietly push open the gate to our shop, unlock the glass door, slip inside, and relock the door, waiting until I reached the back of the store to turn on the light, since I was always afraid that someone would notice me. I put some water on to boil and made my first instant coffee of the day with "3 in 1," which also contained powdered milk and sugar. Then I opened the piano lid—and began my journey.

I have no idea how my father never noticed. But one day he went to my high school with Mohammed, my stern uncle, looking for me. The principal took them to my classroom and asked the teacher where I was. The teacher merely shrugged and said he hadn't seen Aeham Ahmad.

And how could he have? I was sitting in the store playing piano. Suddenly, my cell phone rang.

"Aeham, where are you?"

"Um . . . at school?"

"Where? We're standing outside your classroom with the principal."

"Oh . . . I'm in the bathroom," I said. "I'm not feeling well!"

"What are you talking about? Come here, at once!"

My thoughts were racing. I had to get to school, I had to protect my secret.

"I don't feel well," I said, moaning dramatically, as I locked up the store.

"Why didn't you tell your teacher?"

"I'm coming!"

I started biking. I ran several red lights, and I must have cut off countless cars. Seven minutes, eight minutes. After ten minutes, my father called again.

"Aeham! Where are you?" he snapped.

"The bathroom! I couldn't get the door to open!"

"What?"

"It's open! I'll be right there."

I locked up my bike, ran toward the wall, climbed to the top, swung myself over it—and found myself looking straight into the principal's face. He stared back at me, completely dumbfounded. He'd been searching for me out in the schoolyard and now approached me, menacingly tapping his cane.

"So, you're not feeling well," he growled. Then he grabbed my ear and dragged me to his office. Tears welled up in my eyes. It's over, I thought. They'll find out, and I'll never get out of this hell-hole again.

We entered the office, where my father and uncle were waiting for me. "Your son Aeham is a liar," the principal said. "He wasn't in the bathroom. I caught him climbing over the wall."

"Why have you been lying to us?" my father said, furious. "Where have you been?"

In my despair, I immediately confessed. I told him that I'd been hiding in our store. "You have no idea what it's like here. I can't take it anymore. People pick fights all the time, everyone smokes hash. I have no idea why I'm even here."

"What were you doing in our store?" my father asked.

"Playing piano."

"Do you do that often?"

"Yes."

Now the principal chimed in. Not to respond to my outburst, no, he was curious about the music. "What kind of store do you have?" he asked my father, who told him. Within minutes they were discussing wedding music, and realized—to everyone's delight—that they had a mutual friend from back in their university days. Not only that, but in two days they'd all be at the same wedding.

The principal reached for his phone and called the custodian. "Some tea, please!" he said. "Tea for the gentlemen!" Then we sat in his office and shared several cups of sweet black tea. I supposed that meant we were no longer enemies. While my father chatted ami- ably with the principal, my uncle whispered into my ear, "You're a bad person."

"Why?"

"You're not supposed to skip school, you're supposed to learn."

"You can't learn anything here."

When it came time to say good-bye, my father and the principal hugged each other. It was almost noon. I didn't have to go to class that day. The three of us went home.

"Why are you doing this?" my father asked.

Once again, I told him everything. About the bullies, the drugs, the inept teachers. How I hated this school!

"I won't punish you," my father said. "But you have to continue going to school. Please promise me you won't skip class anymore."

I thought about it for a moment, then I said, as diplomatically as I could, "I can't promise. But I'll try."

— CHAPTER EIGHT —

I continued to lead a double life. At school, I was still the pathetic little radish, avoiding the bullies as much as I could, smiling at them to avoid their cruel power games. But when I entered our store, I entered a new world. My world. A place full of discoveries.

Of course, I kept skipping school. I was much more careful now, but that was about the only thing that changed. From that day on, the principal regularly checked my attendance. Thankfully, he wasn't in school most of the time. I had no idea where he went, but all I had to do was casually walk past his office door and see if it was closed. If so, I was in the clear and could make my way toward the wall, then, as quick as lightning, climb over it, get on my bike, dash to our shop, and make myself a hot cup of 3 in 1. And finally take a deep breath.

I began to explore music more and more, some days playing for hours. I learned the names of certain chords and began varying the intervals: I'd play a note and explore different chords built on it, a seventh, a ninth, or an eleventh. Then I'd start rearranging the chords to see how that changed the effect.

Sometimes I just sat there, lost in thought. Imagining what life would be like if I were like the boys in my class, giving in to peer pressure, smoking hash and chasing after girls. Sometimes I thought of what it would be like to have my own family, a wife and children, and wondered if I would be a good father. Other times, I imagined being a famous musician, admired by others, flirting with women. Someone who wasn't a radish.

There were days when I simply listened to music. For hours and hours. The Taksim Trio, three gifted musicians from Istanbul, who blended Gypsy and Arabic music with jazz. Marcel Khalife, the virtuoso oud player and composer from Lebanon, who managed to play the ancient instrument in a stunningly new way, and who used music to rage against injustice. And time and time again I listened to Ziad Rahbani, my hero.

As an artist, he was overtly political, full of poetry, and without restraints. Rahbani came from a Lebanese family of famous artists. His father and uncle's band, the Rahbani Brothers, had appeared in musicals and movies, and were widely admired. And his mother— Fairouz—was a legend in the Arab world, whose music was the soundtrack of several generations. When Ziad Rahbani was ten, he wrote his first poems, and when the Lebanese Civil War broke out in 1975, he had already released three solo albums. He was only nineteen years old.

I was spellbound. He was a free spirit, a free man. An eccentric, who was infamous for canceling concerts on the spur of the moment if he didn't feel like performing. He criticized the hateful rhetoric you hear in too many churches and mosques, and exposed injustice wherever he saw it. One of his songs is called "Shou Hal Ayyam," "What Are These Days?" and is available on Spotify. One of its lines goes like this: "They say the rich give money to the poor. How come, then, so few have so much, while so many have so little?" And it ends with: "All this hidden money, can't be counted, pulled from people's pockets, where it belongs."

If you want to know how I felt in those years, how melancholy I was, how saturated in music, please go to Spotify and type in "Bala Wala Shi," "Without Anything Else," the title of Rahbani's famous love song. He sings: "I love you, only you, without anything else. Without your fancy clothes, without anything tacky, without the friends of your friends, be they annoying or nice, without your parents' sermons, without fake eyelashes, without lipstick and heavy makeup, without any of that nonsense. Come, let's sit in the shade, for the shade belongs to no one."

How I loved this song. I was impressed by how Rahbani merged Arabic folk music with pop and jazz, creating something completely new. That was where I wanted to go. That was what I wanted to do.

One day, an acquaintance gave me a poem he had written and asked me if I wanted to set it to music. I decided to do it, to take the risk. For me, that was unprecedented.

At the music school, we had been taught that music was something overpowering. Something that made you feel insignificant in the face of towering geniuses. You weren't supposed to simply write a song—no, you were expected to go to a conservatory for five years and study composition first. That's what I had been taught. Ziad Rahbani helped me rid myself of all that.

The name of my first song was "Meen Illi Allak," "Who Told You That?"—a love song. For days I pondered what key I should set it in, then thought about a melody, and came up with a series of chords: G minor, C minor, D minor, based on the harmonic minor scale, as it is referred to in Western music, a scale most closely resembling Arabic tonality.

Whenever someone came into the store, I slammed the piano lid shut, feeling as if I'd been caught. Even though there was nothing to see.

When my little song was finished, I played it for a few friends. But not for my father. I was terrified of his critique. I could only imagine what he might say: That it would get me nowhere. That it would only distract me from classical music. He might have sneered at my song. I didn't want that; it would have killed me.

I wrote only two other songs during that period. Later, in the midst of the war, when the songs just came bursting out of me, I realized one thing: Without these quiet hours in the shop, this time of sowing, I could have never been so productive later on. At the time, I simply immersed myself in sounds and ideas. It took years for them to percolate and break through to the surface. By that time, the war had already broken out.

There's a saying in Syria: The tea has to steep. It takes time. You need to have the patience to let the tea leaves become saturated—

that's the only way to achieve perfection. For me, it was the same. Some musicians tell me that my melodies feel fresh, my chords original. It all started back in that store, when I had the peace and quiet to find myself.

I wasn't singing in those days. I didn't like my voice, didn't think I was good enough. I asked others to perform the songs, and I simply accompanied them on the piano. Even when the bombs were falling, when I composed one song after another, I still wouldn't sing. I preferred to accompany someone, even if they were completely untalented, than to find the courage to raise my own voice.

That was to happen only in the middle of the siege, when the other men stayed at home depressed and I had no one to accompany anymore. Only then did I work up the courage to push the piano out into the ruined city, close my eyes, and sing.

As you might expect, my final grades were terrible. In Syria, your high school degree is called the *baccalauréat*, just like in France. After the Turks had left our country, Syria became a French mandate between 1923 and 1943. Among other things, the French completely changed the educational system. For your baccalauréat, you could achieve a total of 320 points. I had 118 points—three more than the minimum required for graduation, 115. I had graduated, but only by a hair breadth.

How could I have done better? I was hardly ever in class. It's a good thing that I had other plans.

Soon, I was working as a music teacher. Syrian society was changing, and the talent shows were providing the soundtrack. *SuperStar* had been the forerunner in 2003, followed by *Star Academy* and *Arab Idol*. Lebanon's pop culture crashed into our living rooms like a Technicolor wave. We saw images of women in elegant dresses, hunky young men, outrageous hairdos. It turned people's heads and challenged the strict morals. It fed the illusion that anyone could achieve anything, including you! Even if you come from nothing, even if you're a nobody. All you need is talent. One of the guys on TV always said, "We'll see you in Beirut!" And that became our slogan, too.

The next day, my students were murmuring, "Did you see the guy from Gaza yesterday?"

"He's a genius. Now he's in the final round."

"Why are you so excited?" I asked them.

"No one from Gaza ever reached the finals before. And next time it'll be someone from, say, Algeria. Who knows?"

In order to vote on your favorite contestant, you had to call or text a certain number. It cost you ten Syrian pounds.

"I would never waste my money on something like that," I told them. "Just to vote in a song contest!"

No, I wasn't in the least interested in those shows. The music was primitive, the lyrics shallow. But our business profited from the hype. People would watch *SuperStar* and then come to our store the next day, asking about classes. After all, every superstar has to start somewhere, usually with solfège and simple chords. It was a lucky coincidence that we had opened our store during those years.

One day, a few weeks after our store had opened, a man came in and asked about piano lessons for his daughter.

"You're lucky," my father said. "We have a highly respected pianist working for us." He pointed at me. "That's him, Aeham, our piano instructor."

"That scrawny kid?"

"Yes! He went to the state music school; he studied under Vladimir Tsaritzky." That didn't sound too bad.

"How much an hour does it cost?"

"Two hundred pounds," my father said, about forty cents.

"What? That's too much!"

"Well, normally, we charge three hundred pounds per hour," my father said, making his opening gambit. Haggling was in his blood, as it was with everyone in our family. "It's an incredible price! Do you have any idea how much you'd have to pay for a private lesson at the music school? Five hundred pounds!"

They kept going back and forth for a while. Meanwhile, I was wondering what my father was doing. I had no experience as a teacher. Why was he trying to sell me so hard?

"All right, two hundred pounds," the man said, relenting at last. "But the lessons will have to be at my house."

"We can't do that," my father said. "I need him here in the store." That was true. How could a blind man tend to a music store? As capable as my father was, there was one thing he couldn't do—count money. For a blind person, the Syrian bills were indistinguishable. Time and time again my father had been cheated.

But the man kept insisting that the lessons would have to be at his house. Finally, my father relented. "All right," he said, "then we'll just close up the shop during that time and I'll come over with Aeham."

Three times we walked over there, which was half an hour away. After that, my father convinced the family that it would be better for the girl to practice on a real piano, just like we had in our store. Not on the keyboard.

From then on, everything went smoothly. The man referred six other students to us. I enjoyed teaching. After only three months, we had several dozen students.

My father taught the oud, accordion, and violin, while I taught solfège and piano. That was unique in Yarmouk. There were several shops selling violins and guitars, but they didn't offer music lessons, and didn't repair instruments.

After a while I had an idea: I organized my students into groups. Normally, music was something for the elites. Lessons were expensive and out of reach for most people. Not to mention the cost of the instruments. So I began teaching groups of ten. Each student paid five hundred Syrian pounds for eight lessons per month, about one dollar. In addition to that—and this was our second innovation—we started selling instruments on credit. That was my idea: music for all.

My father was strictly opposed, saying it would be impossible to learn an instrument that way. He felt the quality would suffer. "We're talking about classical music here," he said. "We're not making a stew."

But not just that. "They'll take the instruments and run," he warned me, "and you'll stand there, empty-handed." And yes, that did happen. Six or seven students signed up for guitar lessons, we gave them an instrument, and they were never seen again. Still, I insisted on continuing my experiment. And it worked. In fact, it was a great success. Soon, we had two hundred students, all of whom needed an instrument. We had our work cut out for us.

I kept drinking massive amounts of 3 in 1. And one day I realized that this was, in fact, my unwritten business plan: 3 in 1!

First and foremost, the group classes saved me energy. Second, we sold a lot more instruments. And last but not least, the number of students grew rapidly. Bottom line, we suddenly had a good income.

Music for all! In other parts of the world, this might seem trivial. But we lived in a country where classical music was considered a status symbol of the rich. Any form of music—apart from folk music—was something for the one percent. Not with me! Music for all! Mozart for all! No arrogance, no snobbery. My father had opened the world of music to me. I wanted to pass this privilege on to as many people as I could. That was my revolution.

I enjoyed this period very much. I was determined to do things differently than my abusive teachers. The students liked me. I shared little jokes with them and was passionate, trying to ignite their enthusiasm, motivating them with praise and appreciation.

"You're good!" I would say. "If you'd only practice half an hour more each day, you'd be even better. Then you'd be *very* good!"

My father had a friend who was blind, a sought-after studio musician. He was probably Syria's foremost expert in keyboards. Whenever a new model was released, he bought it and took the time to explore its peculiarities. He played in countless bands. He had a five-year-old daughter named Sarah, and he sent her to me: I was supposed to help her pass the entrance exam to the state music school.

Sarah was small and cute and pudgy. Her favorite thing was dancing. But playing piano? No! Boring!

"Why are we practicing piano? Why aren't we dancing?" she asked.

"Look how my fingers are gliding across the keys. Do you know what we're doing here? We're dancing with our fingers. Playing piano is a form of dancing, a finger dance." That made sense to her.

One time we watched *Amadeus* together, the Hollywood movie about Mozart. During one of the ballroom scenes, I said to her, "See? Mozart wrote dance music!" That, too, helped motivate her.

And if she didn't want to play at all, I didn't make her. I gave her time off and sat with her mother in the kitchen. I suggested to her parents that they reward their daughter with chocolate and pocket money. It worked. I always had to chuckle when I saw Sarah. Her blind father, his unending ambition, her lack of interest—I recognized myself in her.

And Sarah persisted. She passed the entrance exam to the state music school, learned solfège, and mastered her semiannual performances. Why? Because her parents persisted, they kept her accountable with the right blend of carrot and stick.

Children have many different dreams. Today they might want to be an astronaut; tomorrow, a ballerina. You can't bend completely to their will. Often, they don't know what's good for them. It's up to the parents to set the course. If it were completely up to the kid, they'd never learn anything. It's good to make children practice an instrument. When I was young, I was upset because my father was so stern—today I am grateful.

The last I heard, Sarah was in Damascus, practicing for her entrance exam to the conservatory. I would be very proud if she made it.

I had only one other student who was more talented than she, a large, heavyset man named Mohammed Munaf. He simply appeared in our store one day, saying he wanted to learn how to play the oud. I liked him at once.

"All right," I said. "But let's start with solfège."

"Really? I'd rather learn to play the oud. I'm not that interested in singing," he said.

"Please, you should listen to your teacher," I said sternly. He relented, and we had our first lesson in solfège.

A few days later, he came back. But he hadn't done his home-work assignment.

"Please don't be mad, but I'd really prefer to play the oud," he said.

This time I gave in. "If you insist," I said. "Do you have an oud?"

"No."

"I think you should buy a used one. They're the least expensive." I showed him a few models. "May I ask where you work?"

"I'm a salesman in a sporting goods store."

I knew how poorly paid such a job was. In Syria, the average salesperson earned four thousand Syrian pounds per month, less than ten dollars. We began talking, and he told me of his dream. He wanted to become a musician and start his own band. In fact, he'd been dreaming about it for a long time. But his parents were poor, he'd been forced to quit school, and now he was selling running shoes.

I picked up an inexpensive oud. "Here, take it. I'm loaning it to you. Just don't tell my father."

He took off, beaming with joy. And from then on, Mohammed Munaf never stopped practicing. He must have been playing day and night. And he was talented, absorbing the instrument as if it were a vitamin he had been lacking all his life.

The Arabic short-necked oud, like the violin, has no frets. That makes it hard to hit the right note. One day, I assigned him a difficult piece by Riad al-Sunbati. From the very beginning, he placed his fingers correctly. Then he played the next section, making almost no mistakes.

"Wonderful," I said encouragingly. "Go on." Half an hour later, he was done with the piece. I was astonished. We still had a few minutes left—our lesson wasn't over. So we went to the computer and I showed him video clips with classical oud performances by Riad al-Sunbati from the '60s and '70s. Munaf was enthralled. This was exactly his kind of music. I explained the various musical references to him.

"Please show me more by Riad al-Sunbati, Teacher Aeham," he asked me. *Teacher Aeham.* That's what my students called me.

"Of course! But don't call me 'Teacher.' I'm your friend."

Within one year, he had surpassed all the other oud students, even though at his age it's much harder to move your fingers quickly enough. Children have a much easier time at this. My father, too, had taken a liking to Mohammed Munaf.

I had an idea. "If you're really serious, I can get you a few private students. You can quit your job and you'll have more time to practice."

He almost gave me a bear hug. I managed to get him three private students. This way he made as much money as before—and he had all day to practice. He quit his job as a shoe salesman.

His dream had come true. Today Mohammed Munaf is the bandleader of his own orchestra, with a dozen musicians and two dozen singers. They play traditional Syrian music and can often be seen on Syrian state television.

But Mohammed Munaf's orchestra is also a fig leaf for the regime. The government likes to use them to show how vibrant, wholesome, and beautiful life in Syria is.

We lost touch after 2012, when the war began. Until then, we were the best of friends, and sometimes he would spend the whole day in our shop. But after that our worlds drifted apart. He appeared on television; I was left behind in Yarmouk and had no food. He stood in the spotlight, wearing a black suit, conducting his orchestra. I was burning plastic bottles to heat up a stew of clover and grass so that my family had something to eat.

Mohammed Munaf and I saw each other only one more time— and all the warmth between us had vanished. Before the war, we had never spoken about politics. No one did—it was forbidden. Only later did I realize he was on the regime's side. He never contacted me again.

— CHAPTER NINE —

When I was seventeen, I applied to the conservatory in Damascus. At first, earlier, upon graduating from the music school, I thought that I'd left classical music behind. Good-bye, Beethoven. Aeham Ahmad would never become a concert pianist.

But now I wanted to continue. It was my own decision, not my father's. I had finally discovered my passion for playing piano. Now I dreamed of a career as a musician. And I wanted to continue my education as well, but since my high school graduation grades had been so bad, I was inadmissible for most other majors.

I signed up for preparatory class with Vladimir Tsaritzky. After all, I already knew him. We picked up where we had left off.

On the day of the exam, the whole conservatory was buzzing with excitement. Nervous applicants paced the hallways, consumed with their little preparation rituals. The tenors warmed up their voices, the violinists fiddled, and I took my place in the long row of pianists. Everyone was waiting to practice the piano for a while, clutching their music sheets.

I nodded at the others. I knew many of them by sight, even though I hadn't really talked to any of them. Sandybell was there, as beautiful and well dressed as always.

One woman stood out because she wore a headscarf, which was unusual. The music school in Damascus was favored mostly by children from Christian or Druze families. And even girls from Sunni families wouldn't be caught dead with a headscarf.

When it was my turn, I entered the room and sat down at the Steinway Model D on the small stage. It was the same kind of piano my father and I had tuned years ago at the defense secretary's house. It's a powerful instrument, as capricious as a racehorse, and difficult to handle when you've only been able to practice on a small Ukraina. It took me ten minutes to get the hang of it.

I had been the last in line. And now I would be the first to perform. As always. After all, my initials were A.A. I remained seated at the piano and waited.

One of the professors came in. He was surprised. "What are you doing here?" he asked, irritated.

I told him that I was up next.

"No, go outside, we'll call you, then you can come back in," he said harshly.

And just like that, it all came back to me, all my former resentment toward the school, with its demands for obedience, its attitude of "we're better than you." It made me feel pitiful. I had been listening to Ziad Rahbani—now I was supposed to knuckle under for these professors? No way!

"Why?" I asked. "I'm up first, why can't I stay seated?"

"Because those are the rules."

I got up, murmuring, "Screw the rules."

"What?" he snapped at me.

"Nothing," I said, and went outside. I was angry. I disliked him and felt small and insignificant, just as I had with my first piano teacher. I didn't belong here. I stood in the hallway in angry silence and avoided looking at anyone.

Then I was called in.

Six people sat in the auditorium. I went to the stage and plopped my sheets on the music rack. The man with whom I'd had the dispute looked up.

"What was that?" he asked.

"That's who I am," I said.

"You'd better show me who you are on the piano," he said. I had prepared pieces by Beethoven and Rachmaninoff, a mazurka by

Chopin, and three études by Czerny. I began with Czerny. I poured all my rage into the piece, playing fast and forcefully, marching through the lines, stomping ahead. . . .

And then I stopped, unable to play anymore. My rage was stronger than my willpower.

"That's it," I said, getting up and gathering my sheet music. I just wanted to escape from there. The other members of the jury looked at me in astonishment.

"Why?" the man asked me.

"I'm angry," I said.

"You're allowed to perform here. You should be happy."

"You're right, I should be happy," I said. "But I'm not."

"You can go now," he said.

I went home in a grim mood.

Needless to say, I failed the test. But at least my prep class had led to something good: I made a new friend. I had been standing in one of the hallways of the conservatory, waiting for something or someone, when a bald man came down the stairs and smiled at me. Why was he smiling? At me? Just like that? Here, in this snobbish place? I was surprised. I looked up again, and, yes, he was actually smiling. So I smiled back. We shook hands and he introduced himself: his name was Feisal Jamal.

Two weeks later, we met again. This time, we went out for coffee. He was from Aleppo; he wore dark, horn-rimmed glasses and had green eyes. The most striking thing about him was his laughter. He laughed like a child, cheerful, carefree, boundless.

I learned that he had studied piano in Italy, that he hadn't been teaching at the conservatory for very long, and that he was about to perform with the Syrian National Symphony Orchestra. He was one of the best pianists in Syria. He told me that he, too, couldn't stand the smug jerks at the conservatory. Their arrogance amused him. I found myself laughing and agreeing with him. It seemed like we could be friends. So we exchanged phone numbers.

The friends I'd had until that point knew nothing about music, and I wasn't acquainted with any musicians. With Feisal, these borders were erased. It didn't take long before we found ourselves spending hours at his apartment, listening to CDs he had brought home from his travels, outrageously good piano concertos, fugues by Bach that were played on a harpsichord. He helped me discover the Finnish composer Jean Sibelius, whose music went right up to the edge of atonality. He explained to me the connection between modern painting and modern music. He pointed out things I had never heard before.

Sometimes he gave me piano lessons. He showed me how to improve my expressiveness, encouraging me to play with more emotion. He taught me to reveal myself through music, to do what I felt was right. Feisal helped me discover new treasures, and as a thank-you, I occasionally tuned his piano. I owe him a lot.

But he was in his thirties, and had no wife or children. This made him suspicious. There were rumors. A casual acquaintance at the conservatory warned me that Feisal was "into men," and urged me to stay away from him.

Ugh! I had no patience for rumors. I didn't care whether Feisal was gay or straight. Whether someone was Jewish or Christian or Muslim, Orthodox or agnostic, gay or not, didn't matter to me. I knew that Feisal was a wonderful human being, and that was the only thing that mattered.

Sometimes there were three of us who went out together. The third person was Flavio, who also taught at the conservatory. He and Feisal drank beer; I drank cola. At other times, the two of them would cook pasta together, "al dente," as Feisal said. I had never heard that term before. Occasionally, we drove to Flavio's weekend house in the hills of Sahnaya, enjoying the view.

One day, Feisal bought a new car. Together, we took the expressway to Homs. I had a driver's license, but I had never driven outside the grounds of the driving school. I didn't own a car, and I had never dared ask someone to borrow one. It was different with Feisal. I stammered for a while, then I asked him—would he mind if I drove for a while?

At first, he wasn't sure this was such a good idea. But then he pulled over to the right and got out of the car. I slipped over into the driver's seat. We took off. The car was an automatic; I had no difficulties weaving into traffic. I continued driving for a few miles, then I pulled over to the right, beaming.

One day, Feisal returned from a concert tour in Ukraine, where he had performed with the Syrian National Symphony Orchestra. He had bought new CDs. We listened to them in his apartment. I asked if I could borrow some of them and burn them onto my hard drive. He shook his head. These were rare recordings, irreplaceable, and he didn't want anything to happen to them. What if they got scratched? Sorry, but no.

I couldn't stop thinking about the music. A few weeks later I asked him again. I promised to treat the CDs with extreme care. I said I'd only burn them and bring them right back. Again, he shook his head.

All right, never mind. I let it go.

A short while later, he had to go to Aleppo for a few weeks. He called me and asked if I could check on his apartment once in a while, and water his plants.

I was surprised. Watering someone's plants wasn't exactly a custom in Syria. Couldn't he find someone else to do it?

"My home is your home," he said emphatically. "I would appreciate it if you could do it."

So I said yes. I went to his apartment and watered the plants. Of course, I couldn't resist the temptation: I burned the CDs and put them back where I had found them, unharmed. But as soon as I was finished, I felt ashamed. How could I go behind someone's back like that? He's your friend, I told myself. He trusts you, and he asked you not to do it. So why did you?

From then on, my inner voice wouldn't shut up. Every time I saw Feisal, I thought, You have to confess. I tried several times— and never managed to finish my sentence.

I just couldn't bring myself to tell him, yet I couldn't remain silent either. For weeks, I struggled with this question. At last, honesty won out.

"Feisal, I need to tell you something."

"That you burned the CDs?"

"Yes! How did you know?"

"That's why I gave you the keys. I'm sorry I said no. I was looking for a way to get you the music."

That's what he was like. That's how wonderful our friendship was.

And then the war drove us apart, catapulted us onto different planets light-years away from each other. Feisal Jamal sat in the Damascus Opera House at a grand piano, accompanying a famous soprano who had a guest appearance in Syria. I sat in Yarmouk and kept pushing my out-of-tune piano around bomb craters. His world went on as before, while mine was broken.

But he didn't forget me. He kept calling me, asking how I was. He might have even put himself in harm's way by doing so. After all, his phone lines might have been tapped. He had a lot to lose, but he didn't care. Our friendship was more important to him. I will never forget that.

It might seem strange, but at eighteen, I tried to get into the conservatory again. It was a bizarre déjà vu. My reasons were the same as last time. My awful high school grades. My father and his unending dream that I should be a concert pianist. My friendship with Feisal Jamal.

I calmed my rage, swallowed my pride, and worked up some motivation. Once again, I registered for the preparatory class with Vladimir Tsaritzky. I practiced as much as I could, but our store was keeping me busy.

On the day of the exam, my father and I got up at 5 a.m. and took the minibus at 7 a.m. We arrived at the conservatory much too early, and went to one of the fancy cafés in the neighborhood, ordering croissants and Italian coffee. My father kept encouraging me, praising me. He told me how far I'd come! Just this one small step and I'd be there! I nodded.

When the time came, I went over to the conservatory, took my place in the long line outside the large hall, then went inside and warmed up at the grand piano. Then I went outside again and waited to be called.

"Aeham Ahmad!"

I entered the hall. Again, I faced a six-person committee, including the man with whom I'd had the argument the year before.

"Ah, you're back?" he asked me.

"Yes," I said, as politely as possible. "I'm here to take the test again."

"You know the rules," he said, hinting at my outburst the previous year.

"Yes," I said. I wasn't going to get upset again. I had promised my father.

"What are you going to play?"

"Two pieces by Chopin, a Beethoven sonata, the Prelude no. 5 by Rachmaninoff, and two études by Czerny."

"Very well," the man said.

I began. And I gave it my all. That was perhaps my mistake. Yes, I hit all the notes, but I played too intensely. My expression was rigid and overly strained.

When I was done, I gathered up the sheet music, nodded to the jury, and left the room.

Five days later, my father and I went across the city one more time to find out the results. I looked for my name on the list. And I read out loud, "Aeham Ahmad—60 percent." Failed.

In silence, we went back home. I was tired and downcast. My father was even more depressed. He did not say a word. In fact, he didn't speak for days. His decades-long dream was over. His son would never be a concert pianist. I could feel his pain, and it hurt.

Thankfully, there was a plan B: In the fall of 2007, I signed up for the University of Homs. They were offering a new degree in music education. It would allow me to teach at any school in Syria. I was surprised when, during the entrance exam, I ran into someone I knew: Cosette Bakir, my former piano teacher at the music school. Now she taught piano here at the university. I still remembered how she had called me a parrot. But when she saw me, she acted as if we were old friends.

I passed the exam with ease. "I already taught Aeham at the Damascus Music School," Cosette Bakir explained to the other jurors. "He'll be my star pupil." I smiled grimly. Back in the old days, she couldn't even get through Mozart's "Turkish March" without hitting the wrong keys. What did she think she could teach me now?

I didn't want to move to Homs. Our shop was booming, and it needed my complete attention. I didn't want to lose my music students, and I wanted to stay near my parents. And, to be honest, I didn't feel like living the life of a student. Many of my classmates played in bands and thought of themselves as rising pop stars. All they were interested in was parties.

That kind of life was unfamiliar to me. I didn't smoke hash, I certainly didn't drink alcohol, and I've never even had a drag on a cigarette. What was I supposed to do in Homs? I preferred to stay in Yarmouk during the semester and commute, even though Homs was two hours away by car.

It was exhausting. My alarm rang at 5 a.m. At 6 a.m., I got on the express bus. I dug myself deep into my jacket, put some earbuds in, and began listening to music. Usually, I fell asleep. From Damascus the bus drove up to Mount Qasioun, and from there to the Syrian highlands. The bus followed a winding road along the slopes. In the morning light, I could see pale rocks, cypresses, mountain pines, and deep valleys. Then I closed my eyes and went back to sleep.

At around 8 a.m., we reached Homs. I entered the university's main building—and was immediately surrounded by my classmates. Whenever they saw me, they'd call out excitedly, "Aeham is here!" There was no music store in Homs, so I had to help out the others with violin bows, sheet music, and strings. If you played the oud or violin, it was important to have a regular supply of strings. Whenever a string broke, you couldn't practice anymore. So, each morning, my classmates waited anxiously for me.

One time, the dean of the university entered the lobby ahead of me. No one paid any attention to him. But when I came in right after him, someone called, "There's Aeham!" and all heads turned. Even the dean turned to look—that's how much of a celebrity I was.

Classes began at 9 a.m. Music history, music therapy, pedagogics, philosophy, counterpoint, and harmonics. Everyone had to choose a second instrument, and I chose drums. But the piano lessons with Cosette Bakir were exactly as I remembered them: She had no clue what she was doing, and she was always in a bad mood. She assigned me difficult pieces that I had no time to practice, then she'd get impatient and call me a dummy.

So what? She had no more power over me. At the music school, she could have expelled me at any time. But here at the university, the only thing that mattered were your final grades. And those were still a long way off.

After the first year, I saw that there was an open position for a second piano teacher. I showed the ad to Feisal Jamal. "If you want me to, I can apply," he said. Of course I wanted him to! And he got the job.

I went to Cosette Bakir. "I'd like to switch to the piano class with Feisal Jamal," I told her.

"That's not permitted," she said.

"Yes, it is. The new teacher has to accept me as a student, and that's all." I was quoting the school's charter.

"Why do you want to switch?"

"I don't feel comfortable with you."

She was angry, but she had no choice but to relent. The other professors were gloating about it. One time, I was walking down the hallway and accidentally overheard Ms. Bakir talking to a colleague of hers.

"I heard that your star pupil has left you," the colleague said sarcastically.

"Yes, he and Feisal are friends, that's why."

Indeed. From then on, I took piano lessons with my best friend.

As soon as classes were over, by 2 p.m., I went to the bus depot and took the express bus back to Damascus. At 5 p.m., I was back in our store in Yarmouk.

In 2009, my father opened an oud workshop. He had bought a second showroom, much larger than the first. Like our old store, it had been empty for years and was sold under value. When we opened the metal gate for the first time, rats scurried toward us.

"What is that?" my father asked. Although he'd heard the rustling, he had been unable to identify its source. We spread several pounds of rat poison around the store and closed the gate again.

This time, my father wanted to do everything the right way. The new workshop was supposed to be his crowning achievement. He didn't want to have to do as much backbreaking work as he did with our first store, where we'd had to cart out the rubble ourselves. My father knew how to make quality ouds by hand. Now he wanted to scale up. Together with a friend, he worked out each step of the process. Then they drove to Darayya, Syria's most important industrial center, and placed orders for saws and grinders.

One of the reasons he wanted to open an oud workshop was my brother. Alaa had left school after ninth grade and finished an apprenticeship as a carpenter. He built all the windows and doors for our workshop. My brother was almost eighteen, muscular, with close-cropped hair. He wore tight-fitting modern T-shirts and a necklace made of wooden beads. He lived a restless life, sometimes vanishing for days. He probably had a girlfriend. Or several.

Production began. The workers started cutting the wooden

ribs—the backbone of an oud—gluing them together to form the pear-shaped body. Afterward, they glued the neck and soundboard onto it. After that is where my father came in. He sat in a sound-proof room and tested the ouds.

Each oud cover had three sound holes. My father would gently tap against them and listen. Then he tapped some more and listened again. I'm not sure what he was listening for, but he could effortlessly determine the sound quality, and knew exactly what category to place the instrument in. Our best ouds were made on preorders. The body was made of mahogany, the soundboard of rosewood, the tuning peg and pegbox of ebony. The sound holes were covered with rosette-like grilles, and the soundboard was surrounded with decorative purfles that matched the patterns around the sound holes. The body was coated with a thin layer of shellac and then a protective wax coating, before finally being stringed with six pairs of nylon strings.

We made up to fifty of these high-quality ouds per month and shipped them, for two thousand Syrian pounds each (about four dollars), to a wholesaler in Lebanon. From there, they were sold all over the world, in Berlin, Amsterdam, and Los Angeles. Even today I sometimes come across some of our ouds.

Our least expensive ouds—approximately sixty dollars—had hardly any ornaments and were intended for students, beginners, and occasional players. They were used in several music schools. Our standard instrument, which cost a little over 120 dollars, was carefully decorated and had a finer sound than the student version. It was intended for intermediate students. Our instruments were sold at the Damascus airport and in souvenir shops all over the country.

Some months, we made up to 450 ouds. They were sold under the simple name "Damascene ouds." Since we were Palestinians and thus had no Syrian passports, my father decided to forgo a website or brand name. Whoever ordered our ouds would first transfer the money via Western Union, and a short while later, they'd receive their shipment.

Our store was always full of music students. We sold twelve kinds of oud strings and six kinds of violin strings. We had guitars by Fender, keyboards by Korg, dozens of violins, countless guitars, and several pianos.

Sometimes we made five hundred thousand Syrian pounds—about a thousand dollars—in a single month. And still we had no bank account. No, my mother was old-fashioned: she simply hid the money in a pillowcase. Later, my father invested our income in real estate, apartments that he then rented out. Refugees crave stability. But it's an illusion to think that real estate can offer security.

My father bought a 2,100-square-foot apartment in Yalda, an area at the southeast border of Yarmouk. At last, my brother and I had our own rooms. The living room was large enough for us to host dinner parties. The apartment cost seven million Syrian pounds, about thirteen thousand dollars. Papa then bought two more apartments, smaller and at half the price, for my brother and me.

If things had continued like this, I would be a wealthy man today. I would own several music stores and a nice apartment, and I'd be able to take my family to the beach on weekends. But the war put an end to all that, taking everything from us.

We still owned the apartment in Duma, outside the gates of Damascus and bordering on the vineyards, where we used to spend weekends. Duma would be one of the first cities to rise up against the Assad regime, and a unit of the FSA, the Free Syrian Army, ended up confiscating our apartment and turning it into their headquarters. After an army helicopter dropped a barrel bomb onto the building, a neighbor sent us a photo. Nothing but rubble was left of it.

My parents' new apartment would also be bombed, two rooms remaining intact but uninhabitable, since the building could collapse at any moment. My parents would eventually seek shelter in our old apartment, which was only attacked one time, when a grenade splinter tore a hole in a wall and we patched it up again.

Our two stores in Yarmouk are now walled up, a mad attempt

that we made to protect what was inside, the machines and all the instruments we'd been able to save from the war: twelve hundred ouds, six hundred guitars, three hundred violins, two dozen keyboards, five pianos.

To this day, ISIS fighters are holed up in Yarmouk. I hope they don't find our instruments. They hate music.

— CHAPTER TEN —

During all the time I spent at the store, I had never flirted with any of my music students, nor with the women at the University of Homs, all those girls who partied with my classmates. They weren't my type. I wanted to start a family.

When I was at the piano, my mind often drifted off and I thought of girls. Of course. But I also thought of children. That's what it was like for me: I didn't just dream of a woman, I dreamed of a whole family. I couldn't separate them. In my imagination, my future wife and I were already playing with our kids.

One night, shortly after my twenty-third birthday, I went to my mother and told her that I wanted to get married.

"What? Why?" she said, staring at me with big eyes. "You're so young."

"I don't think so. I think it's time I stand on my own two feet. I'd like to move out and start my own family."

"Aeham, you're twenty-three! You're much too young to be a father!"

"I think I'm just the right age. I'd like to have a family."

She kept raising objections, and I kept waving them away. We went on like this for a while. Then she said, "Let's talk to your father about it tomorrow."

The next morning, when the three of us were together, I raised the issue again.

"Do you have any idea what's involved in starting a family?" my father asked. He then launched into a lengthy speech about having a regular income and your own apartment, standing on your own two feet, not straying from the straight and narrow, being a good person at all times.

"You don't think I'm a good person?"

"Of course you are, but—"

"It's not just about the money," my mother interjected. "Getting married is a big step. You have to be understanding of your wife, you have to address her needs, you have to get along with your family, and you have to be a good father and take care of your children every day."

For hours the two of them lectured me, without getting anywhere, so we postponed the discussion until later. My mother suggested that she and I talk alone again.

That night, the two of us sat down in the kitchen together. "Being married means that you always stay together," my mother said. "Divorce is out of the question. And if you're too young to get married, if you don't have enough life experience, you might make mistakes that can't be erased."

"I'm sure I'll be a good husband."

"When you're married, you can never argue."

"You're not exactly a shining example," I said.

"What are you talking about?"

"You remember the day when Papa smashed all the cups and glasses in our kitchen? He was mad because you'd asked to be transferred to a different school district."

"Oh . . . you remember that?"

"Or the way you argued when Papa forgot the pan on the stove and almost burned down the kitchen?"

"That's not important right now, Aeham. What's important is that you understand your wife's feelings. Women are different than men. They . . ."

She lectured me for a while. Do this, do that, do this. My thoughts drifted off. But finally, my mother said, "I'll think about it."

Three days later, she and my father and Uncle Mohammed visited me at the shop. We drank coffee.

"We thought about it," my mother began. "You're right. You're old enough, and you're very responsible. You have our consent. You're allowed to marry."

I hugged her tightly. Then my father went into a lengthy speech about being a good father, while Uncle Mohammed sat there nodding as he listened. Here and there he added, "Just like your father," and I nodded obediently. Then they left.

My mother took action and started asking around. Where could she find a good match for Aeham? She visited several families. She met the parents, spoke to the young women, looked at them without headscarves. Then she made her decision.

"I found the right girl," she said one morning before work.

"Who?"

"Before I tell you, Papa and I have to meet with her father. Then we'll see."

When they came back from the visit, my father was beaming. "You will have a wonderful wife," he raved.

"What's her name?"

"Tahani," my mother said. "Her family is from Palestine, like ours. Her dream is having children."

Now I, too, was beaming. "What does she do?"

"She teaches art at an elementary school."

"Is she pretty?"

"You bet," my mother said. "After all, I want pretty grandchildren, with big eyes and beautiful black hair." She was obviously very proud of her choice.

"Where does she live?"

"You know we can't tell you that."

"I'd like to meet her."

"That's impossible. First you have to get engaged, then you'll meet."

Of course, that was the custom. Couples were allowed to meet only after their engagement. The meeting would take place at her home, in the living room. After our engagement and the initial meeting, I would be allowed to visit once or twice per week, to chat with her. With her father there. If Tahani and I didn't get along, we could end the engagement, without either party losing face. But meeting her alone? Before the engagement? Forbidden. *Haram*.

I wanted to follow tradition and act in accordance with our family's customs, but, my God, I was bursting with curiosity! Each passing day made it harder for me. The closer the engagement came, the more excited I was. Who was Tahani? What did she look like? Would I like her? Would she like me?

One day when I was working at the store, I saw a young woman sitting outside our shopwindow, peering in with curiosity. When I looked back, she turned away and walked off. I didn't think much of it. Maybe she was interested in an instrument. Many people looked into the shopwindow over the course of the day.

The next day at the store, I saw the young woman again. She came in through the glass door and approached me.

"I'm Tahani."

That's all. Just these words. I felt hot and cold at the same time. Tahani! My future wife! I liked her at first sight.

"Oh," I stammered, "please, have a seat."

"You know I can't," she said.

"How wonderful of you to come. I'm so glad you did!"

And I was. She had been quite courageous. She, too, had been overcome by curiosity—and had defied convention. She must be very strong-willed. I was impressed. Still, the situation was delicate. At any moment, someone could come in and recognize her.

"Should we make a date?" I asked. "I could pick you up tomorrow after you finish teaching."

"All right. But don't wait for me at the gate. Pick me up at the next corner."

I stared after her as she left. She was so pretty, and so brave!

The next day, I was waiting for her, one block away from the school gate. She was wearing a blue headscarf, a long-sleeved white blouse, and jeans. When we shook hands, I caught a whiff of her perfume—jasmine, the scent of my childhood.

We took a minibus to a café a short way outside Yarmouk, glancing at each other shyly. I told her about myself and what I did for a living, and she told me about herself and her job as an art teacher and an artist. I mentioned that I was dreaming of a family, that I wanted to be a father. I promised I would spend a lot of time at home, looking after the children.

"My mother always said that you can't trust men," Tahani said with a laugh.

She told me about her parents' divorce, but she also said that she was embarrassed to talk about it. Since her mother lived in Dubai and had remarried, she hadn't seen her in years. It was her aunt who had made contact with my family.

I told her that she looked wonderful. I liked that she was so unpretentious, without any hair gel or fancy clothes. Although we were sitting on a busy street with people hurrying all around us, we just kept talking and forgot about the time.

Suddenly, her phone rang. "My father!" she said. She took the call.

Her father's voice was booming from the phone. "Where are you?"

"I had to fill in for a colleague."

"I'm expecting you at home!"

We ran toward the minibus. I got out a few stations before her, so that no one would see us. Once I was at home, I went directly to my mother.

"I would like to marry Tahani," I said firmly.

"Just like that?" she asked in astonishment.

"I thought about it, about what you told me about her. I think she's the right one."

"That's nice, but you'll have to wait just a little bit longer so that we can arrange the engagement party."

— CHAPTER ELEVEN —

During the months preceding my engagement to Tahani, a popular uprising had been taking place in Syria, and it continues to this day. Beyond the hideous violence, beyond the extremism, there was a vast uproar of civil disobedience, a collective indignation over despotism, torture, injustice, and corruption. Aid workers and teachers, doctors and journalists, civil rights activists and artists had been speaking out, though their voices weren't yet heard in the West. The regime didn't want them to be.

In the West, the Syrian conflict is often referred to as a "civil war." Syrians, especially those who consider themselves neutral, call it a "crisis." Both are wrong: it's a revolution.

In those early months of the conflict, the so-called "neutral" outsiders were in fact on Assad's side. It was like Germany in the 1930s, when everyone outside pretended not to know what was happening.

When it all began, I was spending most of my time working. Business was booming, I was ambitious, I was still pursuing my education and about to get married. I gave plenty of private lessons, and some months had as many as 250 students. I came home each evening completely exhausted and had dinner with my parents and my brother in our beautiful apartment in Yalda.

My father would spend hours glued to the television. He also listened to Al Jazeera radio, which was broadcast by the Qatar-based cable news station that had quickly fallen out of favor with the Assad regime. Mesmerized, my father listened as the corrupt governments of the region began to topple. When playing to a Western audience, these regimes pretended to be "democratic," but we in the Middle East saw their true face. The state propaganda kept reiterating what they wanted us to hear—that they would rule "forever." But soon, a chain reaction went through the Arab world, a domino effect that would topple one regime after another.

On December 17, 2010, the Tunisian vegetable merchant Mohamed Bouazizi poured gasoline over himself and set himself on fire. His death, his self-immolation, was the spark that ignited an explosion in Tunisia: Within a few weeks, mass protests gripped the country, sweeping from office the self-aggrandizing president Zine al-Abadine Ben Ali, who had clung to power for two decades. Despite being eighty, Ben Ali had continued to play the role of a playboy.

"This hunger for freedom will touch the entire Arab world," my father muttered as he listened to the broadcast of mass protests in Tunis. Was there hope in his voice?

At that point, I was not particularly interested in Tunisia. But when, in early 2011, the wave of protests reached Egypt, I, too, watched Al Jazeera's live stream from Tahrir Square. I was particularly fascinated by the artists who were organizing sit-ins lasting for days. But whenever we turned to Syrian state television, all we heard were the increasingly desperate platitudes of the Assad regime.

At first, they said, "Syria isn't Tunisia." Then they said, "What's happening in Egypt and Tunisia has nothing to do with us in Syria." Finally, they said, "The Syrian people stand fully behind their government and the wise leadership of President al-Assad. He alone can save our country from a globalist conspiracy."

In February 2011, Egyptian president Hosni Mubarak was forced to step down and Yemen was in turmoil. And when masses of people pushed through the streets of Libya, we began to ask ourselves if these protests could also reach Syria, the "Kingdom of Silence."

Via satellite television, we saw shaky cell phone videos of sporadic protests in Damascus. Students demonstrated at the Libyan embassy, pledging solidarity with the uprising against Muammar Gaddafi. There was a mass demonstration in front of the Palace of Justice. The relatives of political prisoners demanded that their sons and daughters be released. A spontaneous demonstration erupted in the middle of Hariqa market, where a policeman had beaten a merchant.

On March 15, a crowd of about 150 demonstrators made their way through the historic Hamidiyeh market, chanting, "God, Syria, freedom, and nothing else!" This was a stab at the government-organized marches, where people were required to chant, "God, Syria, Bashar, and nothing else."

The demonstrators were members of the educated middle class and by no means "barbaric Islamists," as the regime labeled them in an attempt to discredit them. The protesters had chosen a historic site for their march: The Hamidiyeh market was where the revolution against the French occupation had begun back in the 1930s. The demonstrators knew their history.

Was it on this day that the Syrian uprising began? Or was it three days later, on March 18, 2011, when parents marched in front of a police station in Daraa, in southern Syria, demanding that their sons and daughters be released? The teenagers had been arrested one month before, when one of them had sprayed onto a wall THE REGIME MUST FALL!, a phrase we heard every day via satellite television. And for that, the young demonstrators were tortured, their fingernails torn out.

The parents were outraged. Hundreds of local residents joined their protest. When state security forces shot live ammunition into the crowd, killing four demonstrators, the outrage spread to other towns. Again, the security forces opened fire. In the first month of the protests, more than a hundred people died. But by then, the uprising was unstoppable.

On state television, the spokespeople for the Assad regime denied everything. First, they denied the demonstrations. Then they denied the violence. In the end, they even denied that the protesters were Syrian. Whenever a protest was shown on television, which was rare, it was always "foreign agents of Zionism and American imperialism" who were blamed for the unrest. Or Iraqi Kurds. Or Palestinians. At times, the propagandists claimed that the "fake news" network Al Jazeera had been giving hallucinogenic drugs to thousands of people to instigate unrest.

In June, hundreds of thousands took to the streets of Hama to protest against Assad. But the regime said that the footage, shot with thousands of cell phones, came from a film studio in Qatar. They said that a facade of Orontes Square had been built there. Al Jazeera, BBC, France 24, CNN—fake news! Agents of a globalist conspiracy against Syria!

In Yarmouk, all this arrived with some delay. After all, we were Palestinians. We had to remain neutral. We obediently avoided Syrian politics, just like my parents had always taught me. My students talked about these events as if they were happening far away, and not on our doorstep.

"Did you hear what's going on in Daraa?" one of them asked.

"Yeah, it's messed up," another one replied.

And that was it. Then they unpacked their ouds, and we began our do-re-mi-fa-so-la.

Many Palestinians were in a quandary: On the one hand, we were indebted to the Syrian state, which had welcomed us so generously as refugees, more generously than other countries in the region. Add to that the Syrian propaganda. But on the other hand, many of us sympathized with the demonstrators.

Our local politicians in Yarmouk warned us to remain neutral. "We're keeping out of domestic political conflicts" was the preferred phrasing by left and right, from Fatah to Hamas to Islamic Jihad. "Domestic political conflicts!" A strange thing to say, considering we had been living there for over sixty years.

Many of us realized that refugees could quickly become scapegoats. This was not just the paranoia of an ethnic minority. In March, Assad's media adviser accused us of being "foreign elements," claiming that we were intent on plunging Syria into civil war. So that's why everyone agreed: Yarmouk couldn't afford to speak out against the regime.

But our neighborhood was meant to be a safe haven for refugees. And they came. Palestinians in Daraa and Homs had joined the demonstrations—and paid dearly. State security forces had stormed the camp and "put it through the meat grinder," as the refugees said. State security had stopped at nothing and no one. Time and again, I heard the story of Sheikh Ahmad Sayasina, the blind imam of the historic Daraa mosque. He had offered shelter to some demonstrators. Soon, the security forces had stormed the mosque, firing wildly and gunning down several young men—"in the middle of God's house!"

Tens of thousands of people had found refuge in Yarmouk. They found shelter at the UNRWA schools, and many people in Yarmouk helped wherever they could, bringing blankets and clothing, or taking in entire families.

It was during that time that I was finishing my studies. I still took the bus to Homs on occasion, mostly to take my exams. My finals would have been in July 2011. But as we were approaching Homs one morning, it seemed as if half the Syrian Army was blocking the expressway. The bus tried to swerve around the massive forces carrying heavy artillery—all the instruments of death, meant to crush the rebellion.

As we approached a checkpoint, I held my breath. There was a good chance the soldiers would stop the bus and check my ID. If they did, they would probably detain me, because I hadn't done my military service. Or they might simply arrest me, because any young Palestinian male was inherently suspicious. But I was lucky: the soldiers waved us through, and the bus rolled past the checkpoint without stopping. I exhaled. It was the last time I traveled to Homs.

My friend Michail, an aspiring opera singer on whose couch I had slept a few nights at the beginning of my studies, called me a week later from Homs and told me about the "Clock Tower Massacre." He worded everything carefully, afraid his phone might be tapped. "We lost many friends," he informed me.

Another classmate of mine, a flutist, expressed it more clearly. He wrote to me on Facebook, saying that the soldiers shot at the demonstrators, until "waves of blood splashed against the walls." Then the fire department had come and hosed down the walls and streets. Two hours later, everything was clean again.

Each year, on May 15, Palestinians remember the Naqba, the "Catastrophe," the displacement of more than seven hundred thousand Palestinians in 1948. This year, there were supposed to be more than just the usual speeches and processions, according to a Facebook page. This time there was talk of driving up to the armistice line at the Golan Heights. The meeting point was the mosque in the middle of Yarmouk Street, usually the site of pro-Assad rallies. From there, buses were supposed to bring everyone to the border.

Buses? Clearly, this rally must have been approved by the top levels of the government. Was the Syrian government trying, once again, to redirect people's anger toward Israel? If so, no surprise there. The regime had always justified its repressive policies with the state of cold war with Israel, beginning in 1963. After all, we were at war, and supposed to be wary of the "cunning Zionist enemy"; that's why public gatherings were forbidden, that's why there was martial law.

We Palestinians were only pawns in a game. In those days, the regime kept saying to the world: Without stability in Syria, there can be no peace with Israel. In other words: Leave Israel's security to us. And at home, they incited people against the alleged "Zionist conspiracy." It was cynical and two-faced.

Hundreds of young men joined the rally. When they reached the border at Quneitra, the Syrian soldiers let them pass. The demonstrators cut through the barbed wire and ran across the demarcation line, waving Palestinian flags. Some of them made it to the border town of Majdal Shams. That's when the Israeli soldiers opened fire.

The buses brought the survivors home. Thirteen demonstrators had been killed. Several dozen had their legs shredded by hollow-point bullets, a kind of ammunition that exploded only after it was lodged in your flesh. The wounded survivors were celebrated as heroes and were brought to Mujtahed Hospital, where they received the best medical care available.

But that was only the beginning. On June 6, three weeks later, was the Naqsa, "the day of revenge," in commemoration of the Six-Day War in 1967, during which Israel occupied the Golan Heights, the Sinai Peninsula, and the West Bank. Once again, people were told to go up to the Israeli border. And this time, there was no doubt: the "General Command" was behind it.

The General Command is a radical militia whose full name is "Popular Front for the Liberation of Palestine—General Command." Their program is simple, the "struggle against the Zionist enemy," by any means possible. Even as the Palestinian Liberation Organization, or PLO, was beginning to negotiate with Israel, the General Command was still calling for the extermination of the "Zionist entity." Their headquarters were in Yarmouk. From here, they organized their terror attacks.

The Assad clan, first the father, then the son, allowed the militia to do as they pleased. The regime fueled the hatred of Israel as much as they could, with Syrians and Palestinians alike. As long as the General Command was directing its hate against Tel Aviv, they had a free hand. On top of that, the organization was full of state security spies.

Once again, hundreds of Syrians and Palestinians arrived at the meeting point and took buses to the Golan Heights. Again, they broke through the barbed wire and ran across the border into Israel. This time, even more blood was spilled: 350 demonstrators were wounded, and twenty-three died, among them a young woman. And again, the buses drove directly to Mujtahed Hospital, where the wounded received medical treatment and the dead were cataloged.

The next morning at eleven, there was a funeral procession in Yarmouk. The bodies were wrapped in white shrouds and placed in open coffins. People carried them on their shoulders to the cemetery. But this was not the usual martyr's farewell. The grief turned to indignation. People in Yarmouk started to ask probing questions: Why had these young people been sent to the slaughter? Why were they treated like pawns? Why were they the cannon fodder with which the Assad regime tried to deflect attention from itself and toward Israel?

Soon, people were no longer shouting, "Palestine, Palestine, millions of martyrs!" No, they were shouting, "Freedom!" just like we heard at the protests in Daraa and Damascus. It was the largest demonstration I had ever seen in Yarmouk. Tens of thousands of people were on their feet. The rage was further incited by thousands of new arrivals from Palestinian refugee camps all over the country. They had brought a revolutionary spirit. The old and the young, businesspeople, workers, students, and of course the left—especially the generation that had grown up in the '80s and '90s with the songs of Ziad Rahbani. My generation.

By the way, Ziad Rahbani, the father figure of the freedom marchers, the man who had schooled our gaze for social injustice and who encouraged us to criticize the state and the clerics—with jazz, no less!—had become increasingly cynical over the years. We suddenly found him on the other side: after a long public silence, he revealed in a television interview—to the bitter disappointment of his followers—that he stood with the Assad regime and Hezbollah. Today I can't listen to his songs anymore without thinking of this betrayal.

One morning, my neighbor from the aluminum workshop next door got on his bicycle and told me he was going to a rally. I was curious, so I locked up the store and rode after him. When I turned onto the main street, I saw a seemingly endless parade of demonstrators, waving flags and shouting slogans. The merchants hastily closed the iron gates in front of their shops. And then, in the distance, I heard three gunshots coming from the cemetery.

Later I was told that angry demonstrators had started to insult

Ahmed Jibril, the gray-haired, mustached leader of the General Command. They were throwing trash at one of his aides, which led to a scuffle with his bodyguards, and one of them fired into the air. That enraged people even more.

"What gives him the right to fire off shots like that?" they said. "He ought to be punished!"

Jibril and his bodyguards took off and fled through the alleyways toward their headquarters. Soon, it was surrounded by protesters.

The mob kept demanding that the bodyguard be handed over. "Give him to us!" they shouted. "He has no right to be shooting at us!"

They threw stones at the building, then Molotov cocktails. Soon, smoke was rising from the headquarters. Then the demonstrators tried to break through the doors and windows with metal trash cans. More shots were fired.

I was standing about 150 yards away, in front of Palestine Hospital. I saw the wounded being dragged out on blankets and brought into the emergency room. A few of them had leg wounds, but the vast majority had been shot in the chest, stomach, or head.

I couldn't watch anymore. Upset, I got on my bicycle and rode home. Although I had already seen how embittered people had become, this was the first time I had witnessed violence.

In the following months, the Palestinian groups splintered. The larger militias mostly joined the Syrian protest movement and remained in Yarmouk, at least for the time being. I heard that Ahmed Jibril had been rescued from the roof of his burning headquarters by an army helicopter. Now he commanded his militias from outside Yarmouk. His men were still present inside Yarmouk, but they barely listened to their commander anymore, and many of them deserted. There were increasing tensions between the militias and the people of Yarmouk, who didn't want to follow any more orders, just because someone had a rifle. "Look at them, swinging their little sticks," some people said mockingly.

The younger generation had different heroes; they were no longer looking up to Fatah, Hamas, or the General Command. Their idols were young people from Italy, Germany, France, or Sweden who had come to Yarmouk to learn Arabic or to support the Palestinian cause. The General Command's calls for neutrality rang hollow to their ears, like music from an old, scratched-up record.

But, for the time being, things in Yarmouk calmed down again. We enjoyed a last respite. It would take another year and a half before the war reached our neighborhood. During that time, the Syrian Revolution turned increasingly bloody. But life in Yarmouk went on as before.

— CHAPTER TWELVE —

On July 7, 2011—one month after the big rally—Tahani and I celebrated our engagement. On that day, sixty of our closest relatives gathered in the living room of Tahani's father. The dining room was reserved for women, the living room for men. The elders were in front, the children all in the back. My grandfather, who had been suffering from Alzheimer's for the past few years, was rocking back and forth in his chair, a distant look in his eyes. I saw Uncle Mohammed and Uncle Sadik, and my cousins Mayad and Tamer, with whom I had played *Tobbeh* and *Dahhal* for so many years. Although I felt happy, I had butterflies in my stomach. I had never made a decision like this, which would define the rest of my life.

The sheikh had come over from the mosque. He was old and fat, with a long beard and a white djellaba that smelled of frankincense. I sat next to him on the sofa as he welcomed the assembled guests.

Tahani's grandfather, who had only one eye, began to talk: "We have agreed on a dowry of one hundred twenty-five thousand pounds." Around 240 dollars, an appropriate sum.

Tahani's father suddenly said, "We should change it to seventy-five thousand pounds." Around 145 dollars.

Everyone was stunned and silent. The sheikh froze.

"We had all agreed to this sum," my father said carefully. "I think we should leave it at that."

"No. Seventy-five thousand pounds. *Challas*, enough," Tahani's father said brusquely.

To this day, I still don't know why he did that. It was an affront. A remark like that could easily cause a rift within a family. Not only was it a snub to his father, repudiating him in public like that, but it was a snub to my father as well. If he didn't have sufficient money to pay it, he might have hinted at that earlier. But what a thoughtless thing to say! Thankfully, no one responded. "Very well," my father said curtly.

The ceremony began. The sheikh made a brief sermon, reading from the Quran and quoting the Prophet. After that, we all recited the Sura al-Fatiha together.

The sheikh asked Tahani's father, "Are you willing to give your daughter as a wife to Aeham Ahmad?"

"Yes, I give him my daughter."

Next, the sheikh read the marriage contract, which stated that this marriage was made before God and all present, and that it was valid for all eternity. In case of a divorce, Tahani would receive two hundred thousand Syrian pounds (almost four hundred dollars). The sheikh asked, "Did everyone hear this? Does everyone agree?"

"Yes," they all murmured.

Then the sheikh rose and went to the half-closed dining room door. Tahani was waiting on the other side.

"Do you also agree?" he asked.

"Yes, I agree," said Tahani, her voice sounding tight from all the excitement.

Three distant uncles proceeded to sign the contract. Our engagement was now official. The room erupted into cheers. People slapped me on the shoulders and called out, "*Mabruk, mabruk!* Congratulations!" I was laughing with joy.

A boy with a tray came through the room, offering glasses of orange juice to the guests. Tahani's grandfather, the man with one eye, missed his glass and knocked everything off the tray. The glasses shattered on the marble floor, and as people began gathering the shards, I slipped next door into the dining room. This was another tradition.

The women were expecting me. They wore their headscarves loosely. I saw Tahani in a dark blue short-sleeved dress. She was wearing makeup and had no headscarf on. It was the first time I saw her beautiful hair. I sat down beside her and barely dared to look at her. She must have felt the same. Every once in a while, we would both look up and smile shyly at each other.

A woman came and gave me a *darbuka*, a clay drum.

"Aeham, you're a musician," she said, "sing for us!" I took the drum and without thinking about it much, started singing a song. *"You were fine alone, my heart, what was it that made you blind? I thought I was happy, but then I reached inside and realized how shallow you are. Your way of being is disgusting to me, you are so mediocre, I would be fine without you,"* I sang with a carefree voice.

Tahani looked at me with big eyes. Only then did I realize how inappropriate my choice of song was. Oh dear! I hastily gave back the drum. My mother didn't seem to have noticed. She was too busy asking all her aunts and cousins how they were doing, how their families were doing. Soon, one of the women began playing the drum. Some of the women began to dance; others stayed seated and ate ice cream. Tahani and I sat there and smiled. Neither of us spoke.

After half an hour, the women were getting ready to leave and I was left behind, allowed to stay with Tahani for a little while. We went over to the empty living room and sat down on the couch.

What do you say in a moment like that? We were unbelievably nervous. For a while, neither of us spoke. And then I asked her about the things I already knew: What did she do for a living, where did she work, why was she interested in art? After fifteen minutes, her father came in. We said good-bye and I went home, confused, curious, happy. I was engaged now.

A few days later, I visited Tahani at her apartment for the first time. Her aunt served us orange juice. Her father sat down in an armchair, opened up the newspaper, and pretended to read it. Tahani and I tried to talk. Again, it was awkward. We had so much to say to each other. But not with her father listening!

No, it wouldn't work like this. The next time I came over, I slipped her my phone number. The next day she sent me a text message and we agreed to meet after school. We did this often in the coming weeks. She asked a colleague to take over her last few classes for the day, then we took the minibus to the old town and went for a walk.

I told her of my crazy friend Vladimir Tsaritzky, about the toolbox that I accidentally stole as a little boy, about Feisal Jamal and the peculiar women at my university, about Sarah, my young piano student, and about my brother's escapades. We talked about everything. I told her that I would never boss her around. It was up to her to decide how many children we should have. And whether she would continue working. She said she was looking forward to staying at home with the kids. Her work was poorly paid—she wouldn't miss it.

Every night before we went to sleep, we furtively talked to each other on the phone, sharing secrets and stories. My mother had been right: Tahani was a perfect match for me.

Soon, the wedding preparations began. Together with my father, I went to a print shop to order two hundred invitations. The man who did the typesetting showed me the design. The calligraphy was beautiful. But the invitation mentioned only my name. Tahani was only referred to as the "precious daughter of the Mnawwar family."

"Why isn't her name on the invitation?" I asked.

"Well, that's how we always do it," the man said.

"I don't like it. If my name is on the card, hers should be, too."

"But then every guy in the neighborhood would know she's about to get married."

"So?"

"That's just not done."

"But I'd like to do it that way."

He looked at my father. "Would you consent to put her name on the invitation?"

"I don't see why not," my father said.

The man asked for the phone number of Tahani's father and

called him. Would it be all right if we printed the bride's name on the invitation?

"No," Tahani's father said.

And that was that. His word was final, and there was nothing more we could do.

At the bottom of the invitation, the typesetter added the phrase "The children's paradise is at home." In other words: Please leave your kids at home. People always did this, to avoid having dozens of excited kids running through the banquet hall.

When the two hundred cards were printed, Uncle Mohammed went out and distributed them in the neighborhood. My mother and I bought a black suit and a white shirt. Then my brother, my cousins, and I furnished our future apartment. We carried a double bed upstairs, a sofa, a flat-screen TV, a stereo, a gas stove, and a gigantic fridge. My brother did all the woodwork in the kitchen. A few days before the wedding, Tahani's aunt came by with several suitcases, to check if everything was ready. Then she put Tahani's dresses in the closet.

The wedding took place on September 7, 2011, when life in Yarmouk was still normal. The event was basically a huge concert. I was sitting in a giant armchair on a stage, looking down into the semi-dark banquet hall, which was lit up with disco balls and colorful spotlights. Waiters were serving orange juice, tea, and Arabic ice cream, with a topping made of pistachio sprinkles and honey. Various musicians performed throughout the evening. The band Flowers played kitschy Arabic pop songs, and the band Hope performed revolutionary Palestinian anthems. Mohammed Munaf played the oud, my father played violin, and I played keyboard and sang.

The men were dancing the entire evening, holding each other by the hand as they made their way in an undulating line back and forth through the banquet hall, singing and waving as they snaked along.

The emcee was a relative of Uncle Mohammed. He had done such events often, and talked like a waterfall. Whenever somebody walked up to the stage to present a gift, he zealously praised that person. "God bless you, Abu Ibrahim, you're supporting the young couple with one thousand pounds, praised be the Prophet!"

The larger the sum, the more elaborate the praise: "Three thousand pounds, Abu Said! May God protect you and your family for all eternity! May He hold his loving hand over you and your business! May you and your loved ones live in wealth and peace forever! Praise Allah!"

Another man would discreetly write down the donor's sum, so that I would know how much I'd have to give at this person's wedding one day. My father still has that list to this day.

Around midnight—my head was already buzzing—my father, my father-in-law, my two uncles, and I climbed into a Kia decked out with flowers and we drove over to the women's wedding hall, honking loudly. The city lights passed us by; pedestrians cheered us on. When we entered the hall, it looked like a disco, with dry ice and colorful lights. On a stage, in one of those throne-like armchairs, sat Tahani in her wedding dress.

When we came in, the women leapt to their feet and rushed to greet us. They wore their headscarves loosely, barely covering their hair. They had on makeup and elegant evening clothes. I had never seen my aunts like this before. It was a shock.

I went to Tahani. We shook hands, and I sat down in the large armchair next to her, whispering that she looked lovely. Soon, we were dancing the wedding dance, while everyone formed a large circle around us, clapping.

"I'm proud of you," my mother whispered in my ear. "You will have a beautiful life together." Then she embraced Tahani and said, "From now on, you are my daughter."

Later, we drove through the streets in a five-car convoy, decorated with flowers, honking loudly. Tahani and I were in the first car. "This is wonderful," I whispered to her. "I'm so happy." She smiled. When we arrived at our apartment, we were met—as tradition would have it—by a noisy percussion band, signaling to all the neighbors that a young couple was moving in. Together, we went upstairs, I carrying Tahani's veil, and my mother and Tahani's aunt prepared some food for us: bread, hummus, and grilled meats. Then everybody said good-bye and left.

Me? I was exhausted. Utterly, completely exhausted. I had shaken so many hands, smiled at so many people, received so many gifts and well-wishes. Now that all the strain had evaporated, my eyelids became heavy.

"I'm going to lie down for a minute," I said to Tahani. She looked at me, puzzled.

"Just for a moment. I need a break. I'm totally exhausted."

I lay down on the floor, in front of the television, and propped my feet on an armchair to reinvigorate my metabolism. Taking the remote control, I turned on the TV and saw that *Tom and Jerry* was on. How nice. I'd always liked that cartoon.

Tahani was moving back and forth behind me, rattling dishes. Then she started rattling them a little louder. I could feel her disappointment growing. She was probably wondering what kind of guy she had gotten stuck with. Lying in front of the TV, watching *Tom and Jerry* on our wedding night!

And I wasn't exactly proud of the way I had let myself collapse. But I felt completely wiped out. My mother had explained to me what to do: Light some candles, put on some beautiful music, look deeply into each other's eyes. . . . But I could barely keep my own eyes open, lying semiconscious on the floor, grinning at the exploits of the silly cat and the clever mouse. The minutes ticked away. Tahani was clattering the dishes even louder as I smiled at the TV, almost falling asleep. . . .

But then, I don't know how, my body received a last tiny jolt of energy. I leapt to my feet, went into the kitchen, splashed water onto my face, chugged a glass of cola, and went back into the living room. I smiled at Tahani. . . .

The next morning, my parents and Tahani's aunt came over for breakfast. A few days later, I started going back to work each morning. I would come home at noon to have lunch with Tahani, who was still on school vacation. Sometimes she visited me in the store to make sure that I wasn't flirting with pretty piano students, not realizing that something like that would never have occurred to me.

Our business was still thriving. Many people from other neighborhoods had fled to Yarmouk. The first checkpoints had been set up on some of the access roads, so refugees could no longer get out quite so easily. Which meant they became bored. And I had even more students.

Among them were three female college students. I liked them a lot. They supported the revolution with heart and soul. Two of them were Christians; the third girl was an Ismaelite, a member of a small Muslim faith community. I have no idea how I know this, but it must have come up in the course of our conversations. I certainly didn't ask them, for in Syria it's taboo to ask someone about their religious affiliation.

The three of them continued taking piano lessons with me, even though the journey to Yarmouk became increasingly dangerous. The first girl was from Bab Sharqi, the heart of the old town, and the second girl was from neighboring Zahira, which remains untouched by the war to this day. The third girl was from Taqaddom, south of Yarmouk, where fighting would soon break out. Of course, none of them wore headscarves: they all wore jeans and tight tops. The boys in the neighborhood couldn't stop staring at them. And Tahani was jealous.

I never spoke with my students about politics. It was too dangerous. You never knew which side the other person was on, so I didn't dare reveal my views. In a dictatorship like Syria's, it could cost you your life. We had a saying that summed it up: "Between you and I, there's always a spy."

"Why do you keep coming here?" I once asked the young woman from the old town. "Isn't it dangerous?" Let's say her name was Rania. "I'm sure you could take classes in your neighborhood."

"You're just a good teacher," Rania answered, "and inexpensive, too."

Well, an honest response! I took heart and asked her, "What do you think of the protest movement in Damascus?"

Rania's eyes lit up, and she gave me an earful. "We urgently need change!" she said. "If not now, when? Things can't go on like this!"

It felt good to hear her talk like that. Everyone else was always yelling and cursing, and I could never make sense of it. The two other students chimed in, telling me about their hope for change. Democracy! An end to fear and spying and the corruption that was eating away at our society! Freedom!

Whenever I think back at those first hopeful months of the Syrian Revolution, I think of these three girls. To me, they embody the path we should have taken, away from dictatorship and fundamentalism.

But that's not how things turned out.

A few months after our marriage, Tahani became pregnant. I was burning up with love, thinking about all kinds of things rather than politics. We were about to start a family, and I wanted my children to have a better life than me. At Tahani's sonogram appointment, as the gynecologist ran the transducer over Tahani's belly, we looked at the monitor and for the first time saw the outline of our baby. We beamed at each other, filled with joy. And in that moment, love hit me like a thunderbolt.

From then on, I completely doted on Tahani. We spent every free minute together. "Did you take your vitamins?" I asked her. "Did you drink your *ayran* today?" For a long time, I had dreamed of a family. Now my dream was about to come true.

— CHAPTER THIRTEEN —

Ahmad was born on June 27, 2012—but he entered a world of cruelty. The Syrian Civil War was escalating. Soon after his birth, soldiers would barricade the streets and seal off our neighborhood. Before long, hunger and death would reign in Yarmouk. I begged Tahani to leave, to get to safety, for her and our baby's sake. In those days, women were still allowed to go through the checkpoints. It would take her only a few hours to reach a safe neighborhood. A lot of women did this, escaping to a normal life and leaving their husbands behind in Yarmouk.

Tahani would have none of it. "I was with you when we were doing well," she said. "Now I will stay with you when we are doing poorly. We will live together and we will die together."

Soon, a neighborhood called Tadamon, to the east of Yarmouk, was bombed. Most of the rockets were fired from Mount Qasioun, but some of them came from Damascus Airport or Mezzeh Military Airport. There was a popping sound as they fell onto the buildings, and then we could see a column of black smoke drifting into the sky.

From the very beginning, the uprising in Tadamon had been violent. Probably because a lot of soldiers lived there—and when they deserted, they took their weapons with them. And when the security forces shot at protesters, the former soldiers fought back. That's how the FSA was created, the Free Syrian Army. Wealthy people in Damascus bought large numbers of weapons from the regime and donated them to the FSA.

Tadamon was a newly developed area, full of Sunnis, Alawites, Christians, Shiites, Murshidis, Orthodox, and Ismaelites. In 2012, when the unrest reached that neighborhood, the various faith communities stood together, for in the beginning, the Syrian Revolution wasn't a religious war. That came much later.

The General Command set up checkpoints at the entry points to Yarmouk, assisting the Assad regime. But the FSA kept advancing. Increasingly, firefights between the two militias broke out. Ahmed Jibril was a friend of Assad's, and he soon committed an unpardonable sin: he called the Syrian Army for help.

On July 15, 2012, eighteen days after Ahmad was born, the first tank rolled through Yarmouk. I can still see it: it came from the "Watermelon." That's what we called the large, round fountain at the traffic circle leading to Damascus. The tank turned into the main shopping street and moved toward Palestine Hospital, rattling loudly. Then it turned back. That was its route. Whenever I biked along the main street, my bike tires wobbled over the tank tracks in the asphalt.

At the same time, I was the happiest father in all the world. Ahmad, our son, was now three weeks old. He was born in the al-Bassel Birth Clinic, via C-section. We spent a lot of money so that Tahani received the best medical care possible. One morning, we got into a taxi to drive to the clinic, and the next morning we drove back home, with Tahani holding the baby in her arms.

Now began the wonderful time of young parenthood. I spent as little time in the shop as possible, so that I could be at home. Just so the three of us could lie in bed. My parents were so happy! Their first grandchild! Soon, my father reached for his violin and began playing songs for little Ahmad. He was probably hoping my son would become a musician like me.

Until early August, everything was peaceful. We were able to put our son in a stroller and go out with him. I was still able to ride my bike to Yarmouk. But then everything changed.

Suddenly, soldiers turned up on our street. During the day, they drove around in their cars, with squealing tires and howling engines, just to show everyone who was boss. They began searching houses, looking for militia members, weapons, or sometimes simply people who had been caught on video at rallies. One evening, they searched the apartment below ours. I wasn't home, and Tahani lay trembling in bed, clutching our son. A nightmare! The next day, we heard of mass executions. More and more people packed their things and left Yalda in a hurry.

We needed a plan B. I asked my music students for help, and one afternoon, we carried hundreds of instruments from our store over to the oud workshop. It was only a few minutes' walk, but we had to keep going back and forth. We had intended to turn the oud workshop into our main showroom, since the space was significantly larger. Now, if worse came to worst, we could even live there.

At the same time, we put all the heavy equipment, all the saws and grinding machines, on a trailer and stored it in our old music shop. My brother was going to use the space as his carpentry workshop, to make windows and doors. The oud business was defunct. What good was an instrument in times like these?

I had made a mistake. In the winter of 2011, with all the optimism of a newly married man, I had taken on a large order from one of our best customers, the wholesaler from Lebanon. He wanted twelve hundred ouds. Because he was a good customer, we hadn't insisted on a down payment. We never did with him. Instead, we began buying high-end wood. We must've spent almost fifty thousand dollars on it.

A short while later—and this was my second mistake—we bought a remainder of expensive Yamaha guitars, six hundred pieces at 120 dollars per piece. A bargain, I thought. But no. It was a disaster. All in all, the guitars had cost us seventy-two thousand dollars, and we never sold any of them! Just like the twelve hundred ouds. When they were finished and ready for delivery, the wholesaler pulled out. At first, he kept making excuses, then he canceled the order. When the war came, we were the proud owners of thousands of instruments, but we had hardly any money.

So we moved our inventory, and not a second too soon. On September 4, my cousin Mayad, who lived in the apartment above us, was getting ready to celebrate his birthday. I was out with an uncle of mine who owned a minibus, and we were getting oud parts. Tahani was already dressed and about to go upstairs with little Ahmad and my parents. And that was when the army began shelling Yalda with heavy artillery.

As soon as the first buildings on our street were hit, Tahani grabbed little Ahmad and a bag of cactus figs—I have no idea why—from the kitchen. My father grabbed a small backpack with our savings, my mother a bag full of food, and then the three of them ran toward Yarmouk, away from the hailstorm of bombs, the baby in their arms.

While all this was happening, I was still out with my uncle. We, too, were caught in the middle of it. The mortar shells were raining down all around us. There was a whistling sound and then—bang!—an explosion behind us. Debris rained down onto the road.

"Oh, we're in trouble now!" my uncle yelled. "How are we going to get out of here?"

"God will protect us!" I called. "Drive faster. Faster!"

I talked to Tahani on my cell phone and she told me where she was. In the rearview mirror, I saw a building collapse as my uncle raced toward Yarmouk, hitting the horn. I sent a quick prayer to heaven.

Finally, we met up with the other four members of my family. I jumped out of the minibus and hugged Tahani. Missiles flew above our heads, toward Yalda, howling in the sky. We quickly drove to the former oud workshop.

It was early evening. We had escaped with our lives, but nothing more than that. We didn't even have mattresses. A neighbor, a friendly man named Abu Abed, had seen us enter the store and came out to see how we were doing. He gave us bedding and two large mattresses. We went to sleep in our street clothes.

When we awoke the next morning, bones aching, little Ahmad had a red lump on his hand. A spider had bitten him.

We went out to get some essentials: underwear, toothbrushes, pacifiers, and diapers. Tahani's aunt lent us some cooking pans. The room was about twenty feet high, the walls unfinished, the floor made of concrete. We had torn down two walls. The front area was used as a store, complete with a shop counter. There were keyboards and pianos everywhere, and hundreds of ouds hung from the ceiling like clusters of grapes. Behind the wall was our only room, full of violin cases and huge crates, with ten guitars each. All the way in the back, we had created a makeshift kitchen and toilet.

Each day, we hoped to be able to go to our apartments in Yalda to get a few things, but things simply wouldn't calm down. It took another year before we were able to enter our apartments. All the windows were shattered, and half of my parents' apartment was gone.

We were in for some difficult times. We were constantly arguing. Only a year before, I had moved out of my parents' apartment, and now I was forced to live with them in one room. We slept penned together on the mattresses, like sardines in a can. I was cranky. And Tahani was doing even worse. She was a young mother, nursing her child, and her sleep was brief. During the day, we had to endure my students' attempts at music. It would be a long time before we had any privacy again.

Most people around us still lived in their apartments, just like they had done before. But we, we were already refugees, desperately trying to create some semblance of normalcy. In the mornings, my mother put on music by Fairouz, whose bright voice was full of confidence and clarity. Just like before, just like in the old days. But my mother no longer had the heart to sing along.

— CHAPTER FOURTEEN —

Around noon on December 16, 2012, I was in the shop playing piano when suddenly, there was a heavy explosion nearby. Then a second one. The walls were shaking, and one of the large windows cracked. I ran outside. We had long since gotten used to the sound of nearby artillery fire. Over the past few months, the air force had bombed entire neighborhoods of Damascus back into the Stone Age. So far, however, Yarmouk had been spared. But this explosion sounded much closer than any of the others. In the distance, I heard a fighter jet roaring away.

I got on my bike and scanned the sky for smoke pillars. But those could be deceiving. After Tadamon, the sky was often full of smoke. People were shouting that a MiG jet had shot a rocket at the Mansoura School. My old middle school! I rode over—and found myself in the middle of the war. Cars were burning; black smoke filled the air. The rocket had hit a garden next to the schoolyard. All the windows of the school and nearby buildings were destroyed, and shrapnel had torn holes into the walls.

As soon as I arrived, I was told that another rocket had hit the al-Bassel Birth Clinic, where our son had been born. Out of damn curiosity I went over there as well. People were carrying the dead and wounded out into the streets. Some of the victims were missing limbs. A doctor arrived to see who could be saved.

"Bring him inside," he called. Four men lifted up a blanket, carrying one of the victims. The man's face had been crushed. You could barely make out his features amid all the blood. Another man arrived at the scene, anxious to peek under a sheet that had been placed over a woman's body.

"She's dead!" someone called.

"I'm looking for my mother!" the man called out. He pulled back the blanket and sent a quick prayer to heaven. *"Alhamdulillah."* Then he continued running.

I saw my friend Thaer, a filmmaker, running around with a camera, shivering. Later, he would turn this material into a short film titled *MiG*.

The Husseini mosque, where some of the refugees had found shelter, had also been hit. People were still screaming as survivors wandered through the smoke, looking for relatives. Ambulances arrived. Blood was everywhere.

I saw I was of no use, and went home.

That night, my father and I sat up together for a long time and I told him what I had seen.

"Why Yarmouk?" he asked, full of sorrow. "We wanted to stay out of this. And now we're getting bombed."

And why had a school, a mosque, a hospital, and the registry office been targeted? That was where the refugee centers had been established. There weren't any rebels there. The bomb had dug deep into the basement of the mosque, where dozens of families had found shelter. More than forty people had been killed. Despondent, we went to bed—that is, we lay down next to each other on the mattresses. We were awake for a long time.

The next morning, we got up at six. I wanted to go to the city, and my father said he'd come with me. We had to pass several checkpoints and realized it was best to do so early. At noon, when the sun was burning, the soldiers tended to be irritable. Then anything could happen.

One week earlier, the UNRWA had pulled its employees from Yarmouk, no longer able to guarantee their safety. The UNRWA schools were full of refugees, and regular classes were out of the question. Instead, the UNRWA announced that it would, for the first time, hand out cash to us Palestinians. From now on, each of us would receive three thousand Syrian pounds per month, around five dollars, with the payments issued by a bank in the center of Damascus. That's where we were headed that day.

It was still early—but when we looked out the shopwindow, we saw our neighbors moving bags and suitcases out of the building and into the street.

"Where are you going?" I asked.

"Visiting relatives, just for a few days."

They were carrying mattresses and bedding. This didn't look like a short visit. My father and I stepped out of the building. I held out my hand, he took it, and we were on our way, just like we had always done.

When we turned into Yarmouk Street, I saw a sight that made the blood run cold in my veins: a seemingly endless stream of people with all their belongings, slowly trickling through the heavy traffic, headed for Damascus. Though it was still early, there must have been tens of thousands of people, carrying bags and suitcases, pushing carts, strollers, and bicycles loaded with boxes. The roof racks of cars had mattresses piled on them. This is what it must have looked like during the Naqba, the mass exodus from Palestine in 1948.

I spoke to some of the people rushing past. Where were they headed?

"Visiting family," one of them said.

"Don't know yet," said another. "We just want to get out of Yarmouk."

"Why?"

"Haven't you heard? Yarmouk Camp News ran a piece today: the government is urging all citizens to immediately evacuate Yarmouk. God help us! Who knows what they're planning?"

No, I hadn't read that. Yarmouk Camp News was one of many Facebook pages run by "citizen journalists." Pages like that had been popping up since the beginning of the protest movement. There was something for everyone, for every political affiliation. Some were as useless as the official Syrian media. Others did meticulous journalistic work and offered a valuable alternative to the state-run media. Facebook allowed us to get around the government's outdated 1960s-era assembly ban, at least in the virtual space. The regime kept shutting down various platforms, but we had all learned how to work around the censorship.

Yesterday we'd been attacked by two MiG rockets. Today the army had issued an ultimatum. And now one of the refugees whispered to me, "My uncle works at state security. He said they're going to place Yarmouk under siege." I became even more queasy.

We joined the stream of people. Normally, it took less than ten minutes to walk down Yarmouk Street. On this day, it took us forty-five minutes.

My father's cell phone rang. It was Uncle Mohammed. He asked us where we were. Were we leaving Yarmouk? Should he come get us?

"No," my father said. "We'll wait it out for the time being. We'll see what happens."

We debated for a while—and decided to use our journey to Damascus as a trial run for escape, a "what if" scenario. If it turned out to be feasible, we'd leave Yarmouk before the war could crush us, as so many people had predicted.

I looked at the crowds. Many of them were made up of people who had fled in the preceding months from other neighborhoods, when there was shooting in their streets, when their houses were being bombed. Small wonder they were so quick on their feet. They had nothing left to lose.

We passed the Watermelon, the large traffic circle at the access point to Yarmouk, and a short while later we crossed a bridge toward New Zahira, a new development with well-maintained streets. The buildings here weren't simply concrete shells like in Yarmouk; they had been refitted with bright granite cladding. Cars were parked along the sides of the street, the stores were open—and the refugees were streaming in. The first arrivals here had been housed in schools and mosques, but by now, Zahira was overflowing with refugees.

They had nowhere to go, and many were simply sitting on the sidewalks, completely exhausted. They told us they'd been turned down everywhere.

It was depressing. The refugees stood in stark contrast to the locals. People here ran down their stairs, keys in hand, to hastily lock their entrance doors, not wanting the refugees to spend the night in their stairwells.

Under normal circumstances, the people of Zahira are decent and generous. But the sight of these masses must have scared them. They didn't want Zahira to suffer the same fate as Yarmouk: we had taken in many refugees, and we were now paying a heavy price for that.

In my mind's eye, I went through the options. Did I really want to put myself, my wife, and my six-month-old baby through this? Leave our store behind? How were we supposed to survive? The rents in Damascus were astronomical. We could never afford an apartment there. Our only option would be seeking shelter in a school or a mosque. And then we'd have to anticipate a raid every few days.

I hadn't served in the military. Initially, I didn't have to, because I was a student. But when my student exemption ended, I never showed up for my registration appointment. Now I was married, and I had a child. Would that help? According to Syrian law, you could get married only after having completed your military service. But my father had connections; he had bribed the right person to put a stamp on my draft card, allowing me to marry. But even with a wife and child, I could get snatched up at any time. In those days, nothing was reliable anymore.

If the soldiers didn't scoop me up at a refugee center, then they'd doubtless catch me at a checkpoint. Checkpoints were everywhere now, sprouting like mushrooms. No, for me, the so-called safe neighborhoods outside Yarmouk were anything but safe.

Suddenly, I saw a soldier peeling off from his group and coming toward us. "ID, please!"

I showed him my identification card.

"Where are you going?" he asked.

"To the bank, to take out the UNRWA money." I kept calm. My blind father was with me, and I had my official family document booklet in my backpack—I didn't think I'd run into trouble.

"And then where will you be going?"

"Back to Yarmouk."

He grinned maliciously as he returned my papers.

We quickly hurried along, Papa and I using the same route we had always taken on the way to the music school. Thinking about it made me melancholy. How many hours had we sat together in minibuses chatting about everything? When I was a boy, I had bombarded him with questions. And he had always answered me patiently. I remembered zipping through these streets on my bicycle, back when the future seemed so far away and never-ending. And now? Now we were sleeping on mattresses on the floor, and our future extended as far as the next checkpoint.

At the bank, we took our place in line. Life here in the upscale Malki neighborhood was perfectly normal. And yet, just a few miles from here, a war was raging. It seemed like a bad dream. When it was our turn, I showed my ID and received nine thousand Syrian pounds for Tahani, Ahmad, and myself. We immediately started on our way back. It was past eleven, the sun was high in the sky, and it was about time we got out of there. We walked next to each other in silence. Only here and there my father asked, "What was that?" Or, "What do you see?"

The closer we came to Yarmouk, the more soldiers we saw on the streets. We grew alarmed and started walking faster. What had we gotten ourselves into? Police cars drove past us, personnel carriers, tanks. Two bulldozers were slowly moving toward the Watermelon. Later that day, they would pile up dirt barricades on all access roads. The guy from state security had predicted it: Yarmouk was being sealed off.

And again, a soldier stopped us. "Where are you going?"

"Back to Yarmouk."

"Are you insane?"

We shrugged, and hurried past the group of soldiers, hearing the distinct snapping sound of magazines being loaded into Kalashnikov rifles. At any moment, a firefight might break out. Snipers could be lurking anywhere. We decided to walk through narrow back alleys. As soon as we reached the next intersection, we hunched over and scurried across.

"All that for a measly nine thousand pounds!" my father said, cursing. "Next time, I'll just give you the money."

"I'm sorry!" I said. "I never thought it would be so bad."

My father was a heavy smoker, and not used to walking long distances. He was sweating and wheezing.

"Papa, don't give up," I implored him. "We've got to get through this. We're almost home."

Finally, we were past all the soldiers. The streets of Yarmouk were empty, the shops closed. We were the only ones who had returned. As we rushed down the main street, there wasn't a soul in sight.

After about ten minutes, we ran into a group of fighters from the FSA coming up the street on foot. They didn't pay any attention to us. Their faces were covered by black bandannas and they cheerfully bantered with one another. One of them waved his rifle in the air. "Tonight we'll be in Damascus!" he shouted. The others cheered.

Finally, we were home. Tahani and my mother almost began punching me, that's how furious they were. "What were you thinking?" my mother said, enraged. "Next time you want to get yourself in danger, do it by yourself and not with your old father in tow! We almost died of fear!"

Tahani was so relieved to see us that she had tears in her eyes.

I realized they were right. Despite everything, it was safest to remain in Yarmouk.

My father had completely exhausted himself. He smoked a cigarette, drank a cup of tea, and then lay down.

In the evening, we turned on the news. We learned that the

army had started an offensive against "terrorists who occupied Yarmouk." Then they showed interviews conducted in nice-looking shelters, with refugees who were cursing the terrorists.

But that's not what was really going on. The army had deliberately emptied out the neighborhood in order to draw in the FSA. That way, they could surround the fighters. They didn't care about the people who still remained here.

— CHAPTER FIFTEEN —

By this time, our neighborhood was completely sealed off. Army sharpshooters lurked at every exit point, supported by the militias of the General Command. Yarmouk was turning into a ghost town. The silence was eerie. The shouting of the vendors, the laughter of children, the joyous cries of mothers, the boys whistling after the girls, the girls—seemingly annoyed—speeding up their steps, Abu Mohammed smoking his *shisha* at the corner, Abu Balila hawking his chickpeas—all gone. Just like my students, my customers, my friends. Yesterday, a half million people lived here. And now? There were maybe fifty thousand people left, at most. It was as if a deadly virus had decimated the population.

I aimlessly wandered through the streets with nothing to do. I was depressed, haunted by questions. I knew my family only stayed because of me. Was I asking too much of them? Should we try to escape? Was there any chance we could make it out of here, in the midst of this war? Had we made the right choice? What would become of us now?

For now, Yarmouk was in the hands of the FSA. Every day, I saw their fighters marching through the streets, their faces hidden behind black bandannas. They didn't want to be recognized; perhaps their wives and children lived in Damascus. Like everyone else, they had their own routine. One of their leaders would deliver a speech, then they'd all wave their Kalashnikovs around and shout, "God is great!" after which they'd pile into their beat-up cars—like something out of a *Mad Max* movie—and drive to the front. Usually, that was the Watermelon, where the worst battles were raging. We were lucky—our shop was at the other end of Yarmouk.

With each passing month, the siege got worse. Eventually, only women and old men were allowed to go through the checkpoints, but just at certain times, and they were always thoroughly searched. They were still allowed to bring shopping bags into Yarmouk, but it was getting harder. At first, the army allowed each person ten pounds of food, then only a "one-day ration." And with each passing day, the rations got smaller.

We had heard the reports coming out of Homs, Daraa, and Duma. Hundreds of thousands of people had been encircled by the army and starved to death. In the end, people had been reduced to eating clover and leaves, hoping to stall the inevitable. Was that to be our fate as well? As Palestinian refugees, we were supposed to be neutral, and grateful to the government for allowing us to settle here, back in 1948. So why would our own government, this "fortress against the Zionist occupation," want to starve us?

There were still some shops that sold whatever was available. Hungry mothers could still go to Damascus to buy rice or oil, which they then sold. But they always kept a little for themselves, to feed their own children. With each week, everything became more expensive. Soon, we were starving.

All our relatives had left Yarmouk as fast as they could, including Uncle Mohammed and Uncle Sadik.

Each of the two owned a small general store where they sold beans and rice, sugar and tea, chickpeas and spices. One day around noon, Uncle Sadik made his way through the checkpoints to visit us in Yarmouk. He handed me a set of keys.

"I want you to sell everything we have," he instructed me. "But don't you dare overcharge! That's *haram*." Under no circumstances would the two of them charge exorbitant prices for their food—that would be against our faith. Uncle Mohammed's shop was relatively empty; his business hadn't been going well lately. But Uncle Sadik still had eight tons of food left, including seven tons of red lentils, which he had originally bought as pigeon feed.

I nodded, agreeing to do it, but frankly, it took me a while to get started. I just didn't see myself as a bean merchant.

One day in February when I happened to pass Uncle Sadik's shop, I saw that the iron gate at the entrance was bent up, damaged by a grenade that had exploded nearby. The shop must have been open for days. Anyone could have gone in and looted it. We had to do something. However, we didn't dare move the food during daylight, for if a soldier happened to come by, he might confiscate everything.

So we came back at night, my father, my brother, and I. We loaded the sacks onto a large dolly that we had found in the store, and we began pushing. We went back and forth the whole night. We rested during the day, and in the evening, when darkness fell, we went out again, pushing one load after another through the empty streets. At one point, a man approached us. Of course, right at that moment, a sack fell off the cart and burst open.

"What's this? Beans?" he asked.

"They're my uncle's," I said. "We're about to sell them."

"Give them to me."

"We'll sell them at a fair price. Everyone should get their share. You're welcome to come by." I told him where the shop was, and he left.

What could I do? There was nothing else to keep me occupied, so I started selling the beans. And so, for the next month and a half, I spent every afternoon in the front of our music store, selling rice and wheat instead of violins or guitars. I charged twenty-five Syrian pounds, around five cents, for a half pound of sugar. But prices kept rising, and before long, people paid as much as twenty-five hundred pounds for it. In the end, the price even rose to twenty-five thousand pounds! I was probably naïve, but I just couldn't imagine a siege being effective, especially not in the middle of an urban metropolis like Damascus. I was wrong.

Soon, word of my good prices began to spread. Whenever I opened the store at 1 p.m., there was already a line of ten people. I made sure to give each customer the same amount: I didn't want anyone reselling the food at a higher price. In the beginning, everyone got four pounds. Then two pounds. Then one pound.

The customers were watching each of my gestures with hungry eyes. Everyone was driven half-mad by fear of starvation. Sometimes arguments broke out. "You're giving the others more!" someone complained.

"No," I said. "Look at the scale. Everyone gets exactly the same."

By May, I had sold everything—the sugar, the rice, the cans of tuna, the bulgur, and the clarified butter. The only thing I couldn't get rid of were the red lentils. Even now, no one wanted them. But there was one exception: "I have a pigeon coop," one of my customers told me one day. "I'd like to buy the lentils for my birds." I said no. People were starving. And this fool wanted to feed the lentils to his pigeons? No way!

The only ray of sunshine in those days was little Ahmad. He squeaked and laughed and babbled, and he grew bigger with each passing day. Soon, he would be walking. We had gotten him a baby walker, and now he could roll through the store, propelled by the tips of his toes. He loved digging his fingers into the rough linen sacks. Each day, when I put him on my lap and played piano for him, he swatted at the keys with his tiny hands. Sometimes my father played the violin for him, or my mother would sing to him. But she sang so quietly that none of the adults nearby could hear her.

My brother, Alaa, continued working as a carpenter. In those days, he had plenty of work. Yarmouk was largely depopulated, and that meant ample opportunities for burglars and looters. Entire buildings stood empty. Countless doors had been pried open, and then the owners, who had briefly stopped by to assess the damage, would call my brother. Sometimes he repaired windows that had been shattered by the pressure of nearby explosions. Alaa lived and worked in his carpentry shop, our old music store. He cooked his meals there and hung out with his friends. He rarely visited us.

He still continued working in Jaramana, a new development east of Yarmouk. Many of his friends lived there. Early in the mornings, he went through the checkpoint and then, during the day, he worked on construction sites, building doors. At night, he slept at his friends' places. And when he came back a few days later, he brought us bread and tomatoes.

My father implored him to stay put. "Please, please, please, Alaa, there's enough work for you in Yarmouk," he pleaded. "The checkpoints are too dangerous. Don't go, I beg you!"

"Oh, come on!" my brother said, dismissing his concerns. "I'm not afraid of the soldiers. What could possibly happen to me?" It was true: He had completed his military service. He had served in the army for two years, right after school. And he had never received a draft order.

"No one is safe," my father said. "You know that. They can pin all kinds of things on you. You've heard the stories!"

My brother shrugged. He had never listened to my parents. Why start now?

On June 22, 2013, a Saturday, Alaa left Yarmouk early to go through the checkpoint toward Jaramana. The day before, he had stopped by to say good-bye to us.

Around eleven, a man came to see us.

"I need to talk to you," he said to my father and me. We were standing at the front of the store. "But you have to promise me never to tell anyone my name. Never!"

We promised.

"Alaa has been arrested."

My father collapsed. It was as if all strength had left his body. "What happened? Tell me, please!"

"Dozens of men were arrested at the checkpoint this morning. I was one of them. I was thrown into a prison transport. But I was lucky, I have an uncle at the General Command. He begged the commandant to release me. At the last moment, Alaa shouted, 'Tell my parents!' "

My father was trembling. "Umm, Aeham, come quickly!" he yelled in a high voice toward the back of the room.

My mother stepped through the curtain, closing her headscarf. "What's going on?"

"Alaa was arrested."

It took a moment for her to comprehend. Then she began to sob.

"Quick, quick, let's go to the checkpoint!" my father cried. "Maybe there's something we can do!"

The four of us hurried there. As we were walking, we learned that the "man with the mask" had singled out my brother.

The man with the mask. There was one at each checkpoint. A man with a black balaclava who scrutinized everyone. But every once in a while, he would point at someone and say, "This one." And then the soldiers would grab that person. For whatever reason. It could mean anything. It could mean that you were a suspected FSA member. It could mean that you were drafted. It could mean that you would vanish in the government's torture chambers. It could be your death warrant. The man in the mask was judge and executioner in one.

It could be anyone under that hood. A man from state security. A denouncer. Or maybe just some prisoner. Maybe it was someone they had tortured with electric shocks and then given a black hood to, forcing him to stand at the very checkpoint where he had been arrested. And then, indiscriminately, he singled out people to fulfill his daily quota, hoping that they wouldn't torture him any longer.

So the man in the black mask had pointed at my brother and said, "That one's Alaa." He must have known him. But how? Alaa had often gotten into fights with the guys in our neighborhood. Maybe one of them had denounced him. Who could have taken such brutal revenge on him?

I went with my parents as far as I could and wished them luck. Then they went on without me. I sat down in the shade. Everything collapsed around me as I thought about Alaa. Where could he be? What were they doing to him now? Why hadn't he listened to my father? At least this one time? Why did he always have to have the last word?

I remembered how Alaa had run out into the street one evening when he wasn't yet twelve. The neighbors had complained about me playing piano, and he had shouted, "The next person who complains will get a beating!" I remembered how, during his short stint at the music school, he had fallen into a fountain, ruining his expensive solfège textbook. How he had pushed me to the floor when we were renovating the store. How he had fought with my father, endlessly, it seemed. For five tedious hours, I waited in the shade.

Finally, my parents came back. Without Alaa. They had gone to the checkpoint. A soldier had told them to wait for the commandant.

They had waited for two hours. Finally, the man arrived. My parents were permitted to see him.

"I am blind, I need my son," my father complained. "He is my only consolation, please give him back to me."

"I don't know what you're talking about," the commandant replied.

"He was arrested this morning."

"We haven't arrested anybody."

"But I'm sure. Somebody told me."

"Who?"

"I don't know his name."

"You're a liar. Go away, or I'll arrest you."

So they gave up. However, checkpoints are laid out like one-way streets. Once you're in line, there is no turning back. So they had to leave Yarmouk and line up again, this time in the opposite direction.

We headed home, my mother crying softly to herself. When we got there, Tahani was waiting for us, out of her mind with worry. In all the excitement, no one had thought to tell her what had happened. My father immediately began working the phone. The landline was still working. Did anyone know someone at the General Command? Has anyone heard anything? Was there anyone who might know something?

Early the next morning, my parents went to Damascus to speak to the authorities, hoping to find out more. Alaa Ahmad, born on February 13, 1991, arrested on June 22—do you know anything?

And because the lines at the checkpoints were unbelievably long, they didn't come back until late at night. Then they left again the next morning.

They would be searching for years. Looking for a trail. Just as tens of thousands are doing in Syria every day, on the desperate quest for some trace of a loved one.

Their last shreds of hope and happiness were gone now. At night, my mother lay awake, and when she got up, her eyes were red from crying. My father, normally a cheerful, talkative person, sat brooding for hours on end, smoking cigarettes. Until he suddenly jumped up and said, "Oh God. Oh God, I can't stand it. It's too much. What can I possibly do?"

Five times a day, my parents prayed, the way they always did. They often prayed together. I could hear them loudly begging God to return Alaa to us. To help him in his time of need.

— CHAPTER SIXTEEN —

It happened on July 18, 2013: Yarmouk was completely sealed off. From one day to the next, the checkpoints were closed. No one got out. Nothing got in. No rice, no oil, no milk powder, no sugar. The siege began. The electricity was turned off. Food prices exploded.

I suspect that the siege had been carefully planned. And Yarmouk's particular geography made the task even easier, as if the neighborhood had been designed to be cut off from the rest of the city. It was simple. The army set up a checkpoint near the Watermelon and positioned a few snipers on Palestine Street, the linear eastern border of our neighborhood. And with that, Yarmouk and the southern suburbs were completely isolated.

Soon, people started dying of hunger. On August 18, a six-month-old girl died while her mother was crisscrossing Yarmouk in a desperate search for baby food. The next victim was a man with kidney disease. Their deaths unsettled everyone. "Do I look sick?" people would ask each other. "My eyes are red, what does that mean?"

Perversely, it was a sudden advantage that my father was blind. He was given preferential and respectful treatment. One day, for example, we were told that a small grove of trees in our neighborhood was going to be cut down. If you managed to sign up in time, you could get your share. So we ran to the FSA headquarters and got permission to cut down a tree. It weighed one and a half tons.

We had to push our cart back and forth three times to bring all the wood home.

In front of our building, we cut the pieces into smaller chunks, and then we split them with hammer and chisel. I piled the logs around the oven so that they would dry quicker. Now our store smelled pleasantly of tree sap.

Every day, we could hear artillery fire and rifle salvos in the distance. In the midst of all the fighting, Yarmouk was descending into darkness and silence. Without electricity, we had to improvise. Since the washing machine didn't work anymore, I put Ahmad's dirty diapers in a large metal tub, put on some rubber boots, and waded around in the water. When we ran out of dish soap, we began cleaning our plates with ash. There was hardly any shampoo left. We showered with cold water only. We had hardly any soap, so we washed our hands only once a day. There was no coffee or tea left, so we started brewing hot water with cinnamon, since there was plenty of cinnamon. We almost never had milk, so we gave Ahmad water with sugar. There was no more tobacco, so I used dried mint to make cigarettes for my father.

He smoked them in front of our store, and it smelled terrible. But he just couldn't quit, even if it meant that he—and the rest of us—would have to endure the lingering stench. Whenever he took Ahmad on his lap, our baby ended up smelling like mint smoke.

One day, Tahani had had enough. She griped loudly about Ahmad smelling so badly. Now she'd have to wash him again!

"He's still my grandchild," Papa shot back. "I'll put him on my lap however often I want."

Tahani fell into shocked silence, realizing that she had hurt his feelings.

In the evenings, we went to bed early. What else could we do? What could we talk about? We were living like cave dwellers now. We sat around by candlelight and indoor campfires, our faces blackened with soot.

I couldn't bear this lethargy any longer, this lingering sadness.

I had to do something. One day, I had a crazy idea. I said to my mother, "What if we used the lentils to make falafel?"

"What?" she asked, astonished. "Falafel?"

That being said, I had never cooked before. Impossible, not my thing, I had no talent for it. As a child, I had burned myself with hot oil, and my mother had banned me from the kitchen. When I moved in with Tahani, I cut my finger slicing tomatoes, so she, too, had told me to stay out of the kitchen.

For weeks, I'd been walking past those sacks of lentils, and all that time, people were starving. I had to do something.

Falafel are normally made from chickpeas. You let them soak overnight, then add baking powder, parsley, garlic, and onions. You can add some coriander and cumin to taste, then salt and pepper. You put everything through a meat grinder and end up with a thick paste, which is then shaped into medium-size balls that are fried in oil. But I only knew all that from watching. I had never made a falafel in my life.

But now I was convinced it could be done with the red lentils. They were hard as rocks, so I soaked them for two days. Then I added some clover that grew in the meadows of Yalda, and seasoned it with the only spice still available: a premade Asian spice blend from a nearby ramen factory that had recently been ransacked by a few militiamen. I put everything through the meat grinder, shaped a few falafel, and fried them in oil. When I tasted one, I noticed that the spice blend added a hint of curry to my falafel. But other than that—excellent! Now it was my mother's turn. "These are good!" she said.

I beamed. Finally, I had something to do. A few days later, I opened my makeshift falafel stand. I sat down on the ground a few yards outside our shop, with a small burner in front of me and a tub of lentil dough beside me. Then I got started. I charged ten Syrian pounds for two falafel, the regular price in Damascus. It never occurred to me to charge more, just because people were hungry.

Soon, the locals started lining up at my falafel stand. Driven by hunger, people came from as far as Yalda, and they didn't seem to mind standing in line for an hour. Even FSA fighters stood in line, their Kalashnikovs casually slung over their shoulders. I politely asked them to return unarmed. They agreed.

Tahani and I made at least fifty-five pounds of dough every night. Into the meat grinder we put the red lentils, the clover, and the spice mix—that's all we needed to make our siege-falafel. Tahani asked me not to sit outside all day because it was too dangerous. But I didn't listen. During each shift, I must have made about three thousand falafel. Samer, a distant cousin, helped me. He was the only relative I still had in Yarmouk. He would fish the falafel out of the oil, take the money, and hand the falafel to the customers.

I had plenty of oil. The militia had also looted a potato chip factory; the frying oil was sold on the black market, in lots of fifty-five pounds. I bought ten blocks, to stock up.

All I needed was gas for my burner. But that was available, too. You could simply burn some plastic and then let the black smoke cool down in a flue. You ended up with a liquid resembling gasoline. All you needed to do was burn plenty of furniture, doors, or carpets. Plastic items were the first things people burned. Entire apartment blocks were gutted. After all, plastic pipes were sticking out of the walls, and those pipes made for valuable fuel.

On some days, I made falafel from eight in the morning until seven in the evening. My starving customers were beaming with joy when they bit into the hot falafel. They were singing praises for me. God help me!

Still, I felt miserable. I was angry. What had I become? Not too long ago I had dreamed of a music career. I had thought I'd be an entrepreneur. I had been a regular guest of Feisal Jamal, one of the best pianists in the country. And now I was crouching on the ground, frying lentil dough, my clothes full of oil stains. It felt like a punishment. What had I done to deserve this?

I heard people whisper: He's the piano player. And they nodded toward our store. I saw the surprise in their eyes, the spite. I heard the whispers, the hissing.

"Ah, who have we here?" an acquaintance called out one day as he passed by. I had heard that this man entered empty apartments, searching for food. "If it isn't Mr. Piano Player!" he said. "You have a calling for frying falafel now?"

"Yes!" I said briskly, fuming with rage. "I am a pianist and a falafel salesman! At least I'm feeding my family and not stealing food!" What had become of me?

On one of those evenings, I sat with a few neighbors around the fire in front of our store. It sounds quaint, but it smelled terrible, since all we had to burn were plastic bottles. Wood wasn't worth burning for just a campfire. But at least the plastic bottles gave off a good amount of heat and light.

We sat there exchanging the usual gossip. So-and-so has died. What happened to so-and-so? Who's handing out soup to the needy these days? That soup, by the way, was made with nothing but water and the Asian spice mix.

At one point Tahani came out and asked, "Why don't you play something for everyone? Come, I'll bring you the accordion!"

"Really?" I asked. "Out here, in the middle of the street? At this hour?" After all, it was eleven at night.

Tahani threw me a loving and determined glance. She seemed to say: Who cares? She went inside and brought me the accordion. She could no longer bear seeing me so downcast.

I began to play. A song by Fairouz that everyone knew. The depressed glances brightened; the boys began to sing along. And then another song. And another. Our mood brightened, and the fire from the plastic bottles didn't seem to stink quite as badly. It turned into a beautiful evening.

One day at around noon I was crouching on the ground, as always, ceaselessly frying falafel, with Samer by my side. The line seemed endless: somewhere between fifty and a hundred people stood in a row—I hadn't counted. Suddenly, there was an explosion. The pressure knocked me over, unconscious.

When I came to, my ears were ringing. I saw people running

through the swirling dust. I could hear their screams, but everything sounded dull, as if it were happening far away.

Samer shook my shoulder. "Aeham, Aeham," he said, "are you okay?" His pants were covered with oil.

"Yes, I'm okay," I murmured. I was dazed, and there was no pain. I could feel something wasn't right. But what?

"Are you sure?" he cried. "Your hand is bleeding!"

I looked down. Blood was pouring from my right hand, pumped out to the beat of my heart. "What's going on?" I murmured.

"We were hit by a grenade."

He took a small towel and pressed it against my hand to stop the bleeding. Then he helped me to my feet, saying, "Can you walk?"

I tried. Yes, I could walk. But I still was in a daze.

"Quick, let's get you to the hospital!"

We took off. The grenade had struck the corner of a nearby building. Just a few yards closer and we all would have been dead, dozens of people. Like me, the bystanders had been hit by grenade splinters or debris. Ahead, people were carrying a man on a blanket. His face was covered in blood; his body dangled left and right as if it were made of rubber. I knew him—he often bought falafel from me. He was dead.

I examined my right hand. My index finger and my middle finger were hanging down. When I tried to move either finger, something at the back of my hand moved as well, right under the skin.

That's it, I thought. It's over! My tendons are cut, I'll never play piano again. Just a few days ago, I had been improvising with a piece by Mozart. Had that been my farewell performance? Still, my left hand continued to work. Perhaps I could play with only my left hand, and my three remaining fingers on the right. I remembered a YouTube video about a man who played extravagant piano pieces with only two fingers. And another one where a guy played with only his toes. If I practiced with my remaining fingers . . . And so, with me wrapped in my thoughts, we entered the makeshift hospital in al-Hajar al-Aswad, right behind the men carrying the dead man.

It took me a while to get used to the murky light in there. Back in the old days, this had been a banquet room for weddings, but now the hall had been sectioned with linens and blankets into twelve stopgap exam rooms. The dead man was gently placed on the front left cot. I sat down one cot over. The leather had dark spots that looked like dried blood. There were not many other patients, since there hadn't been as much artillery fire lately.

After a few minutes, a man came to see me. His white coat was full of bloodstains.

"What happened?" he asked.

"I was selling falafel on the street and a grenade exploded. A splinter hit me." I showed him my right hand.

"Okay, I'll take a look," he said. He put on his magnifying glasses and pointed a pen light at my hand, asking me to move the fingers. He tested my reflexes, observing which parts were numb and which were in pain.

"The grenade splinter separated the part of the finger connecting the finger extensors of your index and middle finger. I saw a doctor sew something like that back together once. I could try it."

"You're not a doctor?"

"No, I'm a carpenter."

"A carpenter?"

"But I've worked with our doctor here for the past six months. I've done many operations. Under normal circumstances, I would suggest amputating both fingers."

"Please don't! I'm not really a falafel salesman. I'm a pianist."

He smiled. "I'll try. We're not very busy today. But I can't make any promises. You might not be able to feel those fingers anymore."

"Please, give it your best."

"Close your eyes," he said. "Relax, don't move, and don't look at your hand." He held a piece of cotton with an anesthetic on it under my nose and I drifted into unconsciousness.

Samer later told me that the carpenter had lifted the two severed pieces of tendon with pincers and sewn them back together. Then he had sewn up the wound and bandaged the two fingers, placing a splint inside the bandage. The whole procedure had taken about two hours.

Once I woke up, he asked Samer to take me home. And he told me, "Don't you dare play piano! You have to wait at least two months before you can move your fingers again. Good luck." I nodded and stumbled out of the room. The dead man was still lying on the front cot.

When I got home, Tahani was furious. She had heard the explosion, seen the puddles of blood, and asked everyone about me. But no one had told her I had been wounded. By now, people hated giving bad news. No one wanted to be confronted with another's grief. They preferred to say nothing at all, or they pretended they didn't know.

After four weeks, I took off the bandages to look at my wound, and to check out the black nylon stitches. My fingertips were cold, but the flesh under the fingernails was bright pink. The area was completely numb.

I sat down at the piano and began to play. One—three—two—three—three—four—one—four. And again. Scales. It was painful, but I was able to do it. In the first two days, I played for half an hour, later a whole hour, and then an hour and a half. Years after that, in Germany, I went to a doctor who x-rayed my fingers and examined them. "Your fingers couldn't possibly work," he said. "And you want to play concerts?" He told me that the nerves in both fingers were seventy percent damaged. I had no idea how I was able to play.

Within a week of the operation, I was able to sell falafel again. We set up shop a few streets away, away from the bloodstains. Samer and I switched places. Now he was frying, and I took care of the sales. And again, the line went almost around the block. If your stomach is empty, you don't care that you might be hit by a grenade.

People were so hungry that when it was their turn, they took the hot falafel and looked at them with something akin to love. They smelled them and nibbled a little bit. Then they gently took the first real bite. And finally, they joyfully pushed the whole falafel into their mouths. Some had picked some bitter greens somewhere, a little bit of dandelion, wild arugula, or clover, and they added it to their meal. They ate like it was their only meal that day. And it probably was.

CHAPTER SEVENTEEN

One day, when Samer and I were selling falafel, I saw a small, plump woman rush past. She was wearing a headscarf and a lot of makeup, and was holding her son and daughter by the hand. The three of them looked pretty, with a healthy dark skin tone. But something about them was odd. They seemed from a different time, the time before the siege. They didn't fit here.

Two or three times, I saw the woman come by with her children. Always well-dressed and made-up, she walked in a proud, upright manner. She always came from the same direction, passing our line of customers and then turning right. I started wondering why she was wearing so much makeup and where they were going. Finally, the fourth time she appeared, she lined up for some falafel.

"Hello, Teacher Aeham," she said when it was her turn. Oh, my goodness! My jaw dropped. She must have known me from before. "Three falafel, please."

The children had nice clean faces and looked like perfectly normal children on a perfectly normal school day. Which made it all very strange. When she called me "teacher," she reminded me that underneath all those layers of lentil dough I wasn't just a falafel salesman.

"Do you know me?" I asked, smiling.

"Of course," she said. "You're Aeham, the teacher. I know you. My husband, Raed, knows you, too."

I was bursting with curiosity. "Where exactly are you going

every day? Why do you keep calling me 'teacher'? And who is your husband?"

She told me that a professor named Abu Saussan had opened an elementary school around the corner, in the former al-Andalus Wedding Hall. The woman worked there as a teacher; her husband was the school's technician. That's why she was always dressed up every morning. As we were talking, I forgot to take the falafel out of the oil, completely absorbed in our conversation. I decided that I wanted to see that school.

I closed our falafel stand earlier than usual that day and went to the old wedding hall. When I knocked on its metal door it opened a crack. I pushed it all the way open and stepped into a dark corridor. There was a generator on the floor that didn't seem to be working, and I could hear children's voices in the distance. I followed the voices and pushed a second door open—and found myself on the gallery level of the wedding hall. The room below me was full of children, dimly illuminated by tiny dots of light. When I came closer, I saw that they were LED lights, the kind you can find in some plastic lighters. Whoever had thought of this?

Throughout the banquet hall, bedsheets had been hung over clotheslines, dividing the room into different "classrooms," with one grade on one side of the bedsheet and another grade next to it. The problem was that everyone could hear everything. Ethics classes, math classes, it was all one big mess.

In one of the makeshift classrooms, I saw a man dressed up as a clown, joking around with the kids. He was wearing a colorful woolen toupee and had pushed a pillow under his shirt. He pretended to be eating air. "Oh my God, I'm so full!" he sighed, and patted his big belly. "It's so delicious, all this air. You should try it, too. Fill your bellies with it!" The children giggled and played along. They sucked in the air and rubbed their stomachs. I grinned. This was a lot better than the daily despair.

And then I had a thought: Damn, I have to play piano here! I'm a pianist, not a falafel salesman! I decided to ask Abu Saussan if I could teach a music class for the kids.

I asked around, and when I finally found his office, I knocked on the door. A voice from inside called out, "Come in!" I opened the door—and found myself in a public bathroom. There was a lot more light in here, but I didn't see any toilets. Apparently, they had been removed. Abu Saussan was working on his laptop. His desk was an odd wooden construction that was shared with another colleague.

Abu Saussan was past fifty, small and thin, with curly black hair. He wore jeans and a T-shirt, and had a stern look on his face. He was in the middle of a tirade: ". . . who the hell is downloading from the internet? I'll change the password if this doesn't stop. I can't work if the internet is this slow!"

Internet? Light? Laptop? In days like these, when most of Yarmouk was without power? Unbelievable!

Finally, Abu Saussan greeted me. "What can I do for you?"

"I would like to work here," I said. There was no point beating around the bush.

He looked at me quizzically. "What are you talking about? And how did you get in here?"

Oh, right, I had forgotten. I laid it on a bit thick, telling him that I'd been aware of his school for a long time, and that I'd like to contribute and play piano with the children. Abu Saussan's face brightened.

"Can you come by on Fridays?" he asked.

"Fridays? Why not during the week?"

"I'm afraid that's not possible," he said. "We're a school, we have to stick to our class schedule. Music isn't on the schedule."

I was taken aback. When I had first seen this place, I'd thought people here would be more open-minded and would want to brighten the kids' days a little with music. But I would only be allowed to come on Fridays?

"How about Saturdays?" I suggested.

He shook his head. Fridays or not at all.

I was perplexed. How could he be so pedantic, with all the chaos around him? I didn't want to do it on the holy day. On Fridays, I accompanied my father to the mosque. And I knew that no one would show up for school on a Friday, since it wasn't a school day.

We were both silent for a moment. There seemed to be no compromise in sight. So I addressed a more fundamental problem: Would there be electricity for a keyboard?

"Ask Raed," he said. "He's the technical assistant." The term *technical assistant* could mean anything here in Yarmouk. The job description included not only finding alternate power sources in case of a blackout, but arranging chairs, making coffee, and peeling onions. Basically, a technical assistant was a servant.

After leaving Abu Saussan's office, I asked someone to help me find Raed. I was told that he was working on a video in a small room in the back of the building. I knocked on the door and went inside. Behind the camera stood a broad-shouldered man with a mustache and a happy grin. Raed. I asked if I could speak to him for a moment. No problem. He stepped out of the classroom.

"I know you, you're the falafel guy," he said in a friendly voice.

Under normal circumstances, it drove me up the wall when people called me "falafel guy." But Raed had such a friendly smile, I couldn't be upset.

"I'm also a pianist," I insisted. I told him that I had met his wife and that she'd told me about the school. "I would like to teach music here."

Raed hesitated, and then he said, quite intently, "You better forget about that." He sounded oddly determined.

"Why?" I asked, startled.

"I'll tell you later."

At first, I thought that maybe he didn't want me to be a part of all this. But an inner voice told me that his advice came from the heart. *You better forget about that.* The words echoed in my head. Why did he and his wife work here if this place was so terrible? I had the feeling he wanted to tell me more. We decided to talk at my place, after school.

When he showed up at five on the dot, right after school, I was surprised. In Yarmouk, "after school" can mean anything from four in the afternoon until one in the morning. Raed seemed to respect other people's schedules.

While Tahani served him a cinnamon coffee, I asked him why he had taken videos of the children. "Isn't that dangerous?" I said. "I mean, who knows where the footage might end up? What if state security gets their hands on it? God only knows what they might do with it!"

"But what can I do?" Raed said. "It's my job." He told me that he had to take video footage of just about everything, and then upload it all onto the internet. The school was funded by a wealthy foreign donor, and the donor wanted to see what the teachers and students were doing all day. So Raed had to film everything: the classes, the administration, the children at lunch. The donor wanted to know that his money wasn't going to waste.

"Who's the donor?" I asked.

"The only one who knows him is Abu Saussan. No one else has any idea. All I know is that my wife and I are paid next to nothing."

Then Raed told me that, just a few years ago, he had bought a set of strings in our store. My mind wandered back in time. I remembered how busy our store had been a few years back, how much work we had. I liked Raed. Soon, I called him Abu Rur, a term of endearment. I longed for somebody I could talk openly with. Someone to share my bitter days with, someone to help me ease my burden. Raed had an open, honest way about him.

"How come you have internet at the school?" I asked.

He laughed. "That's the simplest thing in the world. All you need is a router and a little bit of electricity."

I looked at him quizzically.

"You just have to find a phone line that still works. Then you can dial in."

"What? That's insane!"

"Do you need internet access?"

"Of course, that would be incredibly helpful."

"I'll be back in three days with a router. I'll see if I can get it to work."

"That would be fantastic."

"You just need a battery. Do you have one?"

I thought about it for a moment. Then I remembered my old Rama, an electric moped, made in China. Right now, it was in storage at Alaa's carpentry workshop, hidden underneath all kinds of junk. I had bought it five years ago. At that time, traffic in Damascus was exploding. There was an incredibly high tax on any new car, and many people chose to buy electric mopeds instead. All you had to do was plug them in and charge them for a few hours, then you could zoom through the city at around twenty-five miles an hour. You could also charge the Rama by pedaling, but that was only useful in case of emergencies—the vehicle was heavy and clunky.

"You have a Rama?" Raed said. "Great! The engine has five good batteries. You should be online in no time."

Unbelievable! Internet! Electricity! At last, I would be able to chat with my cousins and uncles in Damascus again!

After three days, Raed came back. He tapped a distribution box in my street, pulled out a cable, and connected his router to a battery that he had brought along. Suddenly, my cell phone had internet reception. I cheered. We went over to the carpentry workshop to take the batteries out of the Rama, then we strolled over to Yarmouk Street to take a selfie, which I uploaded to Facebook.

Finally, a sign of life, after so many months.

I got countless comments. "You're so thin!"—"What, Yarmouk Street is so empty! I don't believe it!"—"Over there, on the right, that's where I used to eat falafel. Damn, I miss it!"

In the end, I played at Abu Saussan's school two or three times. But he had been right that music wouldn't be on the schedule. Abu Saussan was curt and had a high opinion of himself. But I have only good things to say about him. He would run his underground school for another year and a half, with money from Europe. Until ISIS came. His school was a ray of hope: What else could the children have done the whole day? Sit around at home? Play on the street? Brave people like Abu Saussan made life in Yarmouk possible. Without him, things would have been even bleaker.

Raed turned out to be my guardian angel. I remember one particular moment, after we had already known each other for a while, when we were at my place, sitting and talking. The afternoon's last rays of sunlight fell onto his eyes, making them sparkle. I can't remember what we were talking about, I just remember the amber glow on his face, and his bright eyes. It seemed as though God was pointing his finger toward him, and suddenly I had a thought: *You're the best friend I'll ever have.*

Whenever I was able to upload videos of myself or my beloved Yarmouk in the following months, and afterward, when I gave interviews to *Süddeutsche Zeitung* and the *Guardian*, and later, when I organized live concerts via Skype—transmitted to Belgrade or Beirut—Raed operated the cameras, the batteries, and the lights. I owe it all to him.

— CHAPTER EIGHTEEN —

Fall was coming. Tahani, little Ahmad, and I had moved into one of the neighboring apartments belonging to Abu Abed, the helpful man who had brought out mattresses, pillows, and blankets for us during our first night at the workshop. He had fled Yarmouk a long time ago and on one of his visits back had offered that Tahani, Ahmad, and I could move into his apartment. Later he had given us the keys to another neighboring apartment as well.

When the fights in Yalda subsided, we took the large dolly and went there to assess the damage. We could see even from a distance that my parents' apartment had been hit. There was a hole in the outer wall, and the windows were missing. The staircase was still intact, but when we unlocked the metal door to the apartment, dust rained down on us. A grenade had exploded inside the apartment, tearing out a supporting beam and blasting concrete off the walls, all the way down to the supports. No one would have survived this.

A wall had collapsed and half my father's library was buried under the rubble. I described to him what I saw: "The left side of your bookshelf is completely gone." "What luck," he said. "My Braille books are to the right." He felt their spines and took out a few volumes, including a book about geography and one about dream interpretation, which he wanted to read during quiet evenings in the workshop.

We carried my parents' double bed downstairs to bring back to Yarmouk so that they wouldn't have to sleep on the floor anymore.

We also took the flat-screen TV and the fridge so that they wouldn't be stolen, as well as dishes and spices. My wedding photos. A childhood picture of Alaa and me. My mother sighed when she took it off the wall. Most important: six canisters of olive oil, which my mother had once bought to stock up. Twenty-five gallons of good, smooth olive oil. A treasure.

We went back and forth twice. We also stopped by the apartment Tahani and I used to share. Everything was intact—only the windows were missing, and one of the outside walls had a hole. We took photo albums and CDs, the fridge and television, pacifiers and bottles for the baby. We had been lucky.

One day, a man approached me, offering to sell rice and sugar, one large sack of each. He wanted to leave the neighborhood, and praised my falafel stand, adding that he knew one of my uncles. He asked a fair price, not the astronomical sums that were common on the black market at the time. I gratefully accepted.

From then on, those two sacks were our last reserves. Once a week, we allowed ourselves some rice. Only Ahmad received a tiny plate full of rice every day. And a bottle of warm sugar water.

All of Yarmouk continued to suffer from extreme hunger. Hardly a week passed without us learning of a new "martyr of hunger." It was always the weakest among us who died, the most emaciated ones, the babies and the old folks. They died from contaminated water or a virus or some other disease, sometimes from a combination of them. A local human rights organization recorded the following:

Mahmoud Alaa al-Din, died on October 26, starved to death.
Aya (baby), died on October 28, starved to death.
Abdelhay Yousef (4 years), died November 2, starved to death.
Omar Hussein (child), died on November 10, starved to death.
Malik Jumaa (baby), died on November 10, starved to death.
Mahmoud Mohammad al-Aydi, died on November 20, starved to death.

One time, they found the spindly corpse of a very old man who had died in his bed, forgotten by everyone. He looked like a mummy. We didn't even have coffins anymore—wood had gotten too expensive. The bodies were brought to the cemetery on a stretcher. During the funeral processions, people carried the body on their shoulders and chanted, "Yarmouk, Yarmouk is neutral! Open your gates, oh Yarmouk. Yarmouk is here!"

The newspapers in Europe wrote that Yarmouk was a "death camp." Only eighteen thousand people—out of six hundred and fifty thousand—were said to be alive there.

One thing was still abundantly available: the Asian spice mix. The needy drank gallons of water mixed with the salty spice mix. It gave you the illusion that you weren't hungry anymore, at least for a few hours. Unfortunately, it seemed that the chemical powder was bad for your health. People's stomachs bloated and they became increasingly haggard, yet they looked swollen at the same time.

Or perhaps it was the clover? We were constantly eating yellow clover, which grows wild from England to Iran. Farmers use it to feed their animals. It has a lot of protein, but it also contains trace amounts of cyanhydric acid. Which is why it is deadly to snails. How bad is it for people who've had no other food for months? I have no idea. I only know that many of us got terrible diarrhea from eating all that grass.

For me and my family, the horned clover was an everyday delicacy. My mother cut up the greens and soaked them twice in salt water, then we cooked them with red lentils. Yes, we still had those. That's what we ate six days a week. Yellow clover with lentils and the Asian spice mix. It was disgusting. If the stems hadn't been soaked enough, they were incredibly bitter. But no matter how much we soaked the stuff, we still kept biting into bitter parts, and it turned our stomachs.

Every few days, I took my bike to Yalda to harvest clover on deserted farms. One of them was subdivided by a row of small cairns. A sniper lurked on the other side of that line, and just recently, someone had been shot. We all knew to stay away from the line, no matter what.

One morning, there were six or seven of us out in the fields, crouching in the grass as we cut clover. A man approached us whom I'd never seen before. He saw that the field looked much greener and juicier on the other side of the line. "I can see radishes over there!" he said. We warned him not to go, pleaded with him, told him it would be his death warrant. But the growling of his stomach was more powerful than our warnings, so he took his basket and went over.

Half an hour passed. He came back, his basket filled with radishes. "And that's not all!" he cried. "There's radishes everywhere!" What could we say?

He went over a second time and crouched down to pick radishes. Then we heard a shot, a popping sound, like a melon bursting open. We threw ourselves to the ground and when we looked up, we saw the man was lying in the grass, covered in blood. The sniper had hit the man's head with an explosive bullet, blowing off his lower jaw. A gruesome sight. My stomach turned.

We discussed what to do. We couldn't just leave him there. One of us got up to look for an iron bar; another man searched for a blanket. Then one of us pushed the bar up the dead man's pant leg and pulled him toward us. Then we laid him on the blanket. Four men were carrying him. I pushed the victim's bicycle. We took him to the makeshift hospital in al-Hajar al-Aswad, where the carpenter had recently patched my fingers up.

We left the dead man outside. If he had relatives who were searching for him, this would be the first place they'd come to look.

Back home, I told Tahani, "This man died for a few radishes. Can you imagine?" Deeply disturbed, we both grew silent.

Being hungry makes you moody. The starving people of Yarmouk shuffled morosely through the deserted streets, or huddled around some campfire, burning clothes and plastic bottles.

People were aging in fast motion. Before the siege, my mother had still seemed young, but now she was gray and haggard, her face lined with deep wrinkles. She had lost a lot of weight—"And all without a diet or gym," she said sarcastically. She still had a scale from her previous attempts at weight loss, and from time to time I would weigh myself. Formerly, I had weighed 143 pounds; now I was down to 108. I could see my rib cage under my skin.

We weren't the only ones who had changed. I knew a large, burly boy in our neighborhood who lost weight so fast, it was as if he'd had his stomach reduced. Or the bodybuilder who used to work as a security guard at one of the large jewelry stores, a guy in a black suit, with shiny shoes, sunglasses, and a stud in his ear. He became as thin and crooked as a burnt match. Soon, he had a long beard, but not because he had found God. No, it was just due to fatalism and lack of shaving cream.

There was only one commercial area left: Oruba Street. Previously, it had been the flea market of Yarmouk; now it became an apocalyptic shopping mall. Some people sold wood, which had been taken from sofas. Other household goods had been stolen from warehouses and shops, like the sacks of cinnamon sticks that had been looted from a spice depot. There were days when a large flat-screen TV was sold for a cigarette, or a cigarette exchanged for a refrigerator or a washing machine. A persistent rumor was that you could get a fifty-five-pound sack of rice for a kidney. With pale, sallow faces, people stumbled from one booth to the next. And no matter where you went, you could never escape the terrible stench of burning plastic bottles.

One day, Tahani and I were walking down Oruba Street, and we heard a woman's panicked screams: "The boy has to get out of here! He'll die! His mother has no milk! He will starve!"

We approached. "What's going on?" Tahani asked.

The woman said that her five-day-old grandson was dying. She told us that his mother was completely exhausted and had nothing to eat anymore. Tahani asked for the address and we went straight there. Tahani entered while I waited outside. When she came back out, she told me that the mother had grabbed her breasts and said, "They're empty. I have nothing left to give him!" Then the mother came outside, carrying the baby. I still remember the little boy's face. All I could see was his wide-open mouth. He could hardly move. Tahani bent down to listen to his breathing, which was very weak. She promised to return, and brought the woman two pounds of rice. We never learned what became of the baby boy, whether he survived.

It was early November. I was frying falafel again, when a man named Abu Mohammed approached me. He was in his mid-forties, large and heavy, with a receding hairline. Before the war, he had been one of my voice students, a baritone who worked hard and was always on time.

"Hello, Aeham!" he said.

"Abu Mohammed!" I called out. "You're still in Yarmouk!"

"Yes, just like you. And now you're selling falafel. I like that."

We talked for a while and finally he said, "Aeham, I would like to start a choir. We need someone to accompany us on the keyboard. I was thinking of you."

"People are starving," I replied. "In times like these, who cares about music?"

"Let me worry about that. I'll get a group together. We even have electricity."

My ears pricked up. Almost no one had power by then. And if they did, there was usually some political party or militant group behind it. "No offense, Abu Mohammed," I said, "but you know that I don't want to be anybody's puppet."

No, no, Abu Mohammed assured me, the group was completely independent. He wanted to call it Samed—steadfast. He said he'd take care of everything. "You just bring your keyboard, I'll get some people together, and then we'll sing. Just like in the old days."

I liked him, and I felt like making music again. So I agreed.

Two days later, Abu Mohammed picked me up at the agreed-upon time. I shoved my keyboard under my arm and we were on our way, walking until we ended up at the headquarters of the Fatah movement, the largest Palestinian party, founded by Yasser

Arafat once upon a time. I recognized their unmistakable yellow symbol—two rifles, a hand grenade, and the outline of Palestine—and immediately wanted to turn back.

But, of course, that was impossible. In a place like Yarmouk, it was all too easy to put your foot in your mouth and get into trouble. So I discreetly took Abu Mohammed aside and politely asked him, "Didn't you say that your choir was nonpartisan?"

"Yes," he insisted. "We're not affiliated with anyone. We're just using a rehearsal space here."

"Sure, and in the end, those guys will want us to do their bidding."

"No, believe me."

"I have my doubts."

After a while, I gave in, deciding to take a leap of faith and not worry about this questionable partnership. In the meantime, eleven men had shown up to sing with us. We all introduced ourselves.

Then the man who had unlocked the door for us turned on a generator. The room lit up and the diodes on my keyboard began to glow. So we began, singing scales, a simple la-la-la to see who could hit the notes. It was all right, but no more than that. My right hand was in pain, the men were humming out of tune—but it still was fun to sit at a keyboard after all those months of serving falafel.

After an hour—bang!—the lights went out. The generator had run out of gas. But the men were happy. "Finally, I know how to sing," one of them said. "Thank you, Professor!"

"Don't call me that," I said. "Call me Aeham." But then I proceeded to lecture them, just like a professor: "It's important that you show up for our rehearsals. That's the only way we can make progress." We agreed to meet again two days later, and I went home in a good mood.

During our second rehearsal, the guys already sounded a little better. I had an idea. Why do cover versions of songs by other people? We should sing about us! About Yarmouk! About the hunger, the bombs, the desolation. I asked around if anyone felt like writing a poem that I could then set to music.

"Oh, you're a composer?" asked Abu Mohammed.

"I haven't written a song in a long time. But I'd like to try."

A young man named Mustafa stepped forward. He said his uncle had studied Arabic and was a poet. But he didn't live in Yarmouk anymore. He had a heart problem and had been allowed to leave.

"How is he going to write about our misery in Yarmouk if he doesn't live here anymore?" I pointed out. "But all right, ask him!"

At our next rehearsal, the third one, Mustafa proudly held out his fists. I was supposed to choose one. I humored him and chose the right fist. He gave me a piece of paper, which I unfolded and read aloud:

Oh, you emigrants, return,
You've been away too long.
We are the men of Yarmouk, we keep the faith.
Yarmouk, you are the path of victory to Jerusalem,
You never surrender.
Come back, oh settlers, and rejoice.
Yarmouk doesn't want to see you gone.
Yarmouk, you womb of heroes,
You shaped our days.

Oh well. I wasn't overly thrilled. Path to victory, Jerusalem, the womb of heroes—it was the same old stuff, all the pathos we've been hearing in Palestinian revolutionary songs for the past sixty years. But what about our current problems? What about hunger, plastic-bottle fires, and grenades? And yet, the poem was well written, in fine Arabic, and it rhymed beautifully. Yes, I'd set it to music.

As I was walking home, I began composing—and soon had the melody in my head. Nothing like that had ever happened to me before. Once I got home, I sat down at the piano, played the motif, added an intro, fine-tuned the rhythm, varied the theme, and then transposed everything from D minor to G minor so that we could all sing it. Less than two hours later, the song was finished. Later, I spent a few more hours working on the intro.

During our next rehearsal—the fourth one—I asked the guys to write down the lyrics for themselves. And then we practiced it, line by line. An Arabic choir always sings in unison. First we sang one line together, then each person sang it individually, then one more time, until it was firmed up, then everyone together, then on to the second line, and so forth.

After a while it got to be too much for some of the guys. "Aeham, why do we have to rehearse so much? Just let the best guys sing, the others can stay in the background."

"No, we need every voice."

"It's too hard. Don't you think it's fine the way it is?"

"Let's practice one more time."

During our break, I discreetly discussed the piece with some of them. They, too, weren't particularly thrilled with all the bombast, the victory marches, and the heroism.

And so, as we said good-bye, I told everyone, "Please, guys, write a poem. About what's going on here. How awful things are for us. Because that's what we should be singing about."

Some of them brought a poem to our fifth rehearsal. The best poem was by Mahmoud Tamim. In general, he stood out, mostly because of his energy, his enthusiasm. He was always in a good mood. He had chin-length, combed-back hair, and most of the time wore a baseball cap. Everyone in Yarmouk knew him. I had seen him often. During demonstrations, he liked to be carried on other people's shoulders, shouting things like "Al-Nusra Front, get out of here!" and "Assad, you killer, get lost!" Mahmoud spared no one, he liked to curse everyone. But he always had good rhymes and rhythms. Whenever he chanted his slogans, it sounded almost like rap music.

He had written a beautiful poem about Yarmouk, about how its people had been scattered to so many other places—Qudsaya, Bahrain, Jaramana, Turkey, Lebanon—and about how Yarmouk misses them, wherever they may be. It was called "Yarmouk Misses You, Brother."

Again, I sat down at the piano at home. This time I composed the piece in a major key. I was thinking of Mozart. I wanted to make it particularly catchy. The notes came flying to me, like birds. After a short while, the song was finished. It would become my greatest hit, if I may say so.

As for me, I contributed "Sidja," one of the two songs I had written as a teenager. It was my first refugee song, full of longing for our lost home. Now I turned it into a song about survival.

"No matter how long the night / the light of the sun is ours."

Our choir was up and running. But during the eighth rehearsal, when we were taking a break, the Fatah guy who always opened the door and turned on the generator approached us, launching into a long speech. He told us that an important day was coming, a meaningful day for all Palestinians: the anniversary of the passing of Abu Ammar, which was what Yasser Arafat was called. They were planning a memorial service in his honor. And then he came out with it: Could we sing at the event?

So I was right! I discreetly took Abu Mohammed aside and whispered to him, "You see, now they're using us for their party!"

"Don't worry, I'll talk to him," he said.

But I could hear the trepidation in his voice. He'd never be able to stand up to the guy. So, throwing caution to the wind, I raised my voice in protest.

"I don't think we should do this," I said loudly. "Let's sing for the hungry people in Yarmouk, or for the bombing victims. Let's invite people and make music together. For Yarmouk. And at the end, we'll commemorate Abu Ammar."

The man was silent.

"Of course, Abu Ammar has achieved a lot for us," I added. "But today we're facing different problems. Every day, people starve to death. That's what we should be singing about."

The man was still silent.

"We're going to sing for Yarmouk, right?" I said, looking at the others. They nodded. "Do you all agree?" More nodding.

"I have a different suggestion," said the Fatah man. "First, we'll do a concert for Abu Ammar. And after that, we'll do one for the hungry people of Yarmouk."

I considered it for a moment. Fine, I thought. I'd swallow my pride and play their songs of heroism, and then we could sing for the people of Yarmouk. We'd sing about the grenades, the starvation, the plastic-bottle fires.

"All right," I said.

The concert took place on November 11, 2013, the ninth anniversary of the death of Yasser Arafat. The memorial service was very crowded, with at least five hundred people squeezed into the meeting hall. The men were wearing the kaffiyeh, the black-and-white Palestinian tassel scarf, and waving flags, just like in the old days. And of course, the Fatah guy gave a boring speech, full of old platitudes:

"One day, we'll tear down the borders and march toward Jerusalem, and then we will . . ."

Blah blah blah. I wasn't listening. I was reminded of my time in school, of the principal's nonsensical speeches. Tearing down borders! Ridiculous! We couldn't even tear down the checkpoints. We couldn't even reach Damascus.

No matter. First, we sang a few of our own songs, the ones of our Samed choir, then we launched into the bombastic revolutionary songs that every Palestinian knew by heart. The songs about Kalashnikovs and spilled blood and victory marches toward Jerusalem. The generator was chugging, the neon bulbs were buzzing, people were dancing, the ceiling fans were whirring—it was just like the old days.

At the end of the concert, I made an announcement: "In exactly one week, there'll be a second concert. For the hungry people of Yarmouk. Please tell everyone, and please come."

As we were packing our things, the Fatah guy thanked us.

"So we'll be back in a week?" I asked.

"Of course. I'll make sure the generator has plenty of fuel."

"Really?"

"Absolutely, even if I have to pay for it myself."

So we came back one week later, the same hall, the same time. But this time only half as many people showed up. The Fatah guy greeted everyone. "The siege continues. Our people are dying of hunger. Let's use music as a protest. This was Aeham's idea. He wanted to do this concert. And here we are!"

The choir lined up next to my keyboard, each guy with his arm around the next one's shoulder. We began, singing "Oh, You Emigrants, Return" and "Sidja" and "Yarmouk Misses You, Brother" and . . . bang! The lights went out. The keyboard fell silent. I couldn't believe it: the Fatah guy hadn't put enough fuel into the generator.

Some in the audience booed. Clearly, the concert was over. We had no more power. People simply got up and went home. I said nothing, sitting behind my keyboard in silence, feeling shame and rage. I didn't show up for the next choir practice two days later.

I vowed never to do anything like that again. But I should have known. First, they made us sing for Abu Ammar, and then they hung us out to dry. Never again! I had to become independent. And that meant independent from electric power. Which meant that I shouldn't play on keyboards. I walked through the streets in a rage.

Then I had an idea. I looked at the large dolly that we had used to transport sacks of beans and tree trunks, sofas, and olive oil. I inspected the large wheels.

"How about," I asked my father, "if we screw the big wheels onto the bottom of the piano? Do you think I could push it out onto the street?"

"No," he said, "it would tip over."

But for the next six weeks, I kept thinking about it. And I had another idea! I went to Mahmoud Tamim, who had written "Yarmouk Misses You, Brother." He shared my sense of adventure. He would be my accomplice. Since I knew where he lived, I went over and knocked on the downstairs door.

"Yes?" I heard a voice from above. I looked up. Tamim looked down at me from the railing on the rooftop balcony.

"Mahmoud, do you have some time?"

"Sure, I'll come down and let you in."

He used to work in his father's hardware store. But the lack of food had hit him and his family very hard. His father had passed away, his mother was a diabetic, and Mahmoud was always searching for food. And yet, his creativity was amazing. He was once filmed leading a sarcastic tour through Yarmouk, showing everyone how "good" we had it: "Do you see how fit and slender people here are?"

While we were sitting on the rooftop terrace, I noticed that Mahmoud Tamim raised pigeons. We are a people of pigeon breeders. Rooftops have a symbolic place within our culture. The hard-drinking, pigeon-loving Palestinian is a legendary figure. During the '60s and '70s, this was part of our youth culture. Back then, the young people of Yarmouk were wearing Afros and bell-bottoms, raising pigeons on rooftops, and fighting for the PLO. Such was the image of the fedayeen, the Palestinian guerrilla fighters, whom my father described to me in his stories.

"Ah, you're breeding pigeons," I said to Mahmoud. "How beautiful!"

"Well, in the old days I used to have more than a hundred," he said, pointing to the many empty aviaries. "Now there are only five left." I didn't ask what happened to the others.

I hadn't seen Mahmoud Tamim for almost two months. This was the first time since our disastrous performance, and he had lost more weight. He didn't seem to be doing well at all. So I talked for a while before I came out with it: "How about we continue with the choir—but without the Fatah? We just take the piano and sing in the streets."

"How are you going to get the piano outside? It's too heavy."

"Let me worry about that. You just get the others, I'll take care of the rest."

He looked at me.

"What do you say?" I said. "Can we do it alone?"

Without thinking further, he said, "Let's try. I'm with you."

That made me happy. Later he asked, "Where are we going to sing?"

I thought about it. "At Mansoura Middle School. Where the

first rocket hit us. That's where we'll sing. Just for us. Under the open sky."

Mahmoud Tamim kept his word. Two days later, he came to our store with five of the Samed guys in tow. Laughing, I greeted them, and then we got to work.

We tilted my Shanghai piano—the cheapest one I owned—onto its back on the dolly, and began rolling it outside.

Tahani and my mother looked at us quizzically. I hadn't told them yet. Only my father knew about my plan, and called out from the back: "Aeham knows what he's doing."

The neighbors gave us strange looks when the seven of us pushed the piano through the street. We went to the middle school and went inside, into the schoolyard. This was where the first rocket had hit. This was where our first performance would be. The symbolic concert at the first bomb crater, the first crack that had run through our world.

We tilted the dolly and piano back upright again. Then I set up a chair, and my mobile orchestra was complete.

I was just warming up when an overweight man came around the corner. Who was that? Mahmoud Tamim said hello and introduced him, telling us he was from the editorial offices of *Bukra Ahla*, which means "A Better Tomorrow." He wanted to make a video of us.

"What?" I said. "A video? No way! Why didn't you tell me?"

"Why are you so opposed to this?" Mahmoud Tamim asked.

"Do you have any idea where this footage might end up? Why don't we just walk over to state security and introduce ourselves? Why does this guy want to film us?"

"To put it on their YouTube page so that anyone can see it."

"Forget it!"

This led to a longer discussion. We decided to take a vote. The others were all in favor. Their argument: We were already trapped. We were starving. What did it matter if they saw our faces on YouTube?

So I gave in.

We started playing. It was our first time making music out amid the rubble. My piano sounded out of tune, echoing through my old middle school. In hindsight, it was an incredible step we had taken, playing "Oh, You Emigrants, Return" out under the open sky like that. But I was worried the whole time. Who's going to see this video? What will become of it?

The guy from *Bukra Ahla* came uncomfortably close with his camera, crawling toward us. Why did he have to be so close? Who would see this video? And what would happen then? The questions kept racing through my head. Only one thought made me breathe a little easier: There were seven of us. It wouldn't be just me who would be arrested. And so I hit the keys. That video is still on You-Tube, even today. Watching it, you can see how tense I was. My right hand was still in pain.

Later, we pushed the piano back to the store. We were in a good mood, because making music makes people happy.

That's how it happened. We began by pushing the piano out into a world of ruins, into the rubble of Yarmouk. The idea didn't just pop into my mind one day. No, it was more complicated than that. I kept thinking about the evening when we were sitting around the campfire, when Tahani suggested that I play accordion for everyone and we began singing together. I wanted to make music when and where and how I wanted. I didn't want to be dependent on electricity or power or money or political groups. When we performed our songs in front of an audience, we had been tricked, and our audience booed us. But in time, our music became a symbol. It was an image anyone could grasp. I played piano to spite Assad. We countered the bombing attacks with satirical songs. We countered violence with art. I wanted to help the people in my neighborhood, but I had no more lentils to sell.

I'm a pianist, not a political activist. My revolution is music. My language is music. Music was going to be my form of protest, even if no one heard me.

It was January 28, 2014.

— CHAPTER NINETEEN —

hree days later, on January 31, at the other end of Yarmouk, a photographer took a shocking picture that counts among the most disturbing images of the Syrian war. If you type the words "Yarmouk" and "hunger" into a search engine, you'll see what we had become after seven months of siege. Our hunger and bitterness and desperation are palpable.

Thousands of people are crowded in between half-collapsed buildings, emaciated and filthy, looking like phantoms that have appeared amid the rubble. They stand in silence, everyone gazing in the same direction, as if spellbound. They're staring at a passageway, and everyone who wants to receive an aid package must pass through it.

In the midst of this sea of despair were my parents. I was waiting for them near the back, by a bare tree. I know many of the people in the picture. The young man in front, with the glasses, was an English teacher at the Amal School. The woman with the black headscarf was Umm Mohammad, a friend of Tahani's. Abu Mazen Abu Aisheh, the white-haired man with the mustache, in the middle, is blind, a friend of my father's—my mother once taught classes with him. The man with the high hairline, a little farther to the right, that's Abu Mazen's neighbor. He had three children, but never enough to eat.

For months, the UNRWA had been asking the Assad regime for permission to help the starving people of Yarmouk. And for months,

the Assad regime had declined. Assad had given us a choice: "Al-Ju'
au al-Ruku'," "starve or kneel." It was the same choice given to parts
of Aleppo and Homs, or to entire cities, such as Moadamiyeh. In
Yarmouk, too, the soldiers had sprayed their awful graffiti on the
other side of the checkpoint: "Surrender or starve."

At last, the government had given in. On January 18, 2014, the
UNRWA attempted for the first time to bring food to Yarmouk.
People had been lining up since two in the morning. But as soon as
the aid workers started distributing their packages, shots rang out
and screams echoed through the streets. The aid workers had come
under sniper fire. I wasn't there, but I heard from people that the
regime had opened fire. That seemed the most obvious possibility.

On that day, seventy-one emergency aid packages were distributed. On January 20, it was forty-one packages. On January 21, another twenty-six had been handed out. Then it was over for a while.

All in all, 138 emergency aid packages had been distributed, as
noted by UNRWA spokesman Chris Gunness in one of his daily
press releases. The phrasing of those press statements was always
neutral, always couched in the language of diplomacy—what else
could he have done? And yet, underneath these sober phrasings you
can catch glimpses of the aid workers' despair. Every day, they drove
up to the Watermelon with a truck full of rice and sugar, and then
they weren't allowed to pass. There were always reasons. Perhaps a
mortar shell had exploded at the distribution point the day before,
or a firefight had erupted the previous night. Or a driver, who had
tried to bring the aid packages to the checkpoint in a small van, had
been killed by sniper fire. Or simply because, for whatever reason,
the powers that be didn't want us to have food.

On January 30, the UNRWA successfully handed out 1,026 aid
packages and on January 31, 980. A success. Each package weighed
about fifty-five pounds, ten days' worth of food for a family of eight.
According to the UNRWA, two hundred packages meant that a
thousand people had a thousand calories per day for a month. At
least they wouldn't starve.

But that was it. Once more, the supplies stopped coming. The

UNRWA volunteers were waiting at the Watermelon. And we were waiting a few hundred feet away, at al-Reyjeh Square. In the following months, my parents and I got up at six every morning, had our cinnamon coffee, and then walked down Yarmouk Street toward the distribution point. At a safe distance from the checkpoints, my father and mother asked me to sit in the shade to wait. They usually returned empty-handed.

Back then, I didn't know why. But today it is possible to read about it, in the daily updates of UNRWA spokesman Chris Gunness:

FEBRUARY 1, 2014
A large crowd has gathered near the distribution point. The situation is tense. Evidently, the people of Yarmouk are lacking even the most essential items.

FEBRUARY 20, 2014
The UNRWA resumed food distribution to civilians in Yarmouk, Damascus, after a break of eleven days. We welcome the support of the Syrian authorities.

MARCH 16, 2014
It's rare that a spokesman is at a loss for words. But after three years of conflict in Syria, words have lost their meaning. They shatter in the face of this tragedy. Their meaning disintegrates. Taking this into account, I am now publishing 17 photos.
[Among them was the picture of January 31.]

MARCH 20, 2014
Chaotic scenes were on display in Yarmouk yesterday, as crowds of hungry and desperate people made it impossible to distribute food.

MARCH 21, 2014
After only two hours, the UNRWA team had to withdraw.

The distribution point was under fire from the Yarmouk side. All UNRWA employees are safe. For several hours, hundreds of civilians were trapped between the shooters. Several people had been killed.

APRIL 8, 2014

Time-consuming inspections of relief supplies slowed the pace of delivery in the early afternoon. The UNRWA calls on the authorities to facilitate an increased distribution rate in the coming days.

APRIL 23, 2014

The UNRWA has been informed by the Syrian government that we can resume our humanitarian work in Yarmouk to-morrow, April 24, after a fifteen-day break. We welcome this step.

MAY 24, 2014

For the first time, the UNRWA has been able to distribute hygiene kits to 690 families. Each kit contains soap, towels, toothpaste, detergents, shampoos, and other hygiene items.

JULY 7, 2014

Today, there have been dramatic and chaotic scenes when the UNRWA distributed food for the first time in six weeks in the beleaguered Yarmouk district.

At the beginning of February, my parents received their first aid package. As usual, I had brought them to Fedayeen Street. When I saw them going through the passageway, I walked on for a few blocks, to a different exit point at al-Reyjeh Square. Everyone going back home would have to pass by here. The square was large. Bare tree trunks stood everywhere. It was a no-man's-land, a death zone, besieged by the snipers of both sides. Time and again, heartbreaking scenes played out here.

But this time everything went well. I saw my parents approaching, my father carrying the heavy aid package, my mother guiding him. Thankfully, I had brought my old bicycle with me, a massive vehicle from China. I joyfully hugged my mother, then I strapped the aid box onto the luggage rack. We hurried home and unpacked our treasures:

Eleven pounds of rice
Eleven pounds of beans
Eleven pounds of sugar
Eleven pounds of oil
Seven pounds of powdered milk
Three pounds of noodles
Five cans of mortadella, each weighing seven ounces

We all treated ourselves to a glass of powdered milk. God, it tasted so good! My body shivered as I drank. It was as if the milk went straight into my bloodstream.

Of course, I would never have dared to line up for an aid package myself. The famous picture doesn't tell the whole story. The UNRWA photographer was facing al-Reyjeh Square from Fedayeen Street. But behind him were three checkpoints. The first one was operated by the General Command, the Palestinian militia. The second was under the command of a Shiite group, and I have no idea what they were doing here. And the third checkpoint was run by the Syrian Army. The United Nations vehicles were parked behind those three checkpoints.

In order to get food, you had to show your ID card three times. And each time, the fighters randomly picked out young men. Perhaps they were hoping to settle some old scores. It was like running a gauntlet.

Hundreds of young men had been arrested during food distribution. The ones who didn't have anyone to stand up for them. The ones who had been driven half-mad by hunger and who ran straight into the arms of their torturers. That's why you see only women and old men in the foreground of that famous photo. They were allowed to pass without any problems. Except for the young man with the glasses, the English teacher. After that day, I never saw him again.

The UNRWA boxes saved us from starvation. But many of the people paid for them with their lives. When you joined the line, anything could happen to you. One time, the soldiers plowed into the crowd with a bulldozer, to push back the starving people. Another time, the throng of people crowded against a badly damaged building and the walls collapsed, crushing half a dozen people. And time and again, sniper shots proved fatal.

I spent endless hours sitting at al-Reyjeh Square, waiting for my parents. I heard the uncontrolled sobbing of all the people who came back empty-handed. I saw women looking for their husbands, running back and forth, asking strangers, "Have you seen him? Have you seen him?" Some were hitting their own faces, screaming in despair. And everyone knew that the husband had been arrested.

One time, I saw a guy who came running with a hand brush and dustpan, to sweep up even the smallest traces of sugar from the dusty road to salvage it for himself.

I saw a woman with blood running down her face. Her teeth and nose had been beaten; her cheek was scraped to the bone. But she was laughing. On her head, she was carrying the heavy box with the light blue UN logo. "I've got one, I've got one!" she cried in triumph.

I saw Abu Omar being shot dead in the no-man's-land of al-Reyjeh Square. I had known him since my childhood, a giant of a man who made granite and marble tabletops. While waiting for my parents in the shadow of the square, I had met up with his nephew, who told me that Abu Omar wasn't doing well; he had diabetes and lived alone in a bombed-out building. Again and again, the young man stood up to look for him—then, finally, we saw him.

Abu Omar had actually managed to snag an aid package, and carried it in his arms like a baby. His walking stick lay on top of it and he was swaying back and forth under the load of the package. Then a shot rang out. Abu Omar fell to the ground. Then panic broke out as masses of people started running back to where they had come from. Four men took Abu Omar and carried him away, bleeding from the head, while his nephew hurried after him crying. There was a fresh trail of blood on Yarmouk Street.

The threat of sniper fire was constant. Once, my parents were in the middle of the crowd when shots came from somewhere. Immediately, everyone ran for their lives, the crowds trampling over people. My father and mother, who always held on to each other, were separated, and my father fell.

He cried out for my mother, but she had long since been pushed aside. Then she, too, fell. And someone stepped on her chest.

She managed to get up again, but had difficulty breathing. Something was wrong. She fought through the crowd to get back to my father. His knee was bleeding, his pants were torn. She helped him, and they started making their way back. When they reached al-Reyjeh Square, I saw them. Throwing caution to the wind, I ran toward them, into the no-man's-land.

From the corner of my eye, I saw a group of soldiers standing on the left, about sixty-five feet away.

"It's Aeham Ahmad!" one of them shouted. During this period my videos were widely seen on Facebook.

I ran to my parents. "What happened?" I cried. "Is everything all right?"

"Aeham, what are you doing here?" my mother hissed. "Get back! Quickly!"

At any time, the soldiers could have rushed forward and grabbed me. Twenty quick steps, and they would have had me. I didn't look at them, but I could feel their gaze on me. My heart was pounding and my mouth was dry. My father was limping along, blood running down his leg. My mother coughed and clutched her chest as we hurried on.

If the soldiers pursued us, however, they risked being shot by a rebel sniper. That's why nothing happened to me. Finally, we crossed an imaginary border and entered the safe zone. Then we stopped.

My mother complained about a sharp pain in her chest. "Your rib is probably broken," my father said. "We have to get it x-rayed."

"How long has it been since you've seen an X-ray machine in Yarmouk?" my mother asked sarcastically.

When we got home, my mother went to bed. She didn't get up for several days. Tahani made herb compresses for her. For the time being, my mother was sidelined. For now, my father would have to rely on Tahani to help him get food. But what if the soldiers asked her questions about me? We came up with a story. She would simply say, "I don't know anything about him. We're divorced. He's probably dead."

The next morning, we tried again. We got up at six, drank our cinnamon coffee, and left. Once again, my father's disability made life a little easier. At least we didn't have to awaken in the middle of the night. When we reached the line, thousands of people were already waiting. But on days when the crowd wasn't too big, people let him pass.

We must have stood in that line about ten times per month. Every few weeks, we managed to snag an aid package. And to celebrate, each of us had a glass of powdered milk.

Despite this hardship, despite these terrors—or maybe because of them?—the first six months of 2014 turned out to be the most productive time of my life. Music was just bubbling out of me. During those months, I composed 160 songs, almost one per day. In the mornings, we lined up for the UNRWA box, then we went to get water or clover. In the afternoons, the "Yarmouk Boys"—that's what we called ourselves—met in the store to rehearse. We briefly practiced a new song, then we pushed the piano out into the streets and used our music to make light of our misery.

The Politician Has Finally Moved His Ass

The politician has finally moved his ass
and sent a delegation from the camp
A delegation left, a delegation came
One delegation brought the next

Oh, what times we're living in
I can't sleep anymore, my stomach growls so much
Oh, what times we're living in
I can't sleep anymore, oh my!

There were more and more delegations
and with them came promises
Promises and more promises
while around us people died . . .

At the end of January—two days had passed since our first performance—the *Bukra Ahla* editor came to my shop. A normal You-Tube video received around several hundred clicks. But we were at over forty thousand, within just forty-eight hours. He was giddy with excitement. He asked if we could do a few more videos.

Over forty thousand! I was elated that people seemed to like what we were doing. I thought about it for a moment—a brief moment—and then I agreed. The next day, we performed again. Mahmoud Tamim suggested playing on Lubiya Street, in Yarmouk's former garment district. We wanted to show how empty and deserted it now looked.

The guy from *Bukra Ahla* tagged along, shooting another video of us. Not too long ago, that kind of thing had made me very nervous. But now? It made no difference anymore. Who cared if there was one video of us or ten? If the regime wanted to arrest us, they already had more than enough rope to hang us with. So why not go on?

Our third performance was in front of the rubble of the Park of Pioneers, where the first barrel bomb had been dropped on Yarmouk. Now it was a no-man's-land, full of debris. Our latest composition was called "Rain," and had lyrics by Ahmad Sallam, the bald-headed, communist friend of my father:

> *You cannot conquer the people, no you can't*
> *You'll choke on your own tear gas*
> *You can break the young man's bones with your batons*
> *But you cannot conquer the people, you invaders*
> *No, you cannot conquer us*
> *When night falls*
> *Dawn is coming*

Everything had gone well so far, but one thing annoyed me. The guy from *Bukra Ahla* kept pushing us. It seemed like our success had gone to his head. He suddenly wanted us to thank the "*Bukra Ahla* film crew." Later, I realized they were putting ads before our videos. That's when I had had enough. What kind of message were we sending here? My friends and I were trying to raise awareness about the siege, about starving to death, and suddenly an ad for sneakers pops up? No thanks!

For a while, we moved our videos to a Facebook page called Photos from Yarmouk. Raed, my IT wizard friend, helped us out. He showed us how YouTube worked and created a Facebook page for us. We moved my old Rama electric moped into my apartment. Now all we needed was someone to push the pedals; then we could upload our songs onto the internet.

When I saw that people in Europe watched our videos, I became giddy with joy. There were comments from people with foreign names—we had viewers in cities like Hamburg and Berlin. It was incredible! Our voice was being heard!

One day, a man approached me on the street. He lived in my neighborhood, I had seen him before. He introduced himself as Marwan. He liked what we were doing and asked if he could join us. "Yes, of course!" I said. And so the Yarmouk Boys had one more voice. It's too bad that Marwan wasn't a great singer. He growled like a bear. But he wrote wonderful lyrics. I must have composed about twenty songs with him.

I very much enjoyed the time with the Yarmouk Boys. We had a lot of fun together. We regularly argued about where we should perform. "In front of *my* building!" someone would say. "No, in front of *mine!*" someone chimed in. And then I would have to decide. Whenever we pushed the piano through the deserted streets, we forgot about our empty stomachs. We felt powerful. We weren't alone anymore. This was our revolution. We had a mission: We wanted the world to see what was going on here. We wanted to show how Assad was killing us, and that we were standing up to him.

One day, I decided to invite all of the Yarmouk Boys over for dinner. I had some rice left over. One and a half pounds, to be exact. It was worth three thousand Syrian pounds at the time, around six dollars. The main course was rice with Asian spice mix. For dessert, Tahani made rice with powdered milk. It was a feast! There is a video of it online. Everyone was sitting cross-legged at a long table, laughing. Just like in the old days.

After a while, the first journalists started approaching us. At first, it was only a few, but their numbers quickly grew. I kept asking the other members of our group if they wanted to be interviewed. But the only ones who volunteered were Mahmoud Tamim and myself. At some point, our videos were broadcast across the Arabian Peninsula via satellite TV. Suddenly, people as far away as Tunisia knew who we were.

Q: Why are you doing this?
A: We're protesting against the siege.
Q: And why else?
A: Life here is very sad. We want to create a little bit of joy.
Q: Have the people from the choir ever sung before?

A: No, this is their first time.

Q: What kind of jobs did you have before?

A: We were carpenters, salesmen, bakers, bricklayers, music teachers.

Q: And why the piano?

A: Because the power is out!

Q: Why do you play in the streets?

A: We want people to see what it looks like.

Q: What's your message to the world?

A: Don't let us starve to death.

Green Mint

You, who's calling out between peoples
"Death is spreading over my land,
Madness and murder, kidnapping and hunger,
It's ripping my heart out of my rib cage.
Bloodshed, fire and light
A tragedy is crossing the sea."

Yarmouk conjures up its children
between the rubble and tombs
plant a flower on the sun
It calls you and screams:
"Come back, my displaced people
The mint is still green
A rose is waiting for you
Come back and water it, poor child
Water it with your tears,
It's waiting for your return."

People started giving me poems all the time. There was even a poem about the UNRWA package that had been written by Hisham Zuawi, a friend of my father's. This frail man, elegant and reserved, was later gunned down by a sniper while returning from picking up his aid package. He was still clutching the UNRWA box when he died.

I got other poems from Mahmoud and Marwan, from friends of my father's, from passersby who approved of what we were doing. I found it inspiring that so many people spoke well of my music, in Damascus and Aleppo, in Algeria and Egypt, in Italy and Belgium. I was composing all the time, as if it were all I had ever done.

For years I had soaked up techniques from European classical music, as well as from artists like Ziad Rahbani and Marcel Khalife. Now those seeds were blossoming. The tea had steeped enough. Sometimes I needed several hours to compose a song. Other times, only ten minutes.

As I walked through the streets with a new poem in my hand, I'd recite it out loud and suddenly a motif would pop into my head. I'd sit down at the piano, play it, change it, adjusting the lyrics and melody. And finally I'd compose an elaborate intro. I owed myself that much. After all, I was a pianist.

I combined European tonal scales with Arabic rhythms, and drew inspiration from some of Mozart's harmonic progressions and accompaniments.

I wanted to create melodies that everyone could immediately grasp, and join to them the seductive power of harmonies. Some of my songs consisted—like Western folk songs—of several stanzas and a refrain. Other songs had longer motifs, interrupted by a bridge, common to the Arabic world.

I composed songs of satire and mockery, sad songs and cheerful ones. I was careful to avoid empty bombast, steering clear of heroic rhythms and victory marches, of blood spilled on the field of honor. Sometimes I blended simple, heartbreaking lyrics with cheerful music, like in a children's song.

Initially, my songs generally had one note for each syllable of text. But then people started giving me poems with no fixed rhyme or meter, and thus harder to set to music. So I started stretching syllables out over several tones. That made the lyrics sound mournful. I wanted people to feel our despair. Our despair over the pregnant woman who died at the checkpoint. Our agony over having to stand in line half the night in hopes of getting one aid package, and then not even getting it in the end!

After only two months, the Yarmouk Boys disbanded. It began with petty jealousies. Three members of our group were wondering why I constantly wrote music for Mahmoud and Marwan but not the others, and complained that Mahmoud was arrogant. So they quit the group.

It didn't take long for the next few men to complain, saying that they didn't have enough time and were exhausted. Getting water in the morning, harvesting clover, looking for firewood—and then, in the afternoon, having to push the piano around, just for a few minutes of singing. It was too much.

They wondered why we weren't getting paid for our music. Why weren't we looking for a sponsor—in Europe, perhaps, or somewhere else? Someone who could pay us?

"The moment we do that, we'll have to dance to their tune," I said. "No, I want us to be independent."

But I was overruled. The complaints grew louder. Finally, they gave me a choice: Either somebody pays us—or we quit.

"Then quit," I said. "I won't be tied down."

We split up, but we remained friends.

I realized that I'd be willing to give up almost anything, but not music. My music kept me alive. I had to go on. From then on, we tried performing as a trio, Raed, Marwan, and I. The two of them were still on my side. But it just wasn't working. It sounded out of tune.

Until that point, I had always accompanied others on the piano. I was a pianist, not a singer. Yes, I had spent years practicing solfège, I had sung in choirs. But I still didn't trust my voice. Or maybe I was just too shy to sing by myself. Only when everyone else had left the group did I overcome my shyness. What choice did I have?

I asked Niraz Saied, the photographer, to take footage of me. Everyone in Yarmouk knew him. He had long hair tied into a ponytail, a goatee, and round metal-rimmed glasses. His pictures were sold around the world by photo agencies, and he had exhibits from Damascus to Ramallah. On April 21, 2014, he took the photo that eventually went around the world. I was sitting at the piano, wearing a green T-shirt, singing by myself for the first time, the pianist amid the rubble. It was an image everyone was able to grasp.

A man I knew named Amer Helwani had a talent for writing particularly beautiful lyrics. One day when he was in the shop with me, he begged me to give him sugar or rice.

"I'd love to. But we only eat clover and lentils all day, so that my son can have the rice. Maybe you should eat grass! That's what we do."

"I hate it!" he said, despairing. "It gives me diarrhea. Just looking at that stuff makes me want to throw up!"

"Don't blame me," I said. "We're all hungry! You should write about it. Let the world know how awful things are in Yarmouk."

"Come with me," he said. "I'd like to show you something."

"What?"

"It's personal. Something that will make you angry."

"I'm already angry. And exhausted. I have no strength left."

"Please, just ten minutes."

I gave in. We walked next to each other in silence. Amer Helwani looked terrible. His face was dark from the smoke of the plastic-bottle fires and his right hand was swollen and blue from a splinter that just wouldn't heal. He had studied Arabic once, then he worked as a housepainter. He was a good poet. What did he want to show me?

His apartment was on the ground floor of a concrete building. One of the rooms had been hit by a grenade; the outside walls were gone. I saw a pot standing on a plastic-bottle fire. He lifted the lid. Some kind of animal was boiling in the water.

"What is it?" I asked.

"A cat."

I flinched back in disgust. "Ugh! How could you do that? Why don't you just eat grass?"

"The grass is killing me."

"Why are you showing me this?"

"I want you to taste it."

So that was why he had asked me to come here! He didn't want to suffer this disgrace alone. I remembered the sheikh of the Palestine mosque issuing a fatwa once, stating that you were allowed to eat dog or cat meat if it prevented you from starving to death. There used to be many strays in the streets of Yarmouk. But no more. They'd probably all been eaten. But I'd never seen a person so desperate that they would eat a pet. I stood there, uncertain. I was disgusted. But then it was as if a switch in my head flipped. An odd craving came over me. I hadn't eaten meat in over a year.

"Just one bite," I said.

Amer Helwani cut off a small piece of meat for me. I put it in my mouth. Almost immediately, I began rummaging around in my pocket: I found a piece of paper and spit into it. It was disgusting! It tasted horrible and bitter. I remember thinking that human meat probably tasted similar.

"How can you eat this?" I said.

"What else can I eat?" he burst out. "I tried everything, I went everywhere. I couldn't get any rice, not from anyone. And believe me, grass gives me the shits."

I stood there, embarrassed and silent.

"And here you are, telling me I'm supposed to write a poem! Great, thank you! Yes, I'm hungry! I want to eat! Screw you and your poems!"

"But it's the only way we can bring about any change," I said sheepishly.

He didn't want to hear it.

But later, he showed me a poem.

Two Little Braids

Two little braids
Are talking on the street
Telling the bitter tale, again and again.

If you can't find a shoulder to lean on
Be it your brother or a helping hand
Don't shed your tear, but keep it alive.

Our hearts are hardened
Harder than steel.

So stretch out your scrawny legs
And stand still, stand still, stand still.
And sigh: Oh, oh, and oh again.

When I asked Amer Helwani what he had been thinking about when he wrote this poem, he burst into tears. Then he explained that the lyrics were about a girl, maybe eight years old, who had gone with her mother to get a UNRWA aid package. They had both lined up in clean clothes, but hours later, they returned, crestfallen, covered in dust from top to bottom.

I sat down at the piano and began composing a melody that was meant to imply a vicious cycle. I imagined that in the first two stanzas, the gods were speaking. I pictured fifteen gods looking into the crystal ball that held the world, focusing on Syria, and then on Yarmouk, and finally, on this small, dust-covered girl. Between each line I played a "basso continuo," which used to be called the "voice of the devil" in the music of the Baroque era. In the last two stanzas, the girl spoke. I called my piece the "Yarmouk Operetta."

— CHAPTER TWENTY —

When our first son, Ahmad, was born, Tahani and I had decided that at age two, he would have a little brother or sister. But then the revolution came. The siege began. Everything was dysfunctional. And I wasn't thinking about children anymore.

But one night, Tahani broached the subject again: Wouldn't it be nice if we had a second child? I looked at her in astonishment. "What do you mean?" I asked.

"Just like we planned."

"But that was during peacetime. Now there's not even enough food for the three of us."

"Life will go on," she said. "The siege can't last forever."

She was right. At the time, we didn't really believe that anything could ever change. Did it really matter if there were three or four, living and dying together? We were all doomed to die, no matter what.

Our first son was brought into this world via C-section, and the doctors told us that our second child would have to be delivered the same way. But there hadn't been a functioning hospital in Yarmouk for a long time. "How is this supposed to work?" I asked Tahani. "We can't risk your life."

"God is on our side," she said. "We've always found a way."

"I said it's your decision, and I'm serious. You decide." I added, "It's not going to be easy."

"We'll never get out of here," Tahani said. "I want a child."

We left it at that. But she kept bringing it up. Finally, I suggested asking my parents for advice. After all, our decision would affect them as well. So, one evening, we asked them what they thought of it.

At first, they were very happy. But then they started thinking of all the problems this would cause. Finally, my father said, "We're happy with Ahmad. We'd be just as happy with a second grandchild. It's your decision."

We decided that, yes, we wanted another child. To spite the war.

One day, Tahani had to sit down suddenly. She was feeling dizzy. She told me she couldn't shake the feeling that she was pregnant. She went to see a midwife, who confirmed it. Tahani was overjoyed. And I was, too. But my doubts grew.

The midwife had given us a lecture about healthy diets. An important topic, no doubt. But it had been an eternity since we'd had fresh vegetables, fruit, or meat. The midwife suggested that Tahani take vitamin pills, calcium tablets, and iron supplements. Those kinds of things could still be had. It was springtime: the UNRWA started delivering their first food packages. Which meant that at least Tahani could have a glass of powdered milk once in a while. And of course, day in and day out, rice and lentils and boiled clover.

Meanwhile, I had always loved making music with children, and continued to do so even during the siege, since there were still a handful of schools. In my time with the Yarmouk Boys, I had appeared in four different schools, one after the other, to sing with the kids. One member of our group had arranged it. But then the Yarmouk Boys split up, and our music lessons were over.

Then Marwan had an idea: we could take the kids out onto the streets to make music with them. So that's what we ended up doing. We started a new group, the "Yarmouk Kids," our own little children's choir. Marwan loved children and had a good way of working with them. He was the one who would wheedle the kids during rehearsals. After all, a group of children can be as jumpy as a sack of fleas. I insisted that the parents sign a piece of paper releasing us from any responsibility in case we were hit by a grenade. Always a possibility.

We sang with the Yarmouk Kids two or three times per week. Sometimes only five kids showed up, sometimes twenty. Sometimes we sang in front of the rubble of my old middle school, other times at a crowded intersection. Whenever we did, passersby stopped and smiled at us. Children singing on the street! This was even better than our all-male choir.

But one day, a group of soldiers came by. As of late, they had grown out their beards. By that time, the secular activists in Yarmouk had been pushed aside, and the revolution had turned into a struggle for "true Islam." One of the soldiers said, "You're singing with girls, brother? Don't you know that's *haram*?" Verboten. Un-Islamic. But they let us continue. For now.

One hyperactive boy simply couldn't stand still and was constantly interrupting—until I asked him to stand next to me and conduct the music with his hands. He did so, and everyone loved it. People smiled at the sight of the little conductor, oblivious to everything else, like a sign-language interpreter.

One day a girl approached us with her handicapped brother, who kept twisting his head and slurring his words, with his tongue at the edge of his mouth and saliva around his lips. The sounds he made were disturbing. But the moment he heard music, he turned into an angel. He became peaceful and, in his own way, tried to sing along as best as he could.

One day, as we were singing, a remarkably pretty woman came around the corner with her daughter. When she saw us, she called out, "Here they are, the famous singers!" Both the woman and her daughter were well dressed; their faces were spotlessly clean. By contrast, we all looked pretty shabby.

I stopped. "What do you mean?"

"Well, aren't you the Yarmouk Kids?"

"Yes. You've heard of us?"

"All of Damascus is talking about you."

I saw how proud the kids suddenly were. Such a nice compliment from such an elegant lady!

"What you're doing is very important," she said intently. "We came from Damascus to see you; we had to apply for a special permit. Do you think my daughter could sing with you?" The girl was about eleven years old.

"Of course, it would be my pleasure!" I said. "Join us, take your place!" Then we continued.

When we pushed the piano back after our rehearsal, Marwan said, "Did you hear what she said? What we're doing is important!" He, too, was beaming.

I don't know where the lady and her daughter had spent the night, but when they sang with us a second time, both were wearing headscarves. They must have run into the men from the al-Nusra Front, a Syrian affiliate of al-Qaeda. The third time I saw them, they were almost as gray and dusty as the rest of us. And then they were gone.

One time I saw an old man observing us—and I recognized him as my former Arabic teacher from high school. He followed us as we pushed the piano back to the store. I approached him. He seemed quite frail, so I asked him inside and offered him a glass of water. When he sat down, he had tears in his eyes.

"Aeham, what you're doing is wonderful."

I thanked him, feeling slightly embarrassed. And I took the opportunity to apologize for the many lessons I had skipped. "I hope you didn't take it personally," I said. "It really had nothing to do with you. I just had different things on my mind at the time."

"Oh, don't mention it, that was a long time ago," he said. "I'm very proud of you." He left. Later, he wrote five songs for me.

The kids' favorite piece was the "water song." Marwan had written the lyrics, which told of their everyday life. Many of them had to help their parents carry heavy canisters of water each day.

The Water's Always Out

The water's always out
It doesn't flow like it's supposed to

We're sick of carrying buckets
But we don't have enough water

Ask Abu Mohammad
He's always worried about it

He's always carrying buckets
And complaining about it

Oh, it'll be fine.
Oh, it'll be fine.

The power's out as well
In case we forgot to mention it!

Then Marwan filmed us, and Raed uploaded the video to our Facebook page. The video got ten thousand likes, five hundred shares, and hundreds of comments. Some of our videos on YouTube had been viewed fifty thousand times.

No wonder that we were constantly approached by journalists. They kept asking more or less the same questions. Can you tell us about your situation? What prompted you to do this? I explained as best as I could. My answers can be found online to this day.

I said things like: "In Yarmouk, we don't have much choice—either we join one of the armed groups or we wait to die. I think it's better to sing while you're waiting for death."

And: "The piano is a symbol of high culture. To play piano out in the streets is a symbol of grandeur, but also of hardship."

Or: "The songs we sing touch everyone in Yarmouk, because

they tell about our daily sufferings, about diseases, about our lack of medicine and food, even about how people are eating grass here."

And this: "I didn't know how else to help, so I took my piano out into the streets and began playing songs, to give people courage."

And: "I'm speaking for the starving people here. I'm trying to paint an image of our everyday suffering. We'll keep singing and singing."

In truth, the past six months had been insane. It was a happy and terrible time. We struggled and had our sorrows, but our music made everything a little brighter. Everything seemed to be happening in a blur. In the mornings, I struggled to fetch water. In the afternoons, I sang with the kids in the streets. In the evenings, I created music for a poem someone had given me. Then I went to bed with an empty stomach.

I'm a pianist. I've never waved flags. My revolution is music. And the world began to listen. It was a miracle.

— CHAPTER TWENTY-ONE —

In late August 2014, with Yarmouk still sealed off from the rest of the world, the bombs continued to fall and snipers were hiding on the rooftops. It was impossible to leave the neighborhood, and we remained cut off from supplies.

On one particular day—the worst day of my life—I had once again gone out to get water, together with my friend and neighbor Marwan. Afterward, I lay down again to get some more sleep.

I had a dream. I was sitting on a stool by the side of the road. People were running past me, panicked. To my right, a short way down the road, was a wolf. It was howling, and its head was stretched upward. That's what people were afraid of. They wanted to get away, but they couldn't. They ran back and forth, a strange and rigid look on their faces. And I sat on my stool, unable to get up. I kept staring at the wolf, watching it as it howled. The panicked crowd swarmed all around me. It was eerie. . . .

Then I woke up. A small stone hit the window. I heard the voices of little children calling from downstairs: "Teacher Aeham! Teacher Aeham! Come on down!"

I got up to look, and saw six girls standing on the street, jumping up and down and waving at me. "Teacher Aeham! Come on down! We want to sing!" That's how they always did it.

Zeinab stood to the right. I had met her a few months ago at a cultural center where I had made music with the kids a couple of times. Zeinab played the drums. She was twelve years old, more cheerful and a lot cheekier than the others. "I like rap music," she once told me in a serious voice, drumming a hard beat on the table with her fingers. I liked her at once, and invited her to join the Yarmouk Kids.

From then on, she came by all the time, and we would all sing together, in my store or out in the streets. With most songs, the kids all sang the chorus together and Zeinab would rap. For her, music was a weapon. That was her idea.

She'd told me that her father was sick and had to leave Yarmouk, and that he'd come back as soon as he felt better. One day, when we were singing out in the streets, Zeinab's mother came by. After I said hello and asked about her husband, she took me aside, telling me he'd died in a bombing attack. But she didn't want Zeinab to know.

On this morning, the girls were looking at me expectantly. I rubbed my eyes, still dazed by that terrible dream.

"Not today, kids. I'm too tired."

"No!" they said. "We want to sing! We're bored. We don't want to sit around at home anymore!"

From the corner of my eye, I saw Marwan looking out the window of his building. He, too, had heard the girls. I waved at him. He shrugged his shoulders. Why not? he seemed to say. I relented— I still curse this day—and went downstairs.

Together, we got the piano and began pushing it. Zeinab told us that she wanted to make a video for her grandmother, who had left Yarmouk. So we decided to shoot our video near the building where the old lady had lived.

We pushed the piano into the middle of the street. The children waited near the building, where it was safer. I opened the piano lid. Marwan was ready and nodded. I closed my eyes and started to play a song. Marwan walked around with his video camera, filming us. At the end of the song I looked up. He gave me a thumbs-up. I closed my eyes again and began playing a second song. Marwan continued filming. Everything was normal.

Then it was time to get the kids involved. Marwan grouped

them around the piano, giving a signal when he started filming. I began playing the first few bars of "Yarmouk Misses You, Brother." I nodded at the kids, giving them their cue to start singing. Their clear, bright voices echoed through the street. It felt good, and I closed my eyes for a moment.

Then I heard a shot. I opened my eyes—and saw Zeinab lying on the ground, to my right. Blood was seeping from her head.

I jumped up and bent over her.

"Zeinab, Zeinab, are you all right? Oh God, what happened?"

Marwan and the other kids had dashed away, crouching in front of a store.

"Aeham, come!" Marwan yelled. "The sniper is going to kill you."

I ran for cover. "Maybe she's still alive!" I cried. "We have to get her!"

The other girls sat there, frozen, staring at us with big eyes. Marwan ran into the building and came back with a long pole. We managed to push the pole up Zeinab's pant leg and pull her toward us.

I cried out to Marwan, "Get the kids to safety!" Then I took Zeinab in my arms and started running.

The blood was still seeping from her head. It ran down my left arm. I was sobbing. People were everywhere, but no one paid us any attention. Sights like this were commonplace. It took me ten minutes to reach the hospital in al-Hajar al-Aswad. This is where the carpenter had fixed my fingers, and where we had dropped off the dead man from the radish field. I stormed in, placed Zeinab on a stretcher, and called for help.

A man in a white coat approached. I didn't know him.

"What happened?" he asked.

"She was hit by a sniper."

He checked her pulse. Then he shone a flashlight into her open eyes. "She's gone."

The world seemed to crumble around me.

"Do you know the girl?" he asked.

"Yes," I said, sobbing.

"Would you like to notify the parents?"

I shook my head. I asked for pen and paper and wrote down the address of Zeinab's mother.

"Who are you?" the doctor asked.

"I'm nobody," I said, and left.

I staggered through the streets in my bloodstained clothes. What had I done? This was all my fault! I never should have brought the children out onto the streets! I should never have led them into this world of rubble!

I went to Marwan. He had brought the other girls home safely. I washed off the blood and he gave me clean clothes. We sat together in silence, hardly daring to look at each other.

"It wasn't our fault," he said. I didn't respond.

After a while, I went back to my apartment.

"What happened?" Tahani asked. I must have looked terrible.

"I don't feel well," I said, and lay down on the sofa. Turning toward the wall, I began to silently cry, all the misery pouring out of me, incoherent and unstoppable. I felt as if this, right here, was the end of it all. Everything was over.

The hours passed slowly. How could I live with this guilt?

That night, I slept on the sofa, not going back to our bed. Sometimes, sleep came over me, but a few seconds later I flinched and in my mind's eye, I saw Zeinab lying in her own blood as I stared into her lifeless eyes.

The next morning, I felt as if someone was choking me. As if my heart was made of stone. I went over to Marwan's. His face was lined with sorrow. We decided to go look for the piano.

No one had touched it. The right-hand side and the dolly were covered with bloodstains. I thought that I would never play it again, vowed never to touch an instrument again.

I had an acquaintance nearby. We pushed the piano over to him and asked if we could leave it there for the time being. I didn't need it any longer. The hell with it.

He saw the bloodstains. "Those are from a cat," Marwan said. "Can you wash them off?"

In a daze, I went back home and lay down again on the sofa.

On the second day, I went up to the rooftop terrace. I didn't want to live. It was over. Yes, I had meant well. And I had put so much effort into it all. I had wanted to sing with the children, to laugh, to forget the war. And now a girl had died, and it was my fault.

I went to the edge of the terrace. I'd been courting death for too long. I had kept playing piano, even though I had known the risks. At any point, a grenade might have killed me. There are videos where you hear shots in between the piano chords. Death was everywhere. And I would have been ready for it. Why hadn't that dilettante of a sniper aimed better? Why hadn't he shot me? Why Zeinab? She was twelve! A young girl!

I sat down on the balustrade, feeling as if my life was over, as if I had died along with Zeinab. I didn't want to keep on living. I couldn't bear this guilt. . . .

At some point, I gathered myself and went over to Marwan. We greeted each other with silent nods. And then we sat down and cried together.

"Dammit!" he yelled, jumping up and punching his fist against the wall. "Why the kids? We were only singing!"

Marwan lived with his mother, who had heard the shouting. She came in and wanted to know what was going on.

"Nothing," he said.

For a week, I could hardly speak or eat. Tahani was worried. I had told her nothing.

But at long last, the pain started loosening its iron grip.

Marwan and I went to get the piano. There was water damage. We had stored it with a friend of mine who had hosed it down to wash the blood off. My friend Raed used to be a housepainter, so I asked him to paint the piano white. Another acquaintance painted the Palestinian colors on it, with a calligraphy in black, red, and green. I sat down at the piano and started playing. It was more out

of tune than ever. I played "Yarmouk Misses You, Brother," the
song that Zeinab never finished singing.

But I had to keep on living.

Two weeks after Zeinab's death, a few children stopped by my
store again; they wanted to sing. I said yes. We made music, but we
stayed in the store. And then, a few weeks later, it was September
already. We pushed the piano back out into the street. But from
now on, we only played in narrow, crowded streets where the snipers couldn't reach us. I sang with children again. With different
children. At a white piano.

My chest was so constricted that I could hardly breathe. You can
see my frozen gaze on the videos we made in those days. My face
was like a mask. The children were singing cheerfully, laughing and
jumping around. They sang with passion, but I was distracted. I
had struggled and lost. I no longer believed in the power of music.

Back in those days, I never talked about Zeinab's death. What
could I have said? And who was to blame? Assad's henchmen? The
snipers of the al-Nusra Front? Perhaps. They had targeted me for a
while, irritated by our music. But I couldn't dare accuse them pub-
licly. Only Marwan and I knew what really happened. We knew the
debt of blood we owed. And we pledged never to tell anyone.

Zeinab's mother never came to see me. I'm not sure she knew
that her daughter had died next to my piano. I didn't dare approach
her. What could I possibly have said to her?

Not a day passed when I didn't think of Zeinab. And whenever
I did, I felt as if I couldn't breathe. Every time I closed my eyes to
sing "Yarmouk Misses You, Brother," I saw it all again, as if it were
happening right here, right now.

But all that came later.

Much later.

When I arrived in Europe, when the fear and the terror were
slowly subsiding—only then was I able to talk about it. Only then
was I able to articulate the awful truth. At first fleetingly, without
any details. Then more and more often. Finally, I told the story to
every journalist, whether they wanted to hear it or not. I thought

perhaps my confession would help me atone for my sin. But no one was interested.

Sometimes people told me that it wasn't my fault. That it wasn't me. That it was a war crime. It's a crime to shoot at little girls singing in the street.

That might be true, but I didn't believe it. I would have to be reborn a hundred times before my guilt was paid off. I am condemned to live always with this guilt.

— CHAPTER TWENTY-TWO —

As the fall of 2014 advanced, we continued to line up for our food rations, I kept composing, and Tahani's baby bump grew larger and larger. Zeinab had been killed in August, but I had to go on living. Tahani was nearing the end of her pregnancy. The midwife had calculated October 25 as the due date. And with each passing day, one particular question became ever more pressing: Where could Tahani go for the delivery?

We asked at the field hospital in al-Hajar al-Aswad. Yes, they could do a C-section there, provided we brought a drip and three doses of Rocephin, a liquid antibiotic. In Europe, each dose cost fifty euros. In Yarmouk, it was worth more than gold. Not to mention that it simply wasn't available anywhere. No one had any antibiotics left, since medicine was vital to the war effort. The regime had cut off not just our food supply, but our medical supply as well.

So there was only one remaining option—we had to bring Tahani to Damascus for her delivery. That summer, a cease-fire agreement between the rebels and the government had gone into effect. Any sick or elderly people, as well as pregnant women, could get registered in Yalda and receive transit papers for Damascus. But no one knew if they'd be allowed to return.

Tahani refused to even think about it. She told me that countless families had already been separated. And the thought of a difficult birth made her nervous. She insisted that I be there.

I would have none of it. Instead, I insisted that she go to Damascus, to a proper hospital. If anything were to happen to her, I'd never be able to forgive myself. We argued for weeks.

"I want to stay. I'm so afraid," Tahani moaned.

"You have to get out of Yarmouk!" I insisted. "There are no antibiotics! They'll need to make an incision, and you can bet they don't even disinfect the scalpels at the field hospital here. Tahani, you have to go!"

She finally agreed. Two weeks before the due date she packed a small bag and said good-bye to my parents. I put Ahmad on my shoulders, and we left for the checkpoint to Yalda. Tahani walked very slowly, stopping every few yards, saying, "Aeham, let's turn back. God will protect us. We'll make it. I need you."

"There are no antibiotics! Please act like a grown-up!"

We continued on our way.

"Papa, where are we going?" Ahmad asked, perched on my shoulders. He knew something wasn't right.

"To visit your great-grandmother. You'll be surprised! She'll have sweets for you, and fruit!" I raved about how delicious chocolate was.

But Ahmad burst into tears. "I don't want to leave you!" he said, crying.

"You see, he doesn't want us to be apart either," Tahani said.

"It's going to end in disaster!" I called out. "I don't want you to risk your life, just because we have to be separated for a few days!"

"What if I'm not allowed to return? I'm so scared."

"I beg you!"

We continued in silence. At the checkpoint, we hugged. As my family walked away from me, I couldn't take my eyes off them. I saw Tahani show the soldiers her passport and transit papers. I saw them nodding at her, then I saw my wife and son turn around and wave at me, and then they were gone.

In the evening she sent me a message: "I can't stand it here. I want to come back to you. Tomorrow I'll apply for transit papers for my return."

I called her up. We argued.

She went to the hospital. They did an ultrasound, and we were told that the midwife had miscalculated the due date. The actual date was a month from now. Tahani called me at once. She didn't want to wait that long. She was coming back.

"Are you insane?" I said. I was fed up. "You're a pregnant woman—what are you going to tell the soldiers at the checkpoint?"

"I'll just have to try," Tahani said.

"Please just wait. It doesn't matter if you come back in a month or two. Your health is more important."

But Tahani wouldn't change her mind. Every night, she wrote me the same thing: "I want to come back. I'm so unhappy. I need you with me. I'll come back."

"Don't risk your life just because of how you feel right now," I wrote back.

Tahani stayed with my maternal grandmother. Once upon a time, Papa had played cheerful violin music for her, to convince her to let him marry her daughter. I knew she was a wonderful person. So I called her.

"Please, please, try and make Tahani happy. I insist that she stay in Damascus."

"I'm treating her like a queen. But she doesn't care. She just wants to get back to you."

What was I supposed to do?

Tahani called me. "I need you."

"Think of Ziad's wife," I warned her, referring to the pregnant woman who had died at a checkpoint.

"It'll be all right. I'm a strong woman."

"In Damascus, you have everything you need. Enjoy yourself! Eat! It's good for the baby!"

"I'd rather eat grass with you in Yarmouk."

"Please, I beg you!"

And then she left for Yarmouk, in secret. I had no idea. She left two weeks before her due date. Her stomach was gigantic. She took little Ahmad by the hand, got into a minibus, lined up at the Beit-Sahem checkpoint where the representatives of the

UNRWA, the Red Crescent, and the Syrian Army were standing guard. It was unbelievable: they let her through.

She went to the second checkpoint. This one was managed by rebels. Normally, they'd never let a pregnant woman into Yarmouk, since it would be a drain on limited and valuable resources. The field hospitals were barely sufficient for the fighters.

Tahani burst into tears. And they let her pass.

Now it was just an hour's walk. She continued, holding little Ahmad by the hand. She over-exhausted herself and could have gone into labor at any moment.

I was in front of our apartment, frying falafel. Raed was filming me; we were working on a documentary about our lives.

"Hello, Aeham, how are you?" she said nonchalantly.

I almost keeled over. "How the hell did you get here? How did they let you through?"

She told me the whole story.

"Are you insane? You're playing with your life! And the life of our child!"

People stopped on the street and glared at us as we were arguing.

"*Challas*, enough," Tahani said. "Let's go inside."

Inside, we continued our argument. When we finally calmed down, I set out to try to find a solution to our problem. I felt panicked, for we didn't have much time. How could we save her life?

The next day, we went to the hospital in al-Hajar al-Aswad. By that time, the hospital had already been under rocket fire three times, but so far, the bombs had missed. We asked for Abu Baraa, the doctor. Tahani had asked around, and he was the one everyone recommended. Before the war he used to be an anesthetist. Now he also did C-sections.

He came out to greet us. He had grown out his beard, like one of the Salafists, the fundamentalist group behind the al-Nusra Front.

Which meant he wouldn't make eye contact with women. After all, that was *haram*. So it was up to me to do all the talking. Abu Baraa tried everything he could to get out of having to do a C-section, but he was the only one who could do it. So he had to make a decision: Which would be the lesser evil, letting a woman die or having to look at her? He grudgingly agreed to do it.

I even found an IV bag, in a small bookstore next to the field hospital. I had to pay a security deposit of thirty-five thousand Syrian pounds, around seventy dollars, and I had to leave my ID as collateral. It was a small plastic card with the words LIMITED RESIDENCE PERMIT FOR PALESTINIANS. Then I had to sign a paper stating that I would return an IV drip with glucose infusion within six months. Otherwise I would lose my money and my ID card.

I had always steered clear of the rebels. But now they were my last chance. There was a guy named Abu Manhal living in our neighborhood. He had a deep, monotonous voice and was one of the few people who didn't seem to lose any weight during the siege. Probably because he was a member of a militia group affiliated with Hamas. He ran their charity outreach, providing himself and his people with plenty of food and medicine. This, of course, was an enormous incentive to join.

Tahani had a friend named Hanin, a distant relative of mine who lived in our building, a very warmhearted and helpful person. Among other things, she often brought a hot lunch over to Abu Manhal. As a result, their relationship was quite friendly. Perhaps she would be able to help me. I went to see her. Together, we walked over to Abu Manhal's office. Hanin entered first; a little later, she waved for me to come in.

Abu Manhal sat behind his desk, which was covered with piles of paper. There was a small television set with a battery and—I noted with astonishment—an ashtray. I explained our situation to him and asked if there was something he could do for us.

"All right, I'll see. I can probably arrange something," he said.

"Really?" I asked.

"I'm sure I'll be able to justify it somehow. I'll mention that your father is blind and that you're in a tight spot."

"How are you going to get the syringes?"

"Let me worry about that. Come back the day after tomorrow."

Two days later, Hanin and I came back. The office looked just like before, with Abu Manhal sitting behind his paper-covered desk. After we entered, he put three syringes and a glucose drip on the table. Suddenly, I felt scared, thinking he might suddenly hand me a rifle and recruit me on the spot. The items on his desk were more valuable than diamonds. Those three syringes with antibiotics were worth as much as a human life. If one of their fighters needed bullets removed or a limb amputated, his life depended on exactly this kind of injection.

When Abu Manhal gave me the items, I started to feel my eyes well up with tears. At that moment, I would have done anything for him. If he had asked me to quit making music and become an al-Nusra fighter, I would have said yes.

"Thank you, thanks a thousand times, Abu Manhal!" I cried. "Whatever you need from me, I am ready."

"There's nothing I need from you. Don't tell anyone about it, praise the Prophet, and pray for us, that's all," he said in Classical Arabic, as is fitting for a Salafist. "I wish your wife a speedy recovery."

"What, you don't want anything? At least let me give you money for the IV!"

"With all due respect, that's enough! I don't want to hear any more about it!" he said indignantly.

"May God protect you, sir," I said. "I owe you a debt of gratitude." I had already started calling him "sir"! Just like a Salafist.

"Take your syringes and your drip and go!" he said.

I left. I had only a transparent plastic bag with me; that's where I put the syringes and the drip. It was about as inconspicuous as carrying gold bullion. People were whispering. At first, I found it strange, then I understood how I must have looked. I quickly hid the bag under my jacket and dashed home right away.

"Look what I found," I said to Tahani, and pulled the bag out from under my jacket.

"God has answered my prayers!" she called out, and hugged me. "He didn't want me to stay away from you!"

I went back to the bookstore to return the first IV drip. The guy couldn't believe it: "How did you manage to do that? I never thought you'd be able to get a drip!"

"Well, I found one," I said.

"If you don't tell me where you got that drip, I won't return your money or your ID!"

Abu Manhal had sworn me to secrecy. Now, I may have been stupid enough to carry all that stuff in a transparent plastic bag, but it would have been a huge mistake to give out his name. I would have been executed for that.

But the guy kept trying to pump me for information. I kept on lying. "Brother, I smuggled it in from outside, from the regime-controlled area," I lied.

"Wait, you have regime connections? Tell me! Where did you get the drip?" His eyes kept boring into mine.

In the end, he returned only twenty-five thousand Syrian pounds—around forty dollars—out of the total amount I had left as a deposit. I insisted that he tear up the note I had signed, but he refused. And when he returned my ID, I saw that one corner of the plastic card was damaged. Damn! A damaged ID card could get you in trouble. The soldiers at a regime checkpoint might mistake you for a Salafist, a follower of Adnan al-Arour, a populist TV preacher with a hook nose and a bushy beard who told his people to destroy their ID cards. From that point on, anyone with a damaged ID card was suspected to be a supporter of his.

If they snatched me up, I could immediately be charged with three violations—desertion, a damaged ID card, and distributing satirical songs. They'd probably think I was some kind of opposition leader, and I'd face certain death.

I was fuming with anger about the damaged ID card and kept complaining loudly, until I finally thought better of it. After all, the guy was armed. So I took my twenty-five thousand pounds and my damaged ID card and went home. Now poor Tahani had to endure my rage. I once again accused her of getting us into hot water. We argued loudly and, yes, in my anger I might have even insulted the Prophet. Our window was open. Our voices could be heard out on the street.

Suddenly, I heard a banging on the building door downstairs. Someone was kicking it! I heard a voice yelling, "You infidel, you dog!"

Oh no! I looked out the window. I saw a man dressed all in black by the door. He had a black turban, black flowing robes, and a long beard. Probably a member of the al-Nusra Front. He must have heard me cursing. Tahani and I silently gestured at each other. She rushed down to the door; I ran up to the third floor. Over the past few months, the al-Nusra Front had instituted a Sharia court. Two people suspected of espionage had already been hung from a tree.

"Yes?" asked Tahani through the closed door.

"Who was cursing here, my sister?" the man asked.

"I didn't hear anything. I swear!" Tahani called out.

The man didn't believe a single word of it. "All right, this time I'll let you off," he said. "But we know the building. If we come by here again and hear someone cursing, we'll execute all of you."

For three days I didn't dare step out of the door.

Tahani's new due date was November 20, 2014. At least that's what Abu Baraa had told us. When the day arrived, my mother accompanied Tahani to the makeshift hospital. She wanted to get there two hours earlier, so that there would be enough time for the generator-powered heaters to warm up the room. Tahani absolutely insisted I be there. My mother was strictly opposed. So, for the time being, I stayed at home. Until I couldn't stand it anymore and walked to the hospital.

Abu Baraa, the doctor with the Salafist's beard, caught up with me and asked me into his office. He gave me a probing, serious look.

"I hope you're aware that your wife might die."

I nodded.

"Here, sign this. I want you to assume full responsibility in case anything goes wrong."

He handed me a sheet of paper, which I signed.

Then we went into the operating room. It was completely unsanitary. Surgical tools were lying out in the open. No one was wearing face masks, scrubs, or plastic coverings over their feet. Tahani was on a stretcher in the middle of the room. I went to her, took her hand, and smiled at her.

Abu Baraa gave her small, localized injections of painkillers into her stomach, the kind you usually get at a dentist's office. It was the only anesthetic she received. But it seemed to have no effect. Tahani was completely aware of everything that was happening. She kept moaning with pain.

"Sister, don't be afraid, we're almost done," Abu Baraa said to her. "I'm sorry I can't give you anything else against the pain. Just five more minutes."

"Aeham, where are you?" she moaned, her eyes closed.

"I'm here," I said, and squeezed her hand. With my other hand I stroked her head.

"Don't go away."

"I'm staying with you."

Of course, there were no drapes that could protect her abdomen from our gazes. But I couldn't bear to look; I just kept looking at Tahani's face the whole time.

Suddenly, Abu Baraa held the crying baby by its feet, detached the umbilical cord, and handed the child to my mother. The room was still cold, so my mother immediately took the baby over to the table and put some clothes on it, despite all the blood. She rocked and comforted the baby, while Abu Baraa sewed the wound. I comforted Tahani, who was crying out in pain.

"Is everything okay with Kinan?" she asked me, referring to our newborn son by name.

"Yes, everything is fine."

And then she, too, was allowed to hold our baby in her arms. She was completely exhausted.

But how should we get home? I asked Abu Baraa if we could borrow the hospital's stretcher. It had wheels, after all. He said no.

So I went looking for Hanin. Together, we went back to Abu Manhal. He managed to organize a minibus through his religious charity. The four of us carried Tahani on a blanket into the minibus. Her belly, freshly stitched, was poking out.

Again, she moaned in pain. Later, she told me that at that moment she had felt like a cow getting slaughtered.

At home, I gently led her up the stairs and put her in bed. Then I heated the apartment with wood. My mother took care of tiny Kinan while I went downstairs to fetch my father and little Ahmad.

"What is that?" Ahmad asked when he saw the baby.

"Your brother," I exclaimed.

"Where did he come from?"

"You know! From Mama's belly."

It didn't seem as if he understood.

My father bent down and whispered a traditional prayer in Kinan's ear, the Muslim's version of a baptism, the words that we hear coming from the minarets five times a day:

God is great. I bear witness that there are no gods, there is only God. I bear witness that Muhammad is the Messenger of God. Come to prayer. Come to salvation. God is great. God is great. There are no gods, there is only God.

Then my father said hello to little Kinan. He gently touched him, from the nose down to the toes, forming his own mental image of the child.

But I couldn't be happy. My concerns were too great. I was scared for Tahani. What if the wound got infected? What if she died? What if little Kinan wasn't healthy? After all, Tahani hadn't been able to eat enough during her pregnancy, and she had constantly worried. But I had to keep on going. I took care of the household, I got us water and wood. I was neither proud nor happy.

After two weeks, Kinan began opening his eyes. He started to move and make little squeaky noises. For Tahani, too, the worst was over. That's when the tension finally left me. Soon, my parents took the baby into the downstairs workshop with them. My father played his violin for Kinan, and my mother sang to him.

A few months later, I sat at the piano and was playing to myself when suddenly Kinan said "dadada," as if he wanted to sing with me. My heart leapt with joy, and I took him on my lap to sing with him. That was when I finally understood: I have another son.

CHAPTER TWENTY-THREE

Late in the previous summer, when Tahani was still in Damascus, a film director from the United Arab Emirates named Aya Osman had contacted me, wanting to make a documentary, tentatively titled *The Pianist of Yarmouk*. She had been inspired by our videos, and asked that we send her as much footage as possible about our everyday life.

I had my doubts, but Raed was all in. He absolutely wanted to do this film, and he didn't want any money for it. The most important thing was to spread our message about what was happening in Yarmouk. So we agreed.

Tahani was still in Damascus—this was right before Kinan's birth. In those days, Raed constantly followed me around, making videos of me with his cell phone and an SLR camera. We were busting our chops, and we ended up with 240 gigabytes of raw footage.

At that time, we kept the Rama electric moped in front of our building, out on the street. We gave our Wi-Fi password to anyone who volunteered to pedal for a while. Of course, we changed the password every day. And so, every day, the neighborhood boys gathered in front of our building. Everyone pedaled for a while, and then they surfed the internet. That allowed us to charge extra batteries and run two routers at the same time. We managed to upload one gigabyte per day. Not bad for a siege, but it wasn't enough. Even if our entire neighborhood had volunteered to pedal, it would take us fifty years to upload all the footage.

But Raed was only getting started. He suggested to the director that we shoot even more material and send it to the Emirates on SD cards. His plan was simple: He was going to enlist a woman to smuggle the memory cards from Yarmouk to Damascus in her bra. From there, the cards could be sent to Beirut via a courier and then by mail to the Emirates. The director was delighted.

Generally, women were not searched very thoroughly at the checkpoints. But I didn't know that the woman Raed had chosen had already gotten busted before, and the soldiers at the checkpoints knew who she was. When she approached the checkpoint—this one was run by an FSA battalion called "Ababil Horan"—they pulled her from the crowd, and a female militia member frisked her. Guess what she found? Our memory cards, hidden in the woman's bra.

But at least Raed had had the foresight to encrypt the material. The fighters tried accessing the cards, but in vain. The woman was now under suspicion. They thought she was trying to pass secret military information about the rebels to the regime, and so they began to interrogate the hapless courier. In no time, she gave up Raed's name. Half an hour later, a strike force showed up at Raed's door and arrested him.

Raed's wife came running to me in tears. We ran over to Marwan. What should we do? We couldn't possibly search for Raed ourselves. The militants would have arrested us all. But we'd made a promise to Raed's wife. We had to do something. And so we began talking to all his friends and neighbors. But no one knew where Raed was being held.

There wasn't much time. Every day, we discussed our options. I kept Aya Osman, the director in the Emirates, up to date. At first, she pretended to be full of compassion: "Oh no, the poor man! What can we possibly do?" And so on. But after a while, she didn't even answer my calls anymore. She was probably terrified of getting involved. I tried calming her down, but there was an open question: What if the battalion asked for a ransom payment? Would she be willing to help? Her answer stunned me: "Well, I'm not sure. It's a low-budget production." After that, there was only silence.

On the fourth day, someone had an idea that finally turned things around: We decided to go to the sheikh, the preacher at the local mosque, to ask him to look into Raed's disappearance. Raed had always been a very helpful person to everyone. And thank goodness for that. He was a man with many friends. We were a group of twenty, knocking at the sheikh's door. He stepped outside to greet us. He was old and heavyset, with a long beard and wearing a white djellaba. We explained our predicament and said we would vouch for Raed. The sheikh nodded and promised to see what he could do. "Come back in two days," he said, then bid us farewell.

Two days later we returned, the same twenty men. The sheikh said he knew where Raed was being held. Come with me, he said. Together, we went to a half-destroyed building in the no-man's-land between Yalda and Yarmouk. Several cars were parked out front. The sheikh went inside. He must have been in there for a good thirty minutes, but finally he came out with the battalion commander. The two men approached us. After a few yards, the commander stopped and looked at us.

"We want Raed! We want Raed!" we chanted, a choir of twenty voices. At first, we spoke hesitantly, then we grew louder and louder. We were looking straight into the commander's eyes. The commander turned to the sheikh. The sheikh shrugged and gestured with both hands toward us, as if to say: See what I mean?

Not a word was spoken. Both men left again. A short while later, the sheikh came out—with Raed! He was walking hunched over; his shoelaces were undone, and his shirt was unbuttoned. We crowded around him, beaming with joy. His hands were swollen, his eyes half-closed from pain and exhaustion. "I can't talk right now," he said, breathing weakly. We slowly walked back with him. This was a small revolution. When we turned into his street, his wife was waiting by the window. She thrust herself into his arms.

The next day, Marwan and I went over to visit. Raed was lying on a mattress, curled up like a baby. He was still too weak to talk.

"Is there anything you need?"

"No, thank you."

"Do you have water?"

We looked at his wife. She shook her head. So we filled up the water tank.

Raed needed another day to recuperate, and only then did we learn what had happened: When he persistently refused to decode the SD cards, the militants began to torture him. First, they whipped his back with an electrical cable, then they whipped the soles of his feet. He still didn't talk. They pressed a gun against his head and threatened to shoot him if he didn't talk! But he refused. They put handcuffs on him and strung him up, so that he was dangling from his wrists. After a few hours, they cut him down and he collapsed onto the ground. And still he didn't talk.

Raed never mentioned my name. He knew that if they caught me, I would give in at the first slap. Maybe they would have started with "music is *haram*," and then . . . Who knows what might have happened?

I couldn't believe it: Raed had endured torture to save me. Truly, this man was my guardian angel. My best friend.

Weeks passed, and Raed recovered. He was tough. But the scars on his back will never heal completely. And guess who called one day? Aya Osman, the film director from the Emirates. She asked how Raed was doing. And, by the way, what about the footage we had promised to send her?

Anyone else would have cursed her and hung up the phone. But not Raed. He was stubborn as a mule. Once more, he risked his life: Grabbing his batteries and his router one night, he snuck toward the Watermelon. There was an internet café with a high-speed connection nearby—but it was within reach of the snipers. Still, Raed managed to tap the line, and then he uploaded the entire 240 gigabytes within two or three nights.

And so, the documentary *The Pianist of Yarmouk* was completed. We were told that it played at some festivals, but it was never shown on TV, and never won any awards. The director sent Raed a copy of the film. After watching it, he said: It's garbage.

On October 18, 2014, an article about me ran in *Süddeutsche*

Zeitung, a well-known German newspaper. I didn't know anything about this paper or where it was published. I had long since lost sight of such things. To me, the woman from *Süddeutsche Zeitung* was another one of the many people who wanted something from me. I was increasingly losing my patience with these European journalists, and had a feeling that they were benefiting from our predicament.

A few weeks later, a woman from Hamburg contacted me, first on Facebook, then on Skype. She greeted me in English, and she sounded like a kind person. When I answered in Arabic, a friend of hers joined in, a Palestinian from Yarmouk. He was now working as a doctor in Germany.

"The lady would like to ask you a few questions."

"And who is she, this lady?" I asked, irritated.

"She's a journalist."

She seemed to sense that I was getting irritated. So she added, "It's true, I'm a journalist, but I'm reaching out to you as a human being."

I was still skeptical. But I grudgingly stayed on the line. I learned that her name was Monika. She told me that she admired what I did and that she wanted to help me. She said that she had been supporting refugees in Germany for a long time and that she found it unbearable that the world was simply watching the tragedy in Syria unfold. She wanted to do something.

But I really wasn't in the mood for such sentiments. "Oh, so there's someone in Hamburg who wants to help me? Why don't you help all of Yarmouk? Everyone here needs help. Why me? I know this much: people don't just help." I truly believed what I said. I asked the translator to translate everything word by word.

"I don't want anything from you," she replied. "I'd like to support you. Your humanity, the things you achieve with your music. Of course, it would be nice to help many more people in Yarmouk. But I am just one person."

Until that point, everyone who had promised to "help" me had wanted to somehow take advantage of my situation. I decided to end the call. I said, "I don't have time to talk right now, I have to go."

When the two of them tried to reach me again on Skype two days later, I began to suspect that they were serious. This time, we turned on our webcams. On my screen, I saw a face framed by blond pixels. Next to hers was a darker face, just as pixelated, with the typically Middle Eastern receding hairline. The translator. I was still annoyed and began lecturing them.

"More than a hundred people have died of starvation here. And now you say you want to help me. Is this some kind of joke? I don't need help." This is how mean I can get if I suspect that someone is trying to take advantage of me. Monika explained to me that she and her husband had traveled through Syria before the war, and that she felt a connection to the country. And she reiterated: She didn't simply want to stand by and watch. Perhaps someone else would follow her example.

So we kept in touch. She began making arrangements for me to emigrate. She contacted the German Foreign Office, aid groups and refugee organizations, as well as the Palestinian National Authority delegation in Berlin. But it was hopeless.

It was a hard winter after Kinan was born. I spent hours gathering firewood, trying to heat the apartment. I used up all my money on plastic fuel. We needed it to cook food and wash the baby's clothes.

It snowed in January. In the morning, when I was getting water with Raed and Marwan, we had a snowball fight, and after that, we built a snowman. Later on, I took a video of my parents walking through the white, unreal landscape of snowy Yarmouk.

We were lucky, and our stomachs weren't quite as empty anymore, since every two weeks now we received an aid package from the UN. During the fall, food distribution had been moved to Yalda, where it was safer. No one had to fear for their life anymore, waiting for a ration of rice. People lined up in orderly lines; everyone waited their turn.

But it was a dull time. For two years we'd been under siege, and there was no end in sight. Since Zeinab's death I hadn't composed any songs. We had no plans for the future. All that mattered now was perseverance and survival. There was a stubborn rumor that ISIS would soon march into Yarmouk. Great. Dazzling prospects for someone like me, who had gone out on a limb . . .

A few months before, an acquaintance of mine had fled to Germany. His name was Ghatfan Samarkand, and he used to own a small music shop. We had paid him a commission to sell our ouds. In January, I called him.

"How are you? Are you safe?" was my first question.

"My friend, this is Germany! Of course I'm safe. Everything's peaceful here."

My second question was: "Your journey, was it dangerous?"

He talked to me for an hour and a half. He told me about the route, the prices, the risks. Setting out across the Mediterranean toward Greece, he said, wasn't as bad as he had thought. Hungary was much worse. People had been locked up in refugee camps there—they'd even been beaten. The Hungarian officials took your fingerprints and then you weren't allowed to register as a refugee anymore, not in any of the European countries.

He ended with the following words: "Sorry, I've got to go. I have to go to school."

"School?"

"Everyone here has to take German classes. You have no idea how hard that is."

"Wow."

"They do a lot for the refugees here. I can go to music school and take piano lessons for next to nothing."

I called him back the next day. And the day after that. All in all, we must've talked for ten hours.

"Is it true that the German government gives everyone three hundred euros a month?" I asked.

"That's true, but do you know how much a pound of tomatoes costs here? One euro!"

"You're joking." In Syria, a pound cost only ten cents.

In the end, he gave me a piece of advice: "Bring your family. Once you're here, it's almost impossible to bring them over." I promised to think about it.

In March, Mahmoud Tamim vanished, the cheerful man who had written so many of my songs. He was the first person I'd told about my idea to push my piano out into the ruins. Now he was gone, from one day to the next. He had been lining up for a food package, and then he was gone. Had the soldiers arrested him? Or had he "surrendered" to the army?

In those days, armed rebels were allowed to leave Yarmouk if they handed over their weapons and joined the "Fatherland's embrace." But the offer didn't apply to civilians. A lot of people were afraid of an ISIS assault and wanted to leave Yarmouk. That's why many people spent a lot of money to buy a rifle or a grenade that they could then hand over at a checkpoint. The soldiers would photograph these people with "their" weapon, and you had to sign a written oath renouncing violence. Most of the people who did this, however, resurfaced later not in the Fatherland, but in Turkey, on the way to Europe.

But not Mahmoud Tamim. He was gone. No one ever heard from him again.

And then, in early April 2015, the unthinkable happened: ISIS conquered Yarmouk. At first, the Hamas militia put up some resistance, engaging in bloody street battles with the black-clad militants. But in the end, ISIS overpowered them. Or perhaps they simply paid more. To this day, I'm not sure how they managed to channel hundreds of fighters into occupied Yarmouk. Did these fighters even come from outside the city? Or had ISIS infiltrated Yarmouk with a small detachment and convinced the militiamen to defect? Soon, we started hearing about the dozens of corpses of decapitated Hamas fighters lying in the hospital in al-Hajar al-Aswad.

ISIS opened a recruiting office—in a neighboring street, no less. There was talk of arbitrary arrests. The mood here changed radically: We all began to mistrust everyone. At any point, some snitch could rat me out, lead ISIS to me and say, Here he is. The idiot who always plays piano out in the streets. No, it was time for another escape. Back to Yalda.

Raed, Marwan, and I loaded up one of our two dollies with suitcases, boxes, household goods, and my parents' bed. We brought it through the ISIS checkpoint to my old apartment. The place was dirty and dusty. We covered the empty window frames with plastic, fixed the hole in the outer wall, and began to scrub everything. Soon, my parents, Tahani, the boys, and I were living here again. Of course, the space was too small for us all.

April 17, 2015, my twenty-seventh birthday, fell on a Friday. Marwan, my father, and I went to Yarmouk. We wanted to save my white piano, and we had a plan: We were going to do it on a Friday afternoon. At that time, any ISIS man worth his salt would be praying at the mosque. While we were there, we also packed three expensive violins and sixteen guitars. We tied everything down and covered the instruments with sheets.

When we approached the ISIS checkpoint to return to Yalda, it was guarded by only three guys. They wore black turbans and black djellabas; their Kalashnikovs were casually slung over their shoulders. Behind them was a sandbag barricade. Next to that, in the last building on the Yarmouk side of the border, a wall had been partially broken open to provide for some kind of office. A black curtain was hanging from a taut line across the street, to protect the checkpoint from the FSA snipers in Yalda. And that was all. The checkpoint was fairly small, not like those elaborate army checkpoints that consisted of cage-like metal structures.

We lined up. Marwan and I kept to the back and let my father go first. Then it was our turn. A small militant with a long beard lifted the bedsheet over our dolly and shot us an astonished look. He began quizzing us in labored Standard Arabic—he was probably imitating his favorite TV preacher. "What have we here?" He wore eyeliner, like so many Muslim men who prided themselves on their extreme religiosity.

He pulled the bedsheet off completely and admonished my father: "Don't you know, brother, that owning musical instruments is an unforgivable sin?"

The man made me nervous. His hands didn't seem to fit with the rest of his body; they were too small for his bulky frame. Maybe he was hiding something underneath his djellaba?

One of the ISIS guys seemed to recognize me. Perhaps he was from Yarmouk. When he saw me behind the pushcart, he called out, "Hold on, aren't you the guy who's always playing piano?"

My father pushed himself in front. "No, no, it's my piano! The boys are just helping me push it."

Suddenly, it all happened very fast. The guy who spoke like a TV preacher went into a nearby shed and came back with two plastic bottles. They were filled with a brown liquid. I slowly backed away from the checkpoint. The man started pouring the liquid over our pushcart.

"He's going to burn it," Marwan murmured very quietly. Only my father and I could hear him.

"What are you doing, my son?" my father called. "This is all I own. I worked my whole life for it!"

Then the ISIS guy flicked open his lighter. I saw a flame shooting out. Then I turned and ran.

"Hey, stop!" they called after me. But I had already run around the corner and was out of range. As soon as I reached our store, I looked for a ladder, pulled the printed plastic foil off our neon sign, crumbled it up, and threw it in the trash. Now the light box was unadorned. Aeham's Music Shop was history.

After an hour, my father and Marwan came back. My father had stubbornly insisted that he didn't know us, saying we were just two guys who helped him push the cart. Finally, they let Marwan and him go. We discussed what to do next. My father decided to ask an old acquaintance for help, a man who had since joined the al-Nusra Front. The man accompanied us to the checkpoint and spoke to the guy in charge. We were waved through.

As we walked past our burnt piano, I barely dared to look. I had played on this old Ukraina for almost twenty years. It felt as if a good friend had died. But at the same time, I was relieved. After all, Zeinab had been shot right next to this instrument. That's why we had painted it white. It was as if, along with the piano, a part of my guilt had vanished in the flames. On that day, my burden felt a little bit lighter.

Two weeks later, Raed and I entered Yarmouk for the last time. I had shaved my head so that no one would recognize me. We passed the checkpoint without incident. As soon as we were in Yarmouk, we looked for cinder blocks and concrete to wall up the shop. Two thousand musical instruments vanished behind bricks.

By now, the news about ISIS burning my piano had gone around the world. On the day it happened, eyewitnesses had posted about it on Facebook. A news site from Yarmouk picked up the story, and then the dam broke and it went viral. Media around the world, from Los Angeles to Tokyo, reported about it. I read things like: "Aeham Ahmad has the courage to fight terrorism with music." Ugh! No, I wasn't that courageous. And I wasn't suicidal either. If these ISIS guys read any of this, they'd kill me.

Not far from our apartment was an area where I had internet reception. It took me about ten minutes to walk there, and then, dozens of WhatsApp messages appeared on my cell phone. Almost every day I was contacted by journalists. I was famous, but I never wanted fame. Yes, it was important to me that my message reached people. But I never wanted to be in the limelight.

But after the guy from *Bukra Ahla* had filmed our first few performances—even though at first I was against it—I became well known in the Arab world. And once Niraz Saied had—without my knowledge—submitted the famous picture of me playing piano to a news agency, my fame had spread to Europe.

And now, to my horror, ISIS had burned my piano. For a brief moment, half the world was looking at me. Even CNN aired a segment on it.

It was a strange journey.

Whenever I spoke to journalists, I knew that each interview made my situation more dangerous. I just wanted to get out, and would have done anything to do so.

At my last few performances, I played keyboard on a rooftop

terrace in Yalda. I even gave live concerts on Skype, including one that was beamed to Berlin. But I no longer believed in the power of music. After Zeinab's death, I had started to feel detached from the people of Yarmouk. I continued giving interviews—but I felt like a newscaster, dispassionately reporting about events that I wasn't a part of anymore. Each day, the terrifying feeling that I was putting my family's life at risk grew stronger. Why take that risk if I couldn't even play piano in the streets anymore?

Monika, too, had heard about the burnt piano. She kept in touch with me via a translator, and she kept trying to instill a new optimism in me. She agreed that it was best if I left Yarmouk as soon as possible. ISIS was too great a threat. We talked about money. She said she would keep her word about helping me emigrate. If need be, she would help me financially. I thanked her exuberantly and offered to play a song for her.

Finally, in early July 2015, I had a lead. One of the former Yarmouk Boys had told me—under the pledge of secrecy—about a man who had saved countless activists from Yarmouk. Let's call him Samir. Samir belonged to a well-known aid organization; they're still active today. But in addition, he wanted to make some extra money. So he made a deal with a guy from state security. Together, they smuggled out people who were at risk of getting killed by ISIS.

I contacted Samir on Facebook. He knew who I was. We agreed to talk on the phone. "Aeham, how are you?" he said cheerfully. I wanted to know how much it would cost to get me and my family out. He promised to look into it. A few days later, he called back: twenty-two hundred euros, about twenty-six hundred dollars. I would have paid any price. But I kept asking: Is it safe?

Now that my escape plan was taking shape, I broached the subject with Tahani. We discussed it endlessly. For a long time, she was strictly against it. But in the end, she agreed. It was too dangerous for me to stay. We would escape, all of us. Traveling as a family was safer. And we had sworn to stay together.

We spoke to my parents. My father was strictly opposed to it. It's too dangerous, he said. My mother said nothing.

I told Monika about my connection. She wired me the money—in three installments, to three different names, so as not to arouse suspicion. An aunt of mine withdrew the money from a bank in Damascus. And almost at once, the people from state security knocked at her door. They wanted to know why she was receiving money transfers from Germany. She told them the money came from her niece who lives in Munich (she did have a niece who lived there) and that she'd needed it to pay her rent in Damascus. This way they didn't ask any more questions about that foreign name on the receipt.

One night, my mother took me aside. "Aeham, I have a feeling that you want to tell me something. I know you. Just tell me!"

"I'm not sure I should talk about it."

"About what?" she asked.

"You know what it is," I said.

"Yes, I know. I've been thinking about it for a while. I'll give you the money. I don't want to lose another son. That's all there is to it."

My mother still had seven thousand euros—roughly eighty-four hundred dollars—in a bank account. It was the last of our savings. She used to teach at an UNRWA school, and a part of her salary had gone into a savings plan. Now she was allowed to withdraw it. With that money, we could reach Turkey. That was our goal. And then we'd see. But the main thing was to get out of Syria.

I hugged her. "I'll pay it back, I promise."

"I don't care. I just want you and your family to be happy."

We packed our things. One bag would have to suffice. We packed our passports, our family record booklet, and our UNRWA certificates, confirming that we were registered as refugees in Geneva. In addition, I packed my report cards from the university and the music school. And Tahani's documents. I packed only the most essential clothing for the four of us. And two keepsakes: my green shirt and a small notebook of Beethoven sonatas, a long-ago gift from Irina Ramadan, the Russian pianist. We were ready.

CHAPTER TWENTY-FOUR

On August 1, 2015, Samir called, telling me to be at the checkpoint at 12:30 p.m. the next day. A guy from state security, Abu So-and-So, would be waiting for us in a car.

I never prayed so much in my life as I did that night. I got dizzy from prostrating myself.

The next morning, Marwan came over to say good-bye.

"Do you want to get out of here, too?" I asked him.

"No. I want to stay with my parents."

"I can try to help you from outside."

"I want to stay. I want to get married soon. Everything will be all right."

There wasn't much left to say. We hugged. He said, "I'll see you again." Tears were running down my cheeks.

A short while later, Raed and his family came over. We sang a few songs together. Raed's children and little Ahmad were plunking on the keyboard. My mother was singing and crying at the same time.

I knew that Raed wanted to get out as well. When we said good-bye, I looked him in the eyes. "I'll get you out of here," I said. "As soon as I can." We hugged.

My parents accompanied us to the checkpoint. First we had to get through the FSA checkpoint, which was difficult for any young man. So my father lied, telling the rebels that he was the one who wanted to leave, and I was just helping him carry his luggage. They waved us through.

We stopped somewhere between the two checkpoints. Without Abu So-and-So, it would have been suicide to go on to the army checkpoint. If the regime arrested you, they'd throw you in a cell and no one would ever see you again, no matter who showed up two hours later.

I got impatient and called Samir. "Where's the driver?"

"He's coming, he's coming. Calm down!"

My parents went ahead and lined up at the army checkpoint to wait for the man. As always, it only worked because of my father's handicap. Normally, the soldiers didn't tolerate someone standing around for hours, witnessing all the arrests and bribe payments.

The August sun was burning; we were sweating, and the wind was kicking up dust. Soon, we were all covered with dirt. There was no shade, except for that provided by one small tree. Tahani sat down under it, holding nine-month-old Kinan in her arms. He was sleeping peacefully. Ahmad, who was almost three, wanted to run around and play in the rubble, and Tahani had to keep warning him not to. The hours passed. I kept calling Samir.

"The driver will be there in ten minutes!" he said. And a half hour later: "Give him another fifteen minutes!" Clearly, he had no idea what was going on.

The two checkpoints were within eyeshot of each other. Syria is full of places like that, a kind of no-man's-land. I've never been able to understand it: For months, the soldiers and the rebels would work facing each other, but then, when the order came, they would start shooting at each other.

I began to think about a plan B: What would we tell the rebels if we had to go back through their checkpoint? The one bright spot was that Samir would only get his money once we were safely in Damascus.

At five in the afternoon, Abu So-and-So finally showed up. We didn't recognize him at first. He was standing near the checkpoint, wearing mirrored sunglasses and a trendy brown shirt. But Samir had mentioned a green shirt. Suddenly, my cell phone rang.

"Dammit, where are you guys?" Samir said. "He's waiting for you!"

"So tell him to give us a signal! What am I supposed to do, walk over to the checkpoint and ask around? 'Excuse me, do you happen to be Abu So-and-So?'"

So we lined up, our knees shaking. I couldn't imagine how we would survive this. It felt like we were going to our execution. I saw the stern-looking soldiers guarding the checkpoint with their heavy weaponry. In the rubble of the surrounding buildings, snipers were aiming their rifles.

When it was our turn, the soldier asked me, "Are you Aeham Ahmad?"

I almost fainted, that's how terrified I was. "Yes, that's me," I stammered.

He looked me up and down. Then he typed something into a computer and, without looking up, he asked, "Aeham Ahmad, born 1988?"

"Yes."

Then came a test question: "By the way, where's your brother?"

I gave the right answer: "He's missing."

"And those kids over there, you want to take them with you?"

"Yes," I said.

"What, they don't have names? Come on!"

All of a sudden, I couldn't think of my children's names! My mind was frozen with terror. My head felt empty and I asked Tahani for help. When the man asked for my father's name, I couldn't think of that either.

Finally, Abu So-and-So stepped in: "Let them through, we're all on the same side here."

All on the same side? His remark felt like a slap in the face. Was I supposed to be cozying up to the regime now? It reminded me of my childhood, back in school, when I had refused to sing the national anthem. Suddenly, the word *no* escaped from my lips.

"What do you mean, no?" the soldier said menacingly. I immediately corrected myself: "No, no, sir. I meant yes!"

My father, who never lost his courage, not even when he was

facing off with ISIS, suddenly turned quiet as he nervously listened to our exchange.

But in the end, the soldier hesitantly let us through. We were "out."

We said good-bye. My mother was crying quietly. My father, who had held little Kinan in his arms, kissed the boy from top to bottom. "It'll be all right," he said to me, his face stoic. "May God protect you, my son." All I saw was my reflection in his dark glasses.

"*Challas*, enough!" said Abu So-and-So. And so, reluctantly we turned away and moved on, grabbing our things and putting them in the trunk of his clean new car. We left my parents behind, as well as Yalda and Yarmouk. From now on, we were at the mercy of strangers. Like cattle. We had no idea whether we were headed to greener pastures or the slaughterhouse.

Abu So-and-So was tall and thin. I could smell his aftershave. He offered me a cigarette.

"Thank you, but I don't smoke."

"Then how about a coffee?"

Dear God, how long had it been since I last had coffee? Still, I turned it down. Music was playing on the car's speakers. A song by Fairouz. Even the smell of his cigarette smoke, something I normally couldn't stand, made my heart beat with joy, as if I was reconnecting with a long-lost friend.

A car, coffee, cigarettes, Fairouz—it all felt like a scene from a propaganda film on Syrian state television. The kind of film where people pretended that our country wasn't broken. Abu So-and-So was cheerfully singing along to the music. I felt dizzy. I looked out the window and saw Damascus . . . old Damascus, the city I had known from before the war. Nothing here had changed. Nothing at all.

We drove across the President Bridge, crossing the Barada River. Memories flashed before my eyes. At this corner, Papa and I used to get off the minibus and walk through Zouqaq al-Jinn—the "Alley of the Jinn"—to the next bus stop. This was a small industrial neighborhood where merchants sold auto supplies. On the other side, Papa and I used to turn left and wait for the next minibus.

One time—I remember it so well—my father and I had run all the way through the pouring rain because we had no money for a taxi. Another time, we breathlessly ran toward the minibus that had just pulled up. As I was running, I almost lost my shoes because they were two sizes too large. My father had bought them second-hand somewhere. A pencil was sticking out of my pocket, and it got jammed into my leg as I ran. I was bleeding, but I kept running anyway, and attended my classes at the music school. At the end of the school day, I went to the hospital.

For some reason, Ahmad started to cry. Abu So-and-So offered him some candy. And little Ahmad, who had spent his entire life in a city under siege, said, "Papa, what's candy?"

We passed the Hamra district. Well-fed people were carrying bags full of flatbread from a large bakery. And people like us? We risked getting shot for a sack of rice. Why, I wondered, hadn't we escaped from Yarmouk on December 17, 2012? Had we made a mistake? But then I remembered playing piano with the kids on the streets. I thought of the kids gathered around me, giggling with joy. For me, the beauty and the terror of it all were intertwined.

The car finally stopped in the elegant embassy district, a stone's throw from my old music school. The secret service and state security stood watch at every corner. This was where Samir's aid organization had their offices. Two security guards were posted at the door. Samir came out, said good-bye to the driver, and let us in. He was tall and fat; he wore glasses and had a mustache. "Thank God everything went well," he said. "What do you want to drink? Coffee? Tea?"

We politely declined. We passed chic offices, where the employees worked. When Samir opened the door to his office, my jaw dropped: I saw Niraz Saied! The man who had taken the famous picture of me in the green shirt. Dear God, how had he managed to get here? Then I saw a second friend of mine: Omar, who had worked for the civil air defense and had pulled people from the rubble when the bombs rained down on us.

There was a courtyard with an orange tree and a small fountain.

About twenty people were sitting there. I recognized a number of activists—the people who had kept Yarmouk alive. One of them had photographed the grenade damage and then uploaded the pictures onto Facebook. By now, everyone had fled from ISIS. Yarmouk was dying out.

I asked around: How long have you been here? Some had been there for twenty days; others had just arrived. Niraz Saied had been there for several months. His girlfriend had fled to Germany, and now was trying to get him to join her.

After an hour and a half, my aunt arrived, the one who had received the money transfer from Monika. I gave Samir the twenty-two hundred euros, then I said good-bye to Tahani and the children. They would stay with my aunt until it was time for us to leave. It was much safer for them.

After they left, I went back to Samir's office and asked how much it would cost to smuggle Raed out of Yarmouk.

"One thousand euros," Samir said. Around twelve hundred dollars.

"Fine. I'll pay for him." I had to write down all his information on a slip of paper.

"Now," I said. "How do I get to Turkey?"

Soon, dusk fell and lights were turned on. Electricity! I hadn't seen that in a long time. Someone brought supper. Cheese! Labneh! Olives! Scrambled eggs! It all tasted absolutely incredible. Later, someone handed me a foam mat and a thin blanket. I lay down under the orange tree and fell asleep.

The next morning, the August sun shone onto my face. I got up and looked around. People were sleeping everywhere, and I could smell coffee inside the office. I got up and poured myself a cup, my first in almost three years. My body was shaking.

Then the phone calls began. Everyone here knew somebody in Europe. Friends or relatives who had already fled. Everyone wanted to get to Europe. The idea was to somehow make it to the Turkish border, cross the sea toward Greece, and then take the Balkan route to Austria, France, or Germany. But how, exactly? How much did the crossing cost? Which boats were reliable? We had heard stories about seventy-one refugees who'd suffocated in a truck on the Austrian autobahn. Two of them were from Yarmouk.

The days seemed to melt away in the August heat. A couple of guys were joking around: "You should try and get a piano. We're probably going to be here a while."

Was that supposed to be a joke? "What do you mean, be here a while? Samir said we could leave in two or three days."

"Right, of course! Two, three days. He always says that."

Just a few days ago, a group that had left before our arrival had been arrested somewhere in Syria. They had been charged with "illegal emigration." The punishment was six months in prison. But in the course of the investigation, the regime was bound to find something else they could pin on you, so they could keep you in jail forever.

Once, the guys loudly asked me to sing something for them. One of them began humming "Yarmouk Misses You, Brother." They were singing passionately out of tune. I thought of Mahmoud Tamim, who had written the lyrics and was probably sitting in a jail cell somewhere. I felt full of bitterness.

Every day I harangued Samir. "When can we move on? Did you find a connection?" With every passing hour, I felt more and more nervous. Many of the guys from Yarmouk had to regularly testify to state security; they had to pass on information about the rebels. One day, Samir asked me to testify. "Never!" I said. And paid him two hundred euros to get me out of it.

I knew all too well that some secret service guy somewhere was making a fortune off us. All it took was one jealous person from another department to blow the whistle. We could be arrested at any time.

On the other hand, Samir, this corrupt, good man, kept his word: he managed to smuggle out Raed. Beaming with joy, Raed and I hugged each other when he arrived. The next day, he snuck out into the city to visit his mother. That had been his greatest wish all these years: to see her one last time.

I decided to go out on a limb. For three years I hadn't heard from Mohammed Munaf, my best music student, who now appeared on state television with his orchestra. I thought: My own war is over—it's time for reconciliation. I dialed his number three times, but he didn't pick up. Finally, I sent word that I was in Damascus. He called back but didn't sound too cordial. Nevertheless, he visited me, looking dazzling, well fed, and clean, his beard elegantly shaved in the latest Turkish fashion.

"Aeham, how nice to see you!" he said.

"And you!" We hugged each other.

"You look exhausted," he said.

"At least I'm alive."

I told him that his old building had been bombed. Yes, he said, he had known already. We asked about each other's parents. And what about so-and-so? But we didn't have much to say to each other, since there were too many sensitive topics we had to avoid. Luckily, he had brought his oud. And I had been loaned a keyboard by a former student who lived around the corner. So we made music together, both realizing it would be for the last time.

Finally, after eleven days, Samir called Raed and me into his office. After closing the door, he said, "You're leaving the day after tomorrow. Get ready."

Again, my aunt brought money: The journey to the Turkish border cost twenty-four hundred euros for Tahani, the boys, and me. Raed had borrowed the eight hundred euros he needed from relatives.

I called Tahani. We talked about where we could hide the rest of our travel fund. Sew it into a pants hem? Hide it in her underwear? Both ideas seemed unfeasible. And then Tahani had a thought. She carefully opened a diaper and slipped the forty hundred-dollar notes inside. Then she stitched up the diaper. This way, if they searched us, they wouldn't be able to feel the bills. Hopefully. For now, our journey would continue.

— CHAPTER TWENTY-FIVE —

On the morning of August 15, 2015, an SUV with tinted windows stopped in front of Samir's office. On the hood was a sticker with Assad's face. Beneath it was a little heart and the words WE LOVE YOU!—the slogan of his fans.

A small man with blond highlights and dressed in camouflage gear got out, introducing himself as Abu Jolan. He had the deep voice of someone who drank a lot of *arak*, the local anise liquor. Samir called us into his office, one at a time, to pay the driver. Two guys from Yarmouk climbed into the wide passenger seat; Raed and I got into the seat behind them, stuffing our luggage on the two extra seats behind us. Then we drove to the Mezzeh Children's Hospital, where we picked up Tahani and the kids.

As Damascus vanished in the rearview mirror, Abu Jolan shared his plan with us. He was going to drive past Homs and Hama, to the edge of the ISIS-controlled area. There, we'd be on our own, and we'd have to somehow figure out a way to cross the border. He turned around to face us. "If anybody stops us, just say we're on our way to a wedding. Got it?" Then he put on his sunglasses and stepped on the gas. He was silent for the rest of the journey.

We approached the first checkpoint. We were driving in the military lane normally reserved for army vehicles. I hardly dared to look. But Abu Jolan just lowered his window and held up an ID card—and the soldier waved us through. Tahani and I looked at each other in surprise. The same thing happened at the second and third checkpoint. And so on. What was that magical ID card?

I had taken this route hundreds of times, sitting on the bus to the university early in the morning, next to me a backpack full of violin strings and instruments, listening to the Taksim Trio's romantic songs through my earbuds. At that time, I'd dreamed of starting a family. I looked around. Now my family was sitting next to me, Tahani, Ahmad, and Kinan. But this wasn't how I had imagined it. I'd never thought that we'd be sitting in an SUV, trembling with fear, trying to flee our own country.

Five hours later, we reached Homs. There was a checkpoint at a large circle that was operated by Air Force Intelligence, the most powerful of the four Syrian intelligence services. Once again, Abu Jolan slowed down and held up his ID card.

The officer looked at it. Then he looked through the window, glaring at each of us in turn.

"We're on a military mission," Abu Jolan explained.

"Really? A military mission? With children in the back?" the officer asked, stretching out each word.

Abu Jolan became defensive. "Do you have any idea who you're talking to?"

"Yeah, I know," the officer said, his voice dripping with contempt. "We've been waiting for you all morning."

Then he tore open the door, grabbed Abu Jolan by the collar, dragged him to the ground, and started kicking him. It was as if he'd lost his mind. "You're a war profiteer, is that it?" the officer shouted. "This is how you make your money? Is it? You son of a bitch!" Abu Jolan was curled up on the ground, whimpering. The soldier kicked him in the stomach, the face, the back. "How dare you? You son of a bitch!"

Tahani started to cry. Almost immediately, a soldier tore open the passenger door, where Raed was sitting. He grabbed him by the T-shirt and made a fist, as if he was about to hit him. "Show me some ID!" he shouted. "Come on! Get out of the car!"

We got out, our hands raised. "Where were you headed?" the

soldier snapped. I saw five more uniformed men, a few steps back, their fingers on the triggers of their weapons.

"To a wedding in Hama!" we said.

"Liars!" the soldier shouted. He punched each of us—each of the men—in the face. Now the children burst into tears. "Where are your papers?" the soldier asked.

Then he began searching the vehicle. As he flipped down the visor above the passenger seat, our documents fell out. Abu Jolan had taken them at the start of our journey. Four military certificates tumbled to the ground. According to these documents, we were volunteers headed to the front, to fight against ISIS. That's why the soldiers had waved us through. They thought we were cannon fodder. And that's why we'd been allowed to use the military lane.

Abu Jolan was still on the ground. His lip had burst open and blood was trickling from an open wound beneath his eye.

"We've been waiting for you, you bastard!" the officer shouted at him again. "We know what you're up to!" Turning to Raed, he said, "Come with us!"

When Raed came back ten minutes later, his cheeks were red. Apparently, they'd slapped him left and right. "Just tell the truth," he whispered to me.

Tahani and I were holding our crying kids in our arms. We entered a room. We were told to stand in front of a wall. The officer approached us, coming uncomfortably close. "Where were you headed? And don't lie!" he shouted.

I couldn't speak. I felt dizzy. I knew it was over. There were only two options left: Either I'd disappear in a jail cell, like my brother, or I'd have to go to the front, as a soldier. My only hope was that they'd spare Tahani, Ahmad, and Kinan.

"We're from Yarmouk . . ." Tahani began.

"Yarmouk?" the officer shouted. "You're with the FSA?"

"No, no!" Tahani said. "We were starving. That's why we fled."

"You're headed to Turkey, aren't you? Over to Erdoğan? Admit it!" Much of the Syrian opposition's infrastructure was based in Turkey—anyone headed there was a suspected resistance member.

"We just wanted to get out, no matter where," Tahani said.

The officer turned to me and snapped, "Were you with the FSA?"

"I'm a—" I began, but I bit my tongue before the word "pianist" slipped out. Instead, I quietly said, "I'm Aeham Ahmad."

"Where were you headed?"

"To a wedding in Hama!" I said.

"You're lying!" the officer snarled.

What could I say? What had Raed told them? How much did this guy know? I was grasping at straws. "It's true what my friend said!"

"Doesn't matter," the officer grumbled. "We know all about you. Get out!"

Outside, the soldiers tied us up with cables. We climbed back into the SUV. The officer got behind the wheel and took us to the Air Force Intelligence headquarters, just a few blocks away. We all waited in the courtyard, in the shade of a tree, until Tahani, the children, and I were called into a sparsely furnished interrogation room, where two soldiers were waiting for us.

"Take out all your money," one of them said, staring menacingly at us. "If you have dollars or euros, you'd better hand them over, or there'll be trouble."

Getting caught with a foreign currency in Syria could lead to a charge of subversion—which meant you had to spend years in jail.

"If I find any money, you're in trouble," the man said. "You'd better hand it over now."

There was little we could do. I wondered if we had hidden our money well enough. Would he be able to find the bills? On a whim, I decided to take a chance. If he found the money, I'd simply say this wasn't our bag. I would just keep denying it. Even if they hit me. And if all else failed, I could claim that it belonged to the driver. He was already lost. It made no difference anymore.

"All right, we'll start searching you," the soldier snapped. "If we find anything on you, you'll be in a lot of trouble." Then he unloaded a barrage of insults.

He took everything Tahani and I had on us. Our wedding rings, our watches and cell phones. Tahani's jewelry, the two golden bangles she had bought with her dowry, which, even in the days of our deepest hunger, she had been unwilling to exchange for a sack of rice. The USB stick that I had put in my pocket, full of interviews and videos. I cursed myself for being so careless. Then he searched me, my pants pockets, the seams of my jeans, my shoes and socks. Then the children. And then he kicked us out. We sat down in the shade again.

"It's over, my friend," I said to Raed.

At that moment, the soldier approached us with a small pack of diapers. "Hey!" he snapped at me. "Don't you want your things back?"

Where had those diapers come from? They certainly weren't ours. "No, sir!" I said. "These aren't our diapers!"

"Are you kidding?" he snarled. "They're yours, all right!"

"No, they aren't. Why would we have two bags of diapers, sir?" I tried to imitate his Alawite accent.

He grew impatient. "Take your damn diapers! What are we supposed to do with them?" He threw the bag in my face.

Suddenly, it became clear to me: Those diapers must have been left by some unfortunate soul who was here before us. When the soldiers found the bag, they thought it belonged to us. Yes, that was it! Now I could claim that these were, in fact, our diapers—and not the other bag, the bag with the money. If they ever found it.

Shortly afterward, Raed and I were led down into the basement, three levels deep. The soldiers unlocked a cell door. The air was heavy and damp; there was a disgusting smell of mold, sweat, and urine. In the darkness I couldn't see the other prisoners, but I sensed that the cell was full. Raed and I sat against the wall near the door. I rested my head on his shoulder and dozed off. Half-asleep, I thought about how viciously they had beaten the driver. What, then, would they do to us?

Three hours later, a soldier opened the door and called us out. When the light fell through the open door, I saw that there were at least fifty men in the cell, sitting or standing. Outside, we had to climb into a minibus, together with Tahani and the kids. Inside the bus were six men in combat uniforms. They were tied up and blindfolded. I had already given up all hope, and imagined myself in a uniform, with my rifle, in some godforsaken battlefield. I knew I couldn't survive something like that.

We were taken to the National Security Building, and then into an interrogation room, along with our luggage. A man in civilian clothes interrogated us. He had a folder in front of him, probably our file. But I didn't say much. We were searched again. I had to take off my belt and shoelaces, which were put in a bag. They searched my shoes, and I had to take off my pants and underwear for inspection. Then we were brought down to the basement. To some kind of dungeon.

Tahani and the children were put into a women's holding cell; Raed and I were next door, penned in with the men. The air inside the room was moist, and it stank. Water was dripping from the ceiling. It was pitch-black. Every forty-five minutes, a bright light was turned on. This was to happen day in, day out. There must have been about a hundred prisoners there, unwashed, terrified, sitting or standing around idly. From the neighboring cell, I could hear Ahmad and Kinan screaming with hunger and fear. It was unbearable. Here and there, I felt myself dozing off. It was as if I retreated deep inside myself, as deeply as possible.

I spent the next few days in a kind of haze. All my senses and needs had been cut off, it seemed. All hunger, thirst, and even the urge to go to the bathroom. I simply lay there, motionless. Maybe it was the lack of oxygen. We were in an unventilated room far underground. If you stood up, you got dizzy, that's how bad the air was.

Under the door was a two-inch crack. I could feel a breeze coming in through the corridor. That was the most popular place. The men would lie there and breathe the fresh air.

From time to time, inmates were taken from the cell, or new men were brought in, some of them covered in blood. Many of the prisoners had a bad cough, and several of the men seemed already dead.

Twice a day, the soldiers brought us dry bread, half a pita per person. Raed tried to wake me up. "Leave me alone, I want to sleep," I groaned. The soldiers put a tub of water in the cell. Some of the men tilted it up a little, then they began to drink from it. Others dipped their dirt-caked hands in it. It was disgusting.

I was even more disgusted by the toilet. It was no more than a hole in a filthy, foul-smelling corner of the room where the wooden floor was soggy and covered in mold. Around it stood several pairs of worn-out soldiers' boots. I had no idea why.

Next door, little Kinan couldn't stop crying. Tahani later told me that he'd been wearing his dirty diaper for two whole days. When she finally took it off, he began crying from the cold. It was freezing down there, even though outside, the August heat was stifling. Like the men, Tahani and the others were given only bread and water.

After two days, she pleaded with the guards, "Please, let me change my son's diaper."

The other women in the cell took her side: "Give the woman a diaper!" Apparently, the guards felt sorry for her, and she was allowed to briefly rummage through our luggage, looking for diapers. She also grabbed some towels for the kids to sleep on.

On the fourth day, we were taken out of the cells. I hugged Tahani and the boys. They seemed sick, and scared to death. I looked intently at Tahani: Had she been beaten? No, apparently not. At least that. We didn't speak; we just looked into each other's eyes.

We had to climb into another minibus, and were taken to the police headquarters near the al-Waer district, a rebel bastion. The upper floor had been eaten away by artillery fire. All around the building, I saw armored personnel carriers, heavy machine guns, and mortars. When we arrived, soldiers were firing grenades toward al-Waer. The neighborhood was already completely destroyed. A little while later, we heard explosions nearby, probably in response to the artillery fire.

Once again, we were searched from head to toe: First they shone a flashlight into our mouths, then the men had to undress. After we had taken our clothes off, we had to bend forward and cough. But I was relieved that they left Tahani and the children alone.

We were all taken to holding cells downstairs. The men's was somewhat smaller than the previous one, but not too crowded, with about forty men. Sometimes we heard screams from the floors below us, where they were torturing people. For three days and three nights, we brooded in silence.

Every once in a while, we were taken to the central prison for questioning. There was no point in lying. They knew everything about us. "We've been waiting for you," the officer at the checkpoint had yelled at the driver. Clearly, someone had betrayed us. Or perhaps someone had fallen out of favor with someone else, or the smuggling business had been taken over by a different group. I had no idea. And so I told my whole story. Where my family and I came from, where we wanted to go, what we had paid for the trip.

The next day, we were brought into the courthouse for a hearing. We entered a sparsely furnished room. I saw only one man there, who looked like a typical paper-pusher. He had sallow skin and neatly parted hair, and spoke in a flowery Standard Arabic. He must be the judge, I thought. We sat down across from him. Raed and I told him everything, from beginning to end.

When we were done, the judge burst out laughing: "And that's how you wanted to get out? We busted those guys long ago!"

I had no idea what he was talking about.

"I know who you are," he said to me. "You're Aeham Ahmad, the pianist from Yarmouk. Half of Facebook is looking for you."

I was afraid.

"We'd like to release you," he went on. "You'll need to sign an affidavit that you won't try to escape." He looked at us. "But I know you'll be lying. I know you'll try it again."

I became more and more nervous—why in God's name was he telling us that? Maybe he was just bored. Bored to death. He must have seen stories like that play out thousands of times. Maybe he was just sick of it by now.

"I know what you're going to do," he went on. "I know you'll go straight to the Palestinian quarter in Homs. You'll spend a few days with friends or relatives, and then you'll find someone else to take you to Hama. . . ."

This was insane! It sounded almost as if he was giving us advice. We were utterly baffled. "Go on now. Sign it," he said, breaking the silence, and handed us the form.

Tahani began to cry. "Sir, I swear! We're not going to try and leave anymore!"

The judge only waved his hand wearily. "Yes, yes. Sign here." He sounded like a man at peace with himself. Or at least a man who didn't want to deal with this nonsense anymore. Inside my head, a tiny voice whispered that maybe he liked what I had done in Yarmouk.

"All right. You can go," the judge said to Tahani and me. We had to sign an affidavit that we would never try to leave Syria again. Even Ahmad and Kinan, who had been in tears throughout the hearing, had to leave their fingerprints on the paper.

Finally, the judge said sternly, "Don't get caught again. If you do, it's not going to get resolved in a week. Then you'll be stuck here."

He turned to Raed and said, "You have to stay!" He charged him with violating the building code back in 1992. Back then, Raed had allegedly built an unpermitted annex, and he'd never paid the fine of twenty-five thousand Syrian pounds. In the last twenty-five years, the sum had doubled. Until he was able to come up with fifty thousand Syrian pounds, he'd have to stay in jail.

Seriously? Here I was, a known deserter, and I was allowed to go? But Raed had to stay in jail for something so trivial, something that happened long ago? It made no sense to me.

I hugged him good-bye. "I'll get you out of here, my friend," I whispered in his ear. Then he was taken away.

To this day, I don't understand why I was released, along with my family. I hadn't done my military service. The hard drive in my bag was full of videos of me singing about the misery in Yarmouk. We'd been caught by state security! Those guys are like a state within the state: they have top-notch IT systems, vast files and blacklists—

they're the managers of this war. How did I manage to get out of this? Meanwhile, my brother, Alaa, who had served in the military and had never done anything wrong, had disappeared in their dungeons.

Honestly, I can't explain it. Maybe God was looking out for us. Maybe God didn't want to take my blind father's other son from him.

We got our travel bag back. From the courthouse, I called Samir to tell him that his driver had been busted. I let it ring a few times. Oddly, someone else picked up the phone and said Samir wasn't there.

I explained the situation. The man called back a few minutes later. We were supposed to wait by the courthouse. A man named Mohammad would help us. Why didn't Samir want to talk to me?

We stepped out into the sunlight, completely exhausted. Those seven days in jail had been brutal. Ahmad and Kinan were scared and sick. Tahani was at the end of her rope.

After a short wait, a young man appeared and introduced himself as Mohammad. Samir had sent him, he said. We could stay with him and his mother, in Aidin, the Palestinian quarter of Homs. We started walking.

But it wasn't over yet. When we reached the Palestinian area, we saw a checkpoint.

"IDs and military booklet," said the soldier in a bored voice.

"Oh, I don't have it with me right now," I lied. Without another word, he put our bag on a table and began to search it. He tore out everything. I watched him in silent despair. Of course, he found my military record booklet. He opened it. Anyone could see that I was supposed to report for duty back in 2011.

Tahani and I looked each other in the eye for several seconds to say good-bye. That was it. Now they would draft me.

But the soldier simply closed the booklet again. He said, "You've just come from the court, right?" Tahani nodded, and hastily showed him our release notice.

He waved us through. Once again, God had held his hand over us. Once again.

CHAPTER TWENTY-SIX

As soon as Tahani and I were alone in a room, we lunged for the bag. We nervously unpacked, and to our immense relief, we saw that the money was still there. Incredibly, the soldiers hadn't discovered the bills. We were lucky. The journey could continue.

We stayed with Mohammad for almost two weeks. I slowly got my strength back, and one thing became clear to me: Tahani and the children had to get back to Yarmouk for the time being. If we were caught a second time, we wouldn't get off so lightly. I didn't want my kids to have to go through all that again. And I couldn't risk their lives at sea.

It was heartbreaking, but my decision was made: I couldn't take my wife and kids on such a hellish journey. If I made it to Europe in one piece, I'd do everything in my power to have them join me. But if something happened to me—well, at least my family would live.

But how should I break the news to Tahani? I simply decided not to tell her. I knew how stubborn she could be. But this was a question of life and death. I wouldn't discuss it with her.

Of course, Mohammad, my host, knew a local people smuggler. He introduced us. The man had already brought quite a few people over to Turkey. He explained the route to me: I would travel with a tomato merchant from Homs to Hama, then I'd continue on with some Bedouins, then on to Idlib in the rebel-held area. And from there, I'd simply take a minibus to the Turkish border. The rebel-held areas were only eighty miles from here. The journey would cost me thirteen hundred dollars. Time and time again, I asked if the route was safe. In the end, I paid him and simply hoped for the best.

At the same time, I organized the journey back to Damascus for Tahani and the children. A few hours before we were scheduled to leave, I told them of my plan. I simply presented the facts. It was terrible. Tahani collapsed.

"Please, Aeham, let's do this together!" she cried. I didn't respond.

"If something were to happen to you, my life would be over! I'd rather die with you than live alone."

But I shook my head.

"God will look after us—if we stay together!"

"No, Tahani." It broke my heart to tell her this. It cost me all my strength to not give in. "God already helped us once. We may not be so lucky a second time."

It felt wrong to say good-bye. Then a minibus drove up. Mohammad had ordered it for Tahani. With a heavy heart, she got in.

I kissed the kids. And I promised them, "In less than a year, we'll all be together."

SEPTEMBER 4, 2015

Five o'clock in the morning. I go down to the street. After a while, a station wagon full of tomato crates pulls up. Shortly before we reach the first checkpoint, I climb into the back, wedging myself in between the boxes. We make it through, unharmed. I take my seat again. Homs is already behind us. We're driving across a rocky dirt road, olive groves all around.

At noon, I get into a taxi. Before we reach Hama, I curl up in the trunk. It feels like I'm suffocating in the heat. We reach the city. The car stops. I hear a soldier's voice as he speaks to the driver: "Do you have anything for us? How about some tea, and a box of cigarettes?" And I'm thinking: Thank God Tahani and the kids aren't here!

Later, alone in a room, I turn on the TV. On Al Jazeera, I see lines of exhausted refugees crossing through fields in Hungary. "Images of an exodus," the narrator says. Then they show the Munich central station: The locals hand out flowers to the emaciated refugees. There's applause. My thoughts are tormenting me. Ghatfan's words echo in my head: It's incredibly hard to bring your family over. Maybe it would have been better to bring them along with me, while it was still possible?

On the TV, a refugee talks about getting robbed during the journey. I hide my money again: I put fifteen hundred dollars into the back part of my backpack. I slip another five hundred dollars under the insert in my shoe. I tape seven hundred dollars to my upper arm.

SEPTEMBER 5, 2015
We continue at noon with the same driver. This time, there are four of us. After a few hours, the driver drops us off at a rest stop, a grill restaurant. I spend the night in an empty shop across the street.

SEPTEMBER 6, 2015
In the morning, a black SUV with tinted windows drives up. There's the driver, and a man sitting next to him. Both with big beards and black sunglasses. I'm confused: Are these henchmen of Assad? Or are they rebels? Sometimes it's hard to tell them apart.

I look into the car window and give them the code phrase: "Mahmoud sent me."

"I'm your brother Ahmad from the Islamic State," the driver says.

I beg your pardon? He's with ISIS? But we're still in a regime-controlled area! Is this some kind of sick joke? The driver demonstratively puts a Kalashnikov on his lap. The other bearded guy slips a pistol under the sun visor. Is that supposed to calm me down? I get in. We take off.

Then comes the inevitable question: "Tell me, do you pray?"

"Of course, sir!"

"Don't call me 'sir,' I'm your brother."

Someone once told me that if you're in an ISIS area, you have to roll your pants up, just above your ankles; that's what it says in the sunnah of the Prophet. When they question you about Islam, just keep talking about prayer and ritual cleansings.

To placate my drivers, I say, stupidly, "God preserve you, my dear brother. Let's recite the Sura al-Fatiha together, so that God may protect us on our journey." He goes along with it, clearly satisfied. So we pray.

After a little while, we leave the main road. We turn onto a small dirt path, presumably known only to locals. It works. We're able to circumvent the checkpoint.

At around noon, they drop me off at a Bedouin tent in the middle of the steppe. "Wait here," the driver says. "Tomorrow our brothers will come and pick you up." And with that, they're gone.

Inside the tent is an old shepherd with deeply tanned skin. He looks like a man who spent his whole life in the sun. His teeth are rotten—all I see are a few brown stumps. The tent, however, is remarkably new. Later on, I realize that all this—the Bedouin lifestyle—is just a front. I'm at a secret way station for refugees headed to Europe.

The old man gives me water—and fresh goat milk. Dear God! It's been ages since I've had any milk! The last time was before the siege. The man has a peaceful demeanor. He seems good-natured, as desert nomads tend to be. "Would you like to pray?" he asks me. Yes, I would. I really would, this time. With all my heart.

It feels so good to be in his company; it feels safe out here in the steppe. So I open up my heart to him. Tumbling through time, I tell him about my poor father. About my brother, the prison, the siege.

"Oh, oh, that's too much for you, my poor boy," says the old man. "That's too much, that's too much."

SEPTEMBER 7, 2015

I only have a thousand Syrian pounds left, but before I continue my journey, I decide to give it to the old man. "Thank you for all you've done, my friend," I tell him. "Please pray for me."

"Of course," he says. "God be with you."

A car appears. It's the same car as yesterday, but this time, there's a different driver—and another accomplice with a long beard. He wears a short kaftan, like the Taliban in Afghanistan, and speaks Standard Arabic. He introduces himself: "I'm your brother from the al-Nusra Front."

ISIS, al-Nusra, PLO—they all claim to be my brother. I don't care either way. These days, any fool can say they belong to a militia. It doesn't matter: I'm grateful to anyone willing to help me, whoever it may be. So I say, "Please take me with you, my brother. My name is Aeham."

The bearded man climbs into the passenger seat, and I get in the back. The driver steps on the gas. The air is yellow; you can't see anything past twenty yards. A sandstorm is coming.

We turn onto a dirt road—and pass a checkpoint. Did the sandstorm hide us from the soldiers? Or did they recognize the license plate and know to look the other way?

Onward toward Idlib. Suddenly, a cloud of dust comes toward us. It's a pickup truck full of muscular, bearded men who look like they're military, wearing camouflage vests and cartridge belts across their chest. These are the Tiger Forces, Assad's elite unit, his most feared soldiers.

The car is still moving, but suddenly, the passenger opens

the door and jumps out. He rolls down a sandbank on the right-hand side. It's like something out of the movies. He leaves his two Kalashnikovs in the car. *It's over, Aeham!* I think to myself, and not for the first time.

"Go on, hide!" the driver hisses. "Get in the back!"

I climb into the back and press myself against the trunk lid.

I'm in a station wagon with tinted windows. The back seat is folded down. If the soldiers open the hatchback, and they usually do, there'll be nothing to hide me.

"Stop!" the Tigers call out.

The driver starts slowing down. Two men approach our car. They're carrying assault rifles.

"What are you guys doing here?"

"I've got to get to the checkpoint," the driver says. "My shift's about to start." A brazen lie.

Suddenly, a mortar shell explodes nearby. The soldiers throw themselves to the ground. The car is pelted with sand and stones. I hear shots. The men in the pickup return fire, spraying the entire area with bullets, emptying out their magazines. But there's no one there. The men start chanting, "We are the Tigers! God, Syria, Bashar, and nothing else!" The driver steps on the gas, seizing the opportunity, and the Tigers let us pass.

We race through the semidesert for at least twenty minutes. Finally, the driver stops. "Over there," he says, pointing to an isolated shack, about a half mile away. "That's the Ahrar al-Sham militia checkpoint. That's where you have to go. I have to turn back now. Good luck."

I make my way toward the shack, approaching slowly with my arms raised. There's not much to see here. A couple of sandbags, a barricade, some men.

"Who are you?" one of them yells.

"I come in peace! I'm unarmed!"

"Take off your shirt!"

I continue on, bare-chested, my right hand clutching my backpack and my left arm raised. As far as I can tell, there are seven men. Each of them has his finger on the trigger. Once I'm in the shade of the barracks, I can't keep it together any longer, and burst into loud sobs. One of the bearded men asks me what's going on.

"I just can't take it anymore!" I say, sobbing. "I can't go on anymore." I tell them everything. That I was in jail, that I had to send my own family away, that I barely escaped with my life today. "Please, in God's name, help me!" I say. "I just want to leave! I just want to get out of Syria!"

The militiaman tries to comfort me. "Calm down. Be patient. Abu Qutaiba is going to be here soon—he's our leader. He'll help you, he'll know what to do. Sit down. Have some food."

They invite me into their barracks, a small structure consisting of just one room. Outside are empty gas cans and a big machine gun. On a gas burner, one of the men is making scrambled eggs with tomatoes, a traditional Arabic breakfast. In Iraq, they call it *makhlama*; in Syria, we call it *jazz-mazz*. The militiamen offer me some, and I can't stop eating. The others sit a little farther away from me. They look at me with pity in their eyes, and talk about me. They know about the siege of Yarmouk. They realize how hungry I must be.

Three hours later, Abu Kutaiba drives up, a tall, fat man. He calls me "my son," and I explain my situation. He says I can ride with him, in the back of his pickup truck. We take off. Our journey takes us through the no-man's-land between the ISIS- and rebel-held areas. Along the way, he picks up two young men who are walking by the side of the road.

Soon, we see black pipes sticking out of the scorched earth beside the road like rotting teeth. They emit a foul-smelling gas, and the two guys explain to me that these are rebel refineries. They're burning crude oil to get diesel and gasoline. And they buy the crude from ISIS.

They know their way around, those two guys! Little by little, I find out that they used to live close to the border. Now they earn their money as human traffickers, smuggling refugees across. We exchange numbers.

In the evening, in a village, I'm standing in a small mobile phone store when someone suddenly taps me on the shoulder. "Ayhoum?"—a nickname for Aeham. I turn around and see the friendly faces of the two Yarmouk guys I had driven to Homs with. We hug each other and even though I hardly know them, it feels like I'm meeting two old friends. We tell each other how we ended up here. Again, I can barely hold back tears. My nerves are frayed.

"By the way, Abu Jolan, our driver, is doing fine," one of them says. "They picked him up from jail in a Mercedes."

Suddenly, a bearded man approaches us. He's dressed in a black djellaba, and has a mark on his forehead, a blotchy area from prostrating himself countless times during prayer.

"You seem like a good man," he says to me, completely out of the blue. "Let me help you out. Have you had anything to eat?"

I don't quite trust this man. But, on the other hand, I'm starving. "We'd love to eat with you, the three of us," I say, pointing to the two guys from Yarmouk. He agrees, and we follow him.

His house isn't far from here. I see a flag fluttering in the evening breeze. It's the flag of the al-Aqsa Brigades. Aren't they allied with ISIS? Great! Just my luck! It seems like I've run into every militia there is, that I'll have to endure yet another indignity.

When we enter the living room, my throat feels suddenly dry: The room is full of weapons. I see a pile of Kalashnikovs in the corner, and two grenade launchers leaning against the wall. This isn't a home, it's a military barracks!

But then the bearded man serves us dinner. It's unlike anything I've eaten in years. There's cheese and butter and cottage cheese and olives. We dig into our meals. Meanwhile, our host asks us about the siege of Yarmouk. I tell him how we had been starved. But I don't mention the piano.

Would we like to take a shower? Of course! My clothes are stiff with sweat and dust. The bearded man shows me the bathroom, then he hands me a jogging suit. Adidas, in its original packaging, probably from Turkey. And almost exactly my size. Again and again, he says, "You seem like a good man." So far, there's not been any indication that he expects anything in return. As Muslims, our religion demands that we help others. But I'm skeptical. Can he really be that selfless?

That night, about twenty young men arrive. They're carrying Kalashnikovs, with the cartridge belts slung around their chests. I get it: Our host is their leader. He gives a short, solemn speech. "Your attacks were a miracle! And if God wills it, we'll liberate Palestine."

Oh, so that's it! Maybe now would be a good time to leave. Except that we can't really go anywhere. At this time of day, three strangers, in a village in the rebel-held area? We'd have no chance. The militia leader shows us a room where we can spend the night.

Later that night he wakes us up, asking if we would like to join him and his men for prayer. What choice do we have? We stumble into the living room, drowsy with fatigue. The fighters are all gathered here. They start praying, throwing themselves to the ground with gusto. After fifteen prostrations, they're still not finished.

Then comes the obligatory reading from the Quran. I finally understand why they're spending half the night in prayer: One of their men is about to blow himself up with an explosive belt. Himself and probably many innocent people as well. The others in the room are rhapsodizing about the virgins in paradise. What a cliché! They strap the explosives belt onto him and wire it to a battery. The man looks calm and at peace with himself. Obviously, he's been completely brainwashed.

He gets into a car and drives off. He is about to blow himself up in front of a former hospital where a group of Tiger Forces are holed up.

Later, I try to fall asleep. I keep waiting for the explosion, but I hear nothing. The entire time I ask myself: Why did the bearded man show us all this? He was acting so selfless, and meanwhile, he's organizing suicide bombings. Once again, I'm at my wit's end.

SEPTEMBER 8, 2015

The next morning, we take the minibus to Khirbet al-Joz, a border village in the mountains. I call the two guys that we picked up in the steppe. They lead us to a shed in the woods. A roof, some mattresses, a water tank. And Turkish internet!

I was offline for three weeks. Now I can call my family. When I log on to Facebook, I see some three hundred messages from anxious friends and relatives. "Aeham, where are you?"—"Aeham, is everything all right? We're worried!" It feels like the time when our first video got forty thousand clicks. I've got some time to kill, so I briefly respond to each message. "I'm fine! I'm on my way to Turkey!" And to anyone who wrote to me in English, I respond, "No English." It's not safe.

I post a photo on Facebook. Three hundred and fifty people share it. "Aeham is doing fine!" they write. "The pianist from Yarmouk is safe!"

All these worries, all this joy. What's going to become of me?

It doesn't take long before some journalists from the major networks are calling me. CNN and NBC, BBC and

Al Jazeera. And soon, the *Huffington Post*, France 24, and *Süddeutsche Zeitung*. In the coming weeks, as soon as I have Wi-Fi access again, I'll post pictures of my escape on Facebook. An exodus in the internet age.

SEPTEMBER 9, 2015

We leave at eight o'clock in the evening. We're five young men. We're somewhere in the forest between the border crossings Bab al-Hawa and Bab al-Salameh. We walk uphill for several hours, then we reach a brightly lit road. Behind it is a deep ditch. We hide in the undergrowth. We're a few hundred yards from the border post. The plan is to wait until the guards change their shifts, then we're supposed to run across the street. Until then, we have to wait. Two hours. We can't make any sound. Every now and then, a patrol vehicle drives past us.

Suddenly, we see a group of maybe twenty people dashing out of the woods and breaking into a sprint. Four men are carrying an old woman on a stretcher. The soldiers notice them and start yelling at them to stop. But they keep running—until they get stuck in the ditch. It's impossible to keep going, not with the old lady. The soldiers open fire. Two men are shot in the leg. We start running as well. And in all the turmoil, we manage to get across the border.

By morning, we reach a Turkish village. The locals seem to make a meager living by helping the refugees. They give us water. We offer them money to bring us to Antakya.

When we arrive in Antakya, I run into my uncle Jalal, one of my mother's siblings. We fall into each other's arms. "Thank you," I keep saying. "Thank you, Uncle, for waiting for me. We're together now! We'll make it—together!" My escape was the first time that I was without any family. Being with Jalal makes me feel more at ease. A weight has been lifted from my shoulders.

I've known Jalal for as long as I can remember. There are

baby pictures of me where he's holding me in his arms. For a few years, he worked in Saudi Arabia, then he became a minibus driver in Damascus. Both his marriages ended in divorce. Just recently, at age forty-five, he received his draft order. Imagine being drafted at forty-five! So he packed his things and escaped.

And someone else is waiting for me: a BBC camera crew. That evening, they bring me down to the seaside promenade to take footage of me walking along the shore. I talk about my two sons, and right in front of the camera I burst into tears. Later, when Jalal and I get on the night bus to Izmir, some six hundred miles from here, the cameras are still rolling.

SEPTEMBER 12, 2015

We're in Izmir. The sea is too choppy to attempt a crossing. So we wait. We're twelve people, crammed into a single room that the smuggler rented for us. There's a bathroom and a kitchenette. We have to sleep on mats. A man from Syria, working for the human traffickers here in Turkey, collects the money from us. Twelve hundred dollars each.

I notice an abandoned bag in the corner of the room. And a nice gray turtleneck. It reminds me of a sweater my brother used to have. Whose bag is this? Whose sweater? I start asking questions. But I don't get any answers.

"Do you know who this belongs to?" I ask one of the guys.

"Does it matter?" he replies. "It's not your problem, is it?"

There's no stopping me now. "Tell me! I want to ask the owner if I can have the sweater."

"All right," he says, launching into a lengthy explanation. "When I got here, I asked the same question. You're only allowed to take fifteen pounds onto the boat. So people only take what they need; they put their phones and papers and whatnot into a waterproof bag, and they carry it around their neck. Most people also wrap their phones in plastic, just to be sure."

"Yes, I know all that! What about the bag?"

"You really want to know?" he says. "He's dead, all right? Drowned! You happy now? We're going to be on a raft. You really want to wear the sweater of some dead guy? It's bad luck, you know."

He's right. No one in Syria would wear a dead person's clothes. It's an ill omen. But I simply shrug—and I take the sweater. I'll wear it later, when we're on the boat. I'm not that superstitious.

SEPTEMBER 13, 2015

A truck takes us to the coast. Seventy people are penned into the back. We hide in the hills near the sea, and can see the Turkish coast guard patrolling the beach. The silhouette of the Greek island of Lesbos is visible, a chunk of land in the blue sea, less than ten miles away. I have a waterproof camera in my luggage: the BBC reporter has asked me to record the crossing. He also gave me a tracking device. I find it soothing to have it on me.

That night, we climb into a large raft and take off. The boat is hopelessly overcrowded. Women and children are perched in the middle. Some of the people are moaning; others are praying. My uncle and I are silent. We have our arms around each other. The sea is choppy, and the man at the tiller looks nervous as he steers the boat through the waves. We're going fast, way too fast. We ride all the way up to the crest of each wave, then we come crashing down the other side. Water splashes into the boat.

Ten minutes later, we reach the open sea. Out here, the waves are even higher, the swells are enormous. Splash! More water enters the boat and sloshes around the bottom. The boat sinks deeper. No, this won't work. Suddenly, the engine stops. Panic breaks out. I can hear people screaming, crying. "Jalal!" I yell at my uncle. "Get ready!" The boat is sinking. People are struggling to get out. Everyone is squirming and screaming and thrashing around. The sea is totally black.

In the Arab world, most people can't swim, not unless they grew up on the coast. In Syria, we don't have swimming classes at school. But I'm lucky. My father, once again, left nothing to chance. After second grade, during the summer break, we took a bus every day to attend a swimming course. Whenever I was in the pool, I could see him on the edge, tense with worry, listening intently, in case there were any cries for help.

Later, we would drive to Latakia for short vacations by the sea. I enjoyed swimming. My parents had never learned it, so they only went chest-deep into the water. One day, when I was fourteen, I heard my mother screaming in fear. I turned to look. My father was gone. I swam to her as fast as I could—and saw my father struggling in the water, senseless with panic. He had lost his footing and was kicking around wildly.

I dove toward him, then I waited for the right moment. When it came, I kicked him as hard as I could, with both feet, pushing him toward the shallow water. It worked. A few seconds later, he could feel the ground beneath his feet. He stood up straight and coughed up water. Our vacation was over. We left the same day.

For many years, he told everyone that I had saved his life, swelling with pride.

Well, on this night, he saves mine.

I swim away from the boat as quickly as possible. I can't risk another person grabbing me, dragging me down. My heart is beating calmly. I'm wearing a life jacket, I'm a good swimmer. The coast is less than five hundred yards away. I know I'll make it.

Back in Izmir, you could buy two kinds of life jackets.

The expensive ones cost 160 Turkish lira, about forty dollars. The other kind cost only half as much, eighty lira, roughly twenty dollars. But they were deadly. They weren't made of Styrofoam. Instead, they were made of some cheap stuff that soaks up water and pulls you down. On the raft, I saw a Syrian couple wearing the cheap version. Only their four-year-old daughter was wearing the expensive kind. Now I hear the girl crying.

I swim toward her, and we call for her parents. I swim around looking for them, I ask the others—nothing. Did the sea swallow them? With my left hand, I'm holding the girl by her life jacket. I'm swimming with my right hand only, dragging her along with me. She's crying the whole time. I never asked for her name. At dawn, we're back at the Turkish shore. I know I can't look after the girl, so I hand her over to the first family I meet. Then I start looking for my uncle. At last, I find him. Once more, we fall into each other's arms.

SEPTEMBER 14, 2015

The Syrian man who works for the human trafficker is unmoved by the tragedy. He writes down the names of all those who want to try again. He never mentions the disaster of the previous night. About seventy people signed up for the first crossing. Now there are only forty names left on his list. What happened to the others?

That night, they bring in a new raft, along with five air pumps. We have to inflate the boat ourselves, then we carefully lower it into the water. The Syrian instructs the tillerman—a refugee like us, without any nautical knowledge—to head toward four red flashing lights. I'm sitting on the bulge on the left side toward the back. The boat starts chugging.

Tonight, the sea is much calmer. People are praying: "*Bismillah, Bismillah*, in the name of God." Others mutter Quran suras to themselves. At the first light of dawn, people calm down a bit. Next to me is a man from Iraq whose face is white with fear.

"I can't swim," he says hoarsely.

"But I can," I say. "I won't let you drown." I put my arm around his shoulder. My uncle, who is filming everything, turns the camera on me.

The beach of Lesbos is closer now. And then we reach it. People jump into the water, wading ashore, weeping with joy. Piles of bright orange life jackets are strewn all around. My uncle and I hug and smile at each other. And all this time, I have only one thought: How could I leave my wife and children behind in Syria?

The BBC reporter has been expecting me and has stationed his crew on three different beaches. One of the guys sees me and calls the others on his cell phone. Half an hour later, the reporter arrives.

"How are you feeling now? Now that you're standing on the soil of freedom?"

"The soil of freedom is in Yarmouk," I answer, but I'm beaming with relief.

And then I say, "Now I don't have to worry about drowning anymore. Hopefully, I can find a place where I'm safe and where my family can join me, Ahmad and Kinan and Tahani. The most beautiful place in the world is wherever my family is." I dig out a picture of little Ahmad and hold it up to the camera. Then the BBC crew accompanies us to the ferry to Athens.

It's the morning of September 15, 2015.

On to Macedonia. Then to Serbia. To Croatia. To Hungary. To Austria.

A Macedonian priest hands out water and cheese sandwiches. "Welcome!" he shouts. We hitch a ride with a Serbian cabdriver; he's racing down the highway at 105 miles per hour. There are six of us squeezed into the back seat. At the Croatian border, we have to wait until nightfall, then we begin an endless march through swamps and barren fields. We're told there might still be land mines here, from the Bosnian War. I have to carry my uncle's backpack; his hernia is giving him trouble. We reach Hungary. The streets are empty. People are peeking out from behind their curtains, giving us grim looks. Things are different in Austria. Here, we are met with friendly smiles, and there are booths with provisions along the route, like at a marathon.

Finally, on the morning of September 23, 2015, I arrive in Vienna. I climb aboard a snow-white train. Four hours later, I'm in Munich. A film crew is waiting for me. A friendly policeman gives me directions, waving his hands around. He's trying, as best he can, to explain where I can get food and shelter, and where I have to register as a refugee.

I'm in Germany!

CHAPTER TWENTY-SEVEN

Yesterday, on May 7, 2017, I gave a performance in Olpe, a small town in Germany's Sauerland region. The director of a local music school picked me up at the Siegburg train station, an hour's drive away. I had met him once before, in Cologne, and he had invited me to perform with him. "Of course!" I'd said, handing him a score by Riad al-Sunbati that I happened to have with me.

And now we were driving down the winding country roads on a Sunday morning, chatting about my German classes, about my two little sons, about Assad's poison gas attacks and Trump's retaliation strike, and about this book. I had been working on it for months.

The town hall in Olpe was filled to the last seat. Three hundred people showed up for the concert "by and for Aeham Ahmad." A local journalist had come to my rehearsal and published a long article and interview with me. That's probably why so many people were there. The concert began with chamber music, performed by the teachers of the local music school. Then I played some of my songs from Yarmouk. We concluded with music by Riad Al-Sunbati, the Beethoven of Arabic music. One of the school's teachers had rearranged the piece. When it was over, the audience leapt to their feet and gave us a standing ovation.

People rushed up to shake my hand. An elderly lady handed me a rose from her garden; others wanted to take pictures with me, and in between, I autographed CDs. I smiled at everyone, and I kept saying thank you. This concert meant a lot to me. It encapsulated my year and a half in Germany.

Afterward, I had some time to myself. I went down to the community sports center and ordered a döner kebab at the snack bar across the street. Just a few months ago, that would have been unthinkable. And I thought to myself: I'm a different man now.

After my arrival in Germany, I lived in Olpe for a month, in the exact same sports center where I was now eating my döner kebab. Back then, I had been placed in a gym with 102 other refugees. I shared a bunk bed with my uncle, in a four-bed square enclosed by a chain-link fence and white tarp. At the time, I thought I'd have to live in the gym for years. Some of the refugees were disappointed: the big welcome had given way to months and months of waiting. But I was fine. After all, back in Syria, the refugees from Iraq and Lebanon had also been forced to live in schools and mosques. I heard that on some days, up to ten thousand refugees arrived in Germany.

We were given three meals per day: at eight in the morning, at noon, and then at five in the afternoon. I didn't particularly like the food. The bread was gray, the potatoes were bland. Still, after so many years of starvation, I couldn't get enough of it. At the time, I dreamed of buying a spicy döner kebab at the snack bar across the street. But I couldn't bring myself to do it. I only had seventy euros left, about eighty dollars. That was the last of my travel fund, my emergency cash.

I kept a plastic bag under my bed, with small plastic containers of honey inside. They were part of our daily breakfast rations, but I didn't eat them. I saved them, in case we ran out of food. I knew, of course, that I was being paranoid, that the thought was nonsensical, but the fear of starvation had seeped deep into my bones, and it would stay with me for a long time.

I spent half the day on the phone, calling Tahani, calling my parents, calling old acquaintances from Yarmouk who like me had managed to escape to Germany. Luckily, the gym had free Wi-Fi. Tahani told me how hard her life had become. She had to pay someone to fetch water, or to hit the pedals on the electric moped to charge the batteries. There wasn't a penny left, since all our money had been spent on my escape. She grew increasingly irritated and asked when I would send her money. I was just as impatient. It was painful to sit there and not be allowed to work.

In the evenings, as I lay in my bunk bed, I watched videos from Yarmouk on my phone. I wondered how the children back home were doing. I felt guilty. "Aeham, are you always going to be there to sing with us?" they had asked. "Of course!" I had answered. "Always." But then I had run away.

In those moments, I desperately missed Tahani, Ahmad, and Kinan. I felt lost. My friend Ghatfan's words echoed inside me: "Once you're in Germany, it'll be very difficult to bring your family over." How could I have left them behind? How could I just be sitting here, doing nothing? My thoughts would keep spinning in circles until, at some point, I'd fall asleep.

The lights came on at seven in the morning. Shortly after that, the kids began romping around and it was impossible to get any more sleep. I didn't like living in the gym. We were all crammed tightly together, our futures were uncertain, our thoughts plagued us. I spent hours walking through Olpe. Sometimes I sat at the Biggesee River dam, lost in thought. I liked it here. I liked the mountains, the forest, the lake. But there was nothing for me to do. I didn't speak the language, I couldn't read the signs—I was a stranger. Germany felt odd to me. So small and quiet and tidy. I wondered if the whole country was like that.

On my walks, I had noticed a white mansion with an odd sculpture in front of it—a flute player. At one point, I heard trumpet music coming from the building, and realized it must be a music school. I spent days lurking around there, then finally gathered my courage and went inside. After all, what was the worst that could happen? I wasn't in Syria anymore.

The building looked empty. I walked down the corridors and

tried to make my presence known, calling out, but nothing. I came across a door with a sign on it. The principal's office? I knocked and heard a woman's voice. When I went inside, I saw a blond woman sitting at a desk, looking at me in complete astonishment. Small wonder: I must have seemed very odd to her. A skinny Arab, with his head shaved, his clothes ragged, and a Palestinian scarf wrapped around his neck.

"*Salaam Aleikum,*" I said, as friendly as possible. "Piano?" I said in English.

She didn't answer, just continued to stare at me. I repeated my question, two simple words in English: "Piano? Play?"

Finally, the woman responded. "From where?" she asked me, also in English.

"*Sporthalle,*" I said in German, referring to the sports center. That was a word I knew by now, as well as *polizei*, "police," *apfel*, "apple," and *guten Tag*, "good day."

The woman looked at me in utter confusion. "From where?" she repeated.

"*Sporthalle,*" I said again, pointing in the general direction of the refugee center.

"From where, where?" she asked again, making a gesture that indicated a wide circle.

"Ah," I said. "Syria! Syria, Damascus!"

She got up and motioned me to follow her. We went up to the second floor. She opened a door. Inside the room was—a concert piano! I was thrilled, and kept saying, "*Shukran*, thank you!" Without sitting down, I played a quick arpeggio, my fingers gliding once across the keyboard. I thought to myself: *You are mine!*

In the previous months, I had only been able to play piano twice, once in Vienna and once in Munich. Both times, I had briefly gone into a music shop and played for a few minutes, under the watchful eyes of the salesman. But this was different. I took off my jacket and sat down. Music was like water to me, and I had been dying of thirst. Finally, I was able to drink. I played a few classical pieces, then I closed my eyes and sang "I Forgot My

Name," "The Water's Always Out," and "Green Mint." I felt as if I was back in Yarmouk, together with Marwan, pushing the piano through the empty streets. I saw Zeinab's blank, dead stare. I heard the kids' bright voices. I could smell the burning plastic bottles. It all came pouring out. I felt as if I was falling through time and space, my eyes closed . . .

. . . until I suddenly remembered where I was. I got up abruptly and turned to the lady. I smiled at her and said, "Oh, I am very sorry! *Shukran, shukran*, thank you! Thank you, thank you very much."

But everything was fine. She must have seen my fervor, felt my thirst. She had allowed me to drink again, and I think she liked what she heard. She returned my smile and just said, "More?"

A few days later, a man named Karim called me, saying he was a translator and asking if I had the time for a performance in Munich the next day. They were organizing a giant concert for the refugees and the aid workers.

"I'd like to," I answered, "but how am I supposed to get there? Besides, I'm not allowed to leave Olpe."

"No problem," Karim said. "We'll take care of everything, David and I. You know him, you performed with him in Munich. He's standing right next to me."

Of course I remembered—a clean-shaven man with glasses and a guitar. He had played for the children who'd managed to reach Munich after their endless journey. We had sung some songs together and then exchanged numbers.

The next morning, the two men showed up at the gym. Before I knew what was happening, we were already on our way, headed south on the autobahn. My uncle came along, as excited as a little boy. Karim and David explained that the concert had been organized by a popular German band called Sportfreunde Stiller. I was also supposed to do a duet with a pop star named Judith Holofernes. After we ate, I fell asleep. When I woke up, I saw that we

were zooming past a shiny white oval building next to the autobahn. A soccer stadium. I had seen it on television.

David drove us straight to a hotel. We went up to a room where
a blond woman introduced herself. Judith Holofernes. There was
a TV crew with her. The ZDF, a German public broadcaster, who
wanted to do a documentary about me. Judith sang and I accompanied her, balancing the keyboard on my knees. It was a wonderful
moment. I liked her voice; it sounded both light and profound.
Although we didn't have much time and the rhythms of this type of
pop music were foreign to me, I felt certain that we could make it
work. Karim translated, but it was hardly necessary. We understood
each other without words.

As she left, she made a quizzical gesture. Could she give me a
hug? I shrugged, feeling embarrassed—and then we had a friendly
embrace. Apparently, that's how it works in Germany, but it was
completely new to me. I had never hugged any woman other than
Tahani. This was something else I had to get used to here.

The stage at the Königsplatz in Munich was huge. Someone told
me that twenty-five thousand people were expected to show up. The
event was called "Stars sagen Danke"—"Stars Give Thanks." Only
then did it dawn on me that the musicians must be very famous.

Karim, the translator, introduced me to Rüdiger Linhof, the
bass player of Sportfreunde Stiller. He had read articles about me in
Süddeutsche Zeitung, and very politely asked how I was doing. All
the people in the backstage area seemed to know one another; they
all hugged each other. I could tell if someone was especially famous
by the way they were received. Suddenly, a blond man entered the
tent and everyone, every single person, went over to say hello. People were gushing and timid, both at the same time. I thought: He
must be the president of Germany.

Then, while the man was talking to Rüdiger, they looked over
at me. The blond man came to my table, shook my hand, and took
a seat next to me. Karim translated, introducing him as Herbert
Grönemeyer. I've since learned that Herbert Grönemeyer is Germany's most famous rock star. He and I chatted for a while, then

he asked me, "Hey, do they have an electric piano at your refugee shelter, something you can practice on?" I shook my head.

The concert began. The mayor of Munich gave a speech, then he played guitar, backed up by a band. After that, Judith and I went on, smiling at each other as we walked onto the stage. First I sang "Green Mint" and "I Forgot My Name." After that, I accompanied Judith. We ended with a duet, a song called "The Heart of the World." She had written it especially for today. She sang in German, I in Arabic:

When you can't stand well-meaning words anymore
We'll wait here, without words
And the birds will sing
The answers to unspoken questions

And the heart of the world will carry your heart
The heart of the world will carry your heart
The heart of the world will carry your heart
Until help arrives

Some people told me later that our duet was the most touching part of the evening, that it managed to express what so many had experienced in those days, so many Germans and so many refugees—that we all belong together.

I was grinning as I played. The crowd was so huge, I could barely take it all in. Was this just a dream? Not too long ago I had been in jail, in the trunk of a car, in a raft. And now I was here, on this huge stage.

I waved for Karim to come forward, but he was too shy. So I picked up the microphone and called out in Arabic, "Thank you for helping the refugees! Peace for Syria! Peace for the children of Syria! Yarmouk is here!" The people in the audience didn't understand a word of it, but they cheered nonetheless. That's what the mood was like there.

At the end of our performance, I hugged Judith and we walked off the stage arm in arm. At the backstage part of the tent, everyone slapped me on the shoulder. Herbert Grönemeyer came over to me and said, "Hey, Aeham, that was quite a performance! Give me your address. I'll send you an electric piano."

Sorry, what? I was more confused than ever. Why would a famous man want to give me an expensive gift? Back in Syria, musicians weren't like that. The more successful you were, the more arrogant you became. I couldn't believe how different it was here, and thanked him effusively.

After that, Grönemeyer took the stage and sang with his band, and then he called everyone out for the grand finale. Together, we sang "Mensch"—"Human"—his most famous song. At the end, Grönemeyer handed the microphone around. People sang "tadada-tada," and the audience sang back. At some point, I had the microphone. Thousands of people responded to my singing. Euphorically, I pumped my fist. I had arrived!

Later, I uploaded a video of the event onto my Facebook page. It didn't take long for Tahani to call. She was angry, and had only one question: "Who's that blonde?"

A few weeks later I received a package: Herbert Grönemeyer's gift of the electric piano. I dictated a thank-you note to Karim. Now I was able to play for the children in my new refugee center—by that time, I was living in a small town called Kirchheim, in the state of Hesse. I took the piano with me to my asylum hearing in the city of Giessen, knowing we would have to stand in line for hours, so—under the watchful eyes of the security people—I played a few songs for those who were waiting there tense and anxious.

It was amazing how helpful the Germans were. In Syria, when people help you, they usually expect something in return. Sometimes, in the evenings, when I was on the phone with Tahani, I would tell her about someone doing something kind for me. She was always suspicious, and would warn, "Be careful. I'm sure they want something from you." But it wasn't like that. There were so many people who helped me, and I'll always be grateful to them.

In early December 2015, I met Elke Gruhn, the director of the

Kunstverein Wiesbaden, the Wiesbaden Art Society. She had invited me to play at an art opening. I liked her right away: she was so cordial, and she had a warm, beautiful voice. A few weeks later, by sheer luck, I was transferred to a refugee center in the same town, in Wiesbaden. It was the last step of my odyssey through the German bureaucracy, a journey that had taken me from Munich to Stuttgart to Bochum to Olpe to Münster to Giessen to Kirchheim and now to Wiesbaden.

On a cold day in January 2016, I stopped by the Kunstverein to test a piano that had been delivered for a performance I was supposed to give. I also simply wanted to escape the shabby refugee center, where five of us were living in a tiny room. When I told Elke how hard life at the center was, she said that from now on, I could come and go at the Kunstverein as I pleased. They offered me coffee, and I was allowed to use their Wi-Fi. She understood the needs of a refugee. I wanted to be able to talk to her, to tell her how much I missed my family, so I started learning English on my own. Using a translator app, I kept listening to each word until I had mastered it. And so, the Kunstverein Wiesbaden became my true refuge in Germany.

A refuge. That was something I desperately needed after rushing from concert to concert, from one city to the next. I didn't get paid for my performances because if you're applying for asylum in Germany, you aren't allowed to earn any money. I was constantly anxious about my family, and must have complained at every performance, "I don't need food, I don't need a bed, I don't need shoes. All I need is my family. My wife Tahani, my sons Ahmad and Kinan." And there was something else that spurred me on: I wanted to keep singing for Yarmouk, to continue where I'd left off in Syria. I know that music can bring people together, and I felt that my songs could build bridges between the refugees and the Germans. I wanted to sing for peace, and for the children in Syria. I wanted to thank the Germans for their hospitality, on behalf of all the Syrians and Palestinians and Iraqis and Afghans. I wanted to let go a little bit of the guilt that gnawed at me every night.

I was very irritable during that period, and often treated people unfairly. Many of my friendships didn't last, and I found myself arguing over money a lot, desperate to be able to save whatever I could for Tahani, my parents, and my relatives. I had to help them survive the war.

I crisscrossed the country like a madman, going from stage to stage, interview to interview. Along the way, I ate cheap fast food. Whenever I returned to the refugee center in Wiesbaden, the tiny room was full of noise and smoke, and I had a hard time sleeping.

By the beginning of March 2016, I couldn't go on anymore. I collapsed, sick and exhausted, at the end of my rope. In my distress I called Elke, who said my uncle and I could sleep at the guest apartment of the Kunstverein for a few days, so that I could get my strength back. She brought me medicine, cooked for us, and, through a friend, helped us find a small apartment.

Not long after that, my asylum application was granted. I submitted a request for my family to join me, but from what I understood, it was nearly hopeless. I met a man from Aleppo who had tried to get his family over for months and was one day told that his wife and six children had been killed by a bomb. All seven of them. The idea that something might happen to Tahani, Ahmad, and Kinan drove me crazy.

One morning, Elke called me and said she had an idea. Tahani was an artist: Perhaps the Kunstverein could invite her to an exhibition? They could contact the German embassy in Beirut, the bottleneck through which most Palestinians have to pass if they want to get to Germany. I was very excited. "What a wonderful idea!" I kept saying. "Wonderful! *Shukran! Shukran!* Thank you!"

Tahani prepared all the necessary pictures and documents in Damascus, while Elke typed up the complex application and sent letters to the German ambassador in Beirut. One morning in July, when I was on a train headed to a concert, Elke called. "We've got an appointment at the embassy!" she said, cheering. "And it gets better—this isn't just the artist's invitation, this is a family reunification! Your family is allowed to come!"

I burst into tears, sobbing so loudly that some of the other passengers came over to ask what was wrong. I told them nothing was wrong, that I was just so happy.

Together, we prepared for my family's arrival. Elke and her countless friends helped me find an apartment, get furniture, and secure everything else I needed for my new life.

Less than a month later, on the morning of August 4, 2016, Elke and her husband picked me up and drove me to the Frankfurt airport. My fingers nervously clasped a bouquet of pink roses. Only ten more minutes, then three, then . . . the plane landed!

From a distance, I can see Tahani. I run through the door, and an alarm goes off. But I don't care, I keep running toward her and wrap her in my arms. I shower her with kisses and clasp my two boys tightly. Finally, I am whole again.

Ahmad, who's almost four years old now, still recognizes me and smiles. "Hello, Uncle," he says. I kiss him and say, "Call me *Baba*! I'm your papa!" Kinan, who's almost two, looks at me in shock. He seems to have no idea who I am. I keep hugging Tahani. She smells of jasmine. Just like the first day we met.

On that day, I was the happiest person on earth. In August 2015, when I had said good-bye to them in Homs, I had made a promise: In less than a year, we'll be together again. I knew that I'd often disappointed Tahani, making promises I couldn't keep. But not this time. This time, I kept my promise.

I finally felt as if I had truly arrived. Elke put me in touch with an artist's agency. I recorded a CD. I was finally earning some money and was able to support my family and my relatives back home in Syria. That meant a lot to me. I was independent, not having to line up at the job center anymore. I was standing on my own two feet now and making my own decisions. For too long I'd felt like somebody else's problem. It was exhausting. But no more.

We now live in Wiesbaden, in a very nice one-bedroom apartment. There's a concert almost every day. Today Dortmund, tomorrow

Carrara, in Italy, then Novi Ligure, then back to Germany, in Arnsberg, then Meschede, then Iserlohn, then Bad Homburg, then Melsungen, then Palma, then Munich, then Kassel. Sometimes I think: Aeham, take a break, slow down, breathe, spend some time with your sons, take care of Tahani. She waited a whole year for you. But then I'm sitting at home—and I can't stand it. The silence terrifies me.

As soon as my schedule calms down, my head starts to spin. It all comes back to me: my fear of starvation, my fear of never being able to play the piano again. The sheer terror of being thrown into prison. The fear of my children getting hurt. I think of my brother, Alaa. Where is he? What happened to him? Why did they arrest him? Why him? Why Syria? Why Zeinab? There is no answer. My despair becomes overwhelming. At times, I feel like I can't go on living anymore. So I get up, I leave, I do something, anything. I give a concert, an interview, I keep running and running and running, always running. And when exhaustion and hunger take over, when my strength goes out at two in the morning, that's a blessing. Then the guilty whispers quiet down a little.

There are bad days, when I hate myself for sitting up on a stage. I feel like a fraud, worthless. What right do I have to be there? How is it that I'm alive when so many have died? Why should I, of all people, suddenly be famous? Am I just feeding on the suffering of others? Do I really belong here? Or do I belong with the dead? The stage I'm on seems like a pile of corpses.

For who gave him the poems? Who helped him push the piano? Who sat sweating on the electric moped? Who has always encouraged him? Who endured torture for him?

On those days, when I'm alone on the train back home, my soul sinks into darkness. I feel so guilty that I can hardly breathe. I think of Zeinab, who was gunned down next to me. I think of my father, who is now tapping through the bombed-out streets without me. I think of Marwan, who has to push the water tank all by himself now. I think of the two girls singing "Yarmouk Misses You, Brother" with me. What about them? What have I done for these children?

It was vital for me to have all the conversations that led up to this book, the endless conversations with my "ghostwriters" Sandra and Ariel. I needed to speak, to have the darkness inside me begin to lift. I needed to empty my lungs, so that I could breathe in again.

Back in Yarmouk, when my life was shrouded in horror, my heart was full of music. Someone would hand me a poem; I would read it out loud, then hum it, and a melody was born, tender and strong, floating through the air. Where did this music come from? Was it a gift from God? Nowadays, I'm sitting at my expensive piano, in my beautiful apartment, and I try to compose . . . but nothing happens. No one is handing me any poems. What do I have left to fight for? So I plunk around on the keys, playing some minor chords, harmonious and elegant. But there is no melody, no clarity. The pieces won't come together and I struggle endlessly. Then I close my eyes and . . .

. . . I can smell the jasmine tree in front of my window. I can hear the soccer ball plopping against our wall. I can taste the salty yogurt ice cream, bought at the kiosk "Honesty" downstairs. I remember endless summers, wonderful lazy days. The power goes out, and we're sitting on the cool steps of our music store, singing together. Life feels easy, gentle. Then it's winter: we're sitting in our store, throwing another log into the stove, roasting chestnuts in the embers. Again, we're singing together; everyone sings one stanza. People outside are looking at us. They come in and start singing along with us. We're dancing with our hands . . .

. . . and then I open my eyes. I'm back in Germany. I miss my home so much. Why can I only compose soundtracks now? Where did my own songs go?

There are days when I'm lonely, days when I'm angry. But, little by little, the light is starting to shine through. I wonder if I can truly build a happier life here in Europe. There are days when I feel redeemed, when my burden is eased, my guilt erased. That's what it feels like after a successful concert. In those moments, it seems as if I've accomplished something, perhaps made the world a little bit better.

There's hope. There's always hope.

Every time I see how healthy our two sons are, how joyful, every time I hear them babbling in German as they come out of their preschool, my heart leaps. I remember how pale Ahmad was when we were starving in Yarmouk and could feed him only rice and clover. Whenever little Kinan wants to show me something, he gently takes my finger and places it on the object in question. He does this because he's lived with my blind father for so long. I can only hope that the horrors of the war and their escape from Syria didn't scar the souls of our sons. I can only hope.

And then I'm drinking coffee with my wife, it's spring, the flowers are blooming, the sky is clear, we're safe. Tahani has to go to her German class, and I ride my bike to the train station and take a shiny white train to my next concert. Wonderful people greet me—they're happy that I've come. We do a sound check, maybe an interview, and in the evening, I'm on a big stage playing my songs from Yarmouk, full of sadness and hope. People are listening. I'm sharing my pain with them, and yet I'm happy, for I feel our hearts beating in unison. That's when I'm truly alive—when my audience has tears in their eyes, when I can express what's in my heart: the certainty that we can accomplish anything . . . together. All borders are erased, if only briefly, and each of us is greater than before, free and full of courage.

This, then, is my story. The story behind the photo that went around the world, of a man in a green shirt playing the piano amid the rubble. And, as anyone who sees it will know, the photo can never tell you what happened before or what came after.

— AFTERWORD —

November 2018

A lot has happened in the three years since I completed the writing of this book. My family and I are now settled in Wiesbaden, Germany, although I still find myself struggling when I'm not keeping busy. It sometimes seems that it's easier for me to travel across Europe for concerts and to keep talking about my experiences, raising both awareness of our situation and money to help other refugees, than it is to sit alone with my thoughts.

The war continues in Syria, and will soon enter its eighth year. How many more will it be? And nobody is winning. More than 5.6 million Syrians have fled the country as refugees, and 6.1 million are displaced within Syria. Half of those affected are children. It is thought that this war has created the largest refugee crisis of our time.

We know we are the lucky ones, to have been reunited as a family and allowed the chance to start a new life in a country where we will be safe. It is a very small proportion of refugees who are reunited with their families after fleeing Syria. A lot of people who had fled to Europe have returned to Syria because they weren't able to bring their families over to join them. If it hadn't been possible to bring Tahani and my sons to Germany, there is no doubt I would have returned to Syria as well—even with the strong possibility that when I returned I either would have been imprisoned, forced into the army, or killed. Families have been torn apart by being separated; it was very hard for Tahani during the year I was in Germany on my own, as she often thought I'd found a better life and didn't need her anymore. This happened with a lot of families who were separated around the same time as us. Many refugees returned to Syria not because it is now safe, but because they *had* to be with their families. This situation is still going on; many people are still returning. It felt like the most important thing in the world for me to keep my promise to Tahani that we would all be together again within a year, and I asked everyone I could to help me.

There is no question that I had to make the journey ahead of Tahani and our sons. When they followed, less than a year later, they had a safe journey by plane. It is also almost impossible to raise the funds for a whole family to leave the country at the same time. Once we had found the money for me to leave, I was then able to try to help them from Germany.

The best thing to have happened to us recently was receiving the news that my parents would also join us in Germany. They arrived in October 2018, and I am so happy to have them here. It was a very long process to enable this to happen, but it is a huge relief to me. They made the same journey as Tahani, on a flight via Beirut. It had been hard since I left Syria to know that my parents were still there.

It is incredible to think that in a journey of one day, the rest of my family had been able to leave Syria and be in Germany. It couldn't be more different from the journey I had to make! But this is why I made that journey—for my family.

There is nothing I can do for Zeinab, or for everybody else I left behind, but I have done what I can for my family.

Ahmad is six years old now, and Kinan is four. They attend school and have settled well into life in Germany. They don't really have any memories of their time in Syria, but Ahmad knows when we talk about it that it means war and hunger, so he must have some awareness of it. He knows that to be in Syria is a scary thing. I think that as he gets older, any memories he does have will grow more concrete.

Kinan is a bit more curious than Ahmad. He is a bit quieter, more considered and thoughtful. Sometimes when I am watching the news, he will sit down to watch it with me. He doesn't talk very much about the past, but his language isn't great—he isn't fluent in Arabic or German at the moment, but perhaps things will start to come out as his speech develops. I think his memories will come to him as he gets older. It is the youngest children I worry for the most; older generations are experiencing all of this now and will process it and be okay, but for the younger victims of the war, I worry that the trauma of it won't come out until much later.

Yarmouk was once home to a hundred and sixty thousand Palestinians but is now a shell of bombed-out buildings and rubble. When I left Yarmouk, there were seventeen thousand people still living there. In the years after I left it became an even more dangerous place, which is almost unimaginable. My parents were forced to move to Yalda, and in April 2018, the Yarmouk camp was completely destroyed.

It is thought that the figure of those imprisoned or missing in Syria now stands at more than eighty thousand, although it's impossible to get an accurate figure because many families are too afraid to report their missing relatives, or don't have the means to do so. Families are going years with no news at all about their loved ones. My father continues to struggle a lot, as we still have no news about my brother Alaa's disappearance. We don't know if we will ever learn what happened to him. Many of those missing or imprisoned are children; some with their mothers, some without. For many children, war is all they have known of life. Many of those missing are being tortured or ill-treated in prisons, which is what my friend Raed experienced.

When I left Raed in the prison to continue my journey out of Syria, I never imagined he might still be there three months later. His story has a happy ending, though—he and his wife now live in Hamburg. The torture he experienced in the prison led to him requiring two operations on his spine when he reached Germany. He is still unable to use his hand some of the time, and he struggles to walk. But we are all safe, and grateful to have access to food, running water, sanitation, and medical care.

This is my politics—what is right for the people, for the civilians. I don't side with politicians, I just want what is right for the human population.

Tahani is involved in the art scene in Wiesbaden and has had her first exhibition. She received some really positive newspaper reviews for it, and has been asked to show her work with another refugee at a prominent art exhibition. She finds the same comfort in art that I find in music: it is an outlet for her to express all her feelings of the past few years.

We've also opened a small music and art school, where we teach both children and adults. We wanted to create a cultural center where we can help integrate Syrian refugees into German society. Tahani looks after this mostly, but when I am there I will play a concert with the students. Her German is much better than mine, so she is able to translate for the children. I also run some workshops to teach about the war in Syria, and we sometimes hold concerts where I will read from this book and then invite attendees to ask questions afterward. It is important to me to help educate children about refugees. We teach both Germans and refugees in the school, although most of those we teach are refugees, as they don't have the money to attend the prestigious music schools in Germany.

I continue to keep busy with my music. That is my revolution. I enjoy using my music to work with various aid agencies. We recently played a benefit concert where we raised twelve thousand euros (almost fourteen thousand dollars), which was used to build a new hospital in Syria. While I play I am always thinking about where this all began: of playing with the children in those streets of Yarmouk and wondering where they are now; of Zeinab standing beside the piano; of my father's determination for me to have an instrument I could play well, and how suddenly Syria changed from the country where I was receiving that education to the place it was when I left. Although I have my family here with me now, I still feel helpless when I think of the people I left behind. And this is where I continue to use my music: to build connections, to raise money to help, to bridge gaps in people's understandings, to create common ground.

This is what is important to me now. This, and family.

My father after his arrival in Germany, with my son Kinan.
(Photo courtesy of the author.)

— ACKNOWLEDGMENTS —

I would like to thank—from the bottom of my heart—all those who stood by my side, who supported and helped me, who encouraged me, and who occasionally endured me.

I'd like to thank the following people: Carmen Elena Belaschk, Suraya Hoffmann, Rein Wolfs, Monika Fabricius, Rita Akkawi Hazboun, Michael Stein, Luisa Imorde, Stephan Zind, Marianne Hoffmann, Katharina Deserno, Hendrick Denker, Kai Schumacher, Fadi Jebaily, Ayham Nabuti, Athil Hamdan, Samir Nashat Sido, Verena Rajab, Montserrat Cabero Pueyo, Don Horenhof, Lukas Narojek, Sakher Al-Mohamad, Roswitha Kacmaczyk, Sonja Arnold, Lelya Lavandula, Steve Schofield, Lothar Pohl, Hans Joachim Hecek, Remon Azar, Jürgen Ney, Sabee Ottima, Ahmad Almasri, Bernhard Felix von Gruenberg, Birgit Apfelbaum, Moira Wachendorff, Susanne Gundelach, Birgit Kiel, Britta Fischer, Elke Gruhn, Hiltrud Fuchs, Torsten Schreiber, Thilo von Debschitz, Mechthild, Hans Karl Henne, Teresita Cannella, Edgar Knecht, Vanessa Ess, Vanessa Schmitt, Nail Odeh, Walter Schumacher, Karim Hamed, and Ernesto Briceño.

If there's anyone I might have forgotten, I apologize! Thank you, all! Without you, I wouldn't be where I am today.

CONTENTS

Praise for *Deep Economy*

"[McKibben] offers both a compelling account of what brought us to this perilous moment in history and a credible vision of a more promising future."
—Salon

"If you fancy yourself on the cutting edge of things . . . you'll want to read *Deep Economy*. . . . McKibben's prose is pithy and approachable [and] hope for our future shines through on every page."
—*Capital Times* (Madison, Wis.)

"To say it plainly: *Deep Economy* should be required reading for every economist and economics student in the developed world; for every elected official on the local, state and federal levels; and for everyone else as well."
—*The Oregonian*

"This wise and oddly optimistic book informs us that there might still be time to scale down and save the world."
—*The Courier-Journal* (Louisville, Ky.)

"A book that reveals not only the way we need to live, but the way we should want to."
—*Monterey County Herald*

"A very important book."
—*Earth Justice*

"McKibben's proposals for new, less growth-centered ways of thinking about economics are intriguing, and offer hope that change is possible."
—*Publishers Weekly* (starred review)

"[McKibben] ably argues [that] growth has increased inequality and decreased human happiness [and] tells stories about ordinary people doing extraordinary things to improve both the local economy and the overall quality of local life."
—*Kirkus Reviews*

"With the threat of energy crises and global warming, McKibben's vision of nurturing communities rooted in traditional values driven by 'green' technologies, however utopian, may provide ideas for constructive change."

—*Booklist*

"I'd like to see *Deep Economy* read in every Econ 101 class. Bill McKibben asks the central human question: What is the economy for? The stakes here are terrifyingly high, but with his genial style and fascinating examples of alternative approaches, McKibben convinces me that economics is anything but dismal—if only we can learn to do it right!"

—Barbara Ehrenreich, author of *Nickel and Dimed*

"The cult of growth and globalization has seldom been so effectively challenged as by Bill McKibben in *Deep Economy*. But this bracing tonic of a book also throws the bright light of McKibben's matchless journalism on the vibrant local economies now springing up like mushrooms in the shadow of the globalization. *Deep Economy* fills you with a hope and a sense of fresh possibility."

—Michael Pollan, author of *The Omnivore's Dilemma*

"How is our nation going to cope with global warming, peak oil, inequality, and a growing sense of isolation? Bill McKibben provides the simple, but brilliant, answer the economists have missed—we need to create 'depth' through local interdependence and sustainable use of resources. I will be requiring this inspiring book for my students, and passionately recommending it to everyone else I know."

—Juliet Schor, professor of sociology, Boston College, and author of *The Overspent American*

"Bill McKibben works on the frontiers of new understandings and returns with his startling and lucid revelations of the possible future. A saner human-scale world does exist—just over the horizon—and McKibben introduces us to the people and ideas leading us there."

—William Greider, author of
The Soul of Capitalism: Opening Paths to a Moral Economy

DEEP ECONOMY

THE WEALTH OF
COMMUNITIES
AND THE
DURABLE FUTURE

BILL MCKIBBEN

DEEP ECONOMY

ST. MARTIN'S GRIFFIN

NEW YORK

FOR WENDELL BERRY

www.stmartins.com

Designed by Kelly Too

The Library of Congress has cataloged the Henry Holt edition as follows:

McKibben, Bill.
    Deep economy : the wealth of communities and the durable future / Bill McKibben.—First ed.
        p. cm.
    Includes index.
    Contents: After growth—The year of eating locally—All for one or one for all—The wealth of communities—The durable future.
        ISBN 978-0-8050-8722-2
        1. Economic development—Social aspects. 2. Community development. I. Title.

    HD75.M353   2007
    306.3—dc22

                                                    2006051100

Originally published in hardcover in 2007 by Times Books

P 1

INTRODUCTION

For most of human history, the two birds More and Better roosted on the same branch. You could toss one stone and hope to hit them both. That's why the centuries since Adam Smith have been devoted to the dogged pursuit of maximum economic production. The idea that individuals, pursuing their own individual interests in a market society, make one another richer and the idea that increasing efficiency, usually by increasing scale, is the key to increasing wealth has indisputably produced More. It has built the unprecedented prosperity and ease that distinguish the lives of most of the people reading this book. It is no wonder and no accident that they dominate our politics, our outlook, even our personalities.

But the distinguishing feature of our moment is this: Better has flown a few trees over to make her nest. That changes everything. Now, if you've got the stone of your own life, or your own society, gripped in your hand, you have to choose between them. It's More *or* Better.

Some of the argument I'll make in these pages will seem familiar: growth is no longer making most people wealthier, but instead generating inequality and insecurity. And growth is bumping against physical limits so profound—like climate change and peak oil—that continuing to expand the economy may be impossible; the very attempt may be dangerous. But there's something else too, a wild card we're just now beginning to understand: *new research from many quarters has started to show that even when growth does make us wealthier, the greater wealth no longer makes us happier.*

Taken together, these facts show that we need to make a basic shift. Given all that we now know about topics ranging from the molecular structure of carbon dioxide to the psychology of human satisfaction, we need to move decisively to rebuild our local economies. These may well yield less stuff, but they produce richer relationships; they may grow less quickly, if at all, but they make up for it in durability.

Shifting our focus to local economies will not mean abandoning Adam Smith or doing away with markets. Markets, obviously, work. Building a local economy will mean, however, ceasing to worship markets as infallible and consciously setting limits on their scope. We will need to downplay efficiency and pay attention to other goals. We will have to make the biggest changes to our daily habits in generations—and the biggest change, as well, to our worldview, our sense of what constitutes progress.

Such a shift is neither "liberal" nor "conservative." It borrows some elements from our reigning political philosophies, and is in some ways repugnant to each. Mostly, it's *different.* The key questions will change from whether the economy produces an ever larger pile of stuff to whether it builds or undermines community—for community, it turns out, is the key to physical survival in our environmental predicament and also to human satisfaction. Our exaltation of the individual, which was the key to More, has passed the point of diminishing returns. It now masks a deeper economy that we should no longer ignore.

In choosing the phrase "deep economy," I have sought to echo the insistence, a generation ago, of some environmentalists that instead of simply one more set of smokestack filters or one more set of smokestack laws, we needed a "deep ecology"